The Kabbalah Haggadah

THE KABBALAH
Haggadah

PESACH DECODED

K
KABBALAH
PUBLISHING

www.kabbalah.com™

The Complete Haggadah,
with Commentary by

YEHUDA BERG

Kabbalah Publishing is a registered DBA of
The Kabbalah Centre International, Inc.

For further information:

The Kabbalah Centre
155 E. 48th St., New York, NY 10017
1062 S. Robertson Blvd., Los Angeles, CA 90035

1.800.Kabbalah
www.kabbalah.com

Third Edition
January 2009
ISBN13: 978-1-57189-618-6

Design: HL Design (Hyun Min Lee) www.hldesignco.com

CONTENTS

INTRODUCTION FROM THE RAV

It is not necessary to be in jail to be a prisoner. Chaos is the real prison. According to the Ari, the word "freedom" has only one meaning: freedom from chaos, or bila hamavet la*Netzach*. For thousands of years, negative consciousness has caused society to believe that the Festival of Freedom is about emigration— the Exodus of the Israelites from Egypt. This consciousness has prevented people from discovering the true meaning of the night of the *Seder* and of the Feast of *Pesach* (Passover).

Kabbalah teaches that every event in the universe is the result of human action. When we are good or bad, we create a positive or negative energy that is the cause of all phenomena. This is exactly what Kabbalah states, even if we don't always see the correlation between cosmological events and human actions.

If we want to control future events, we must control the tape of our lives that we are transmitting, and we can decide from an endless series of possibilities what will be realized. From the moment we insert the tape and turn on the cosmic VCR, subsequent events occur in a prescribed manner, without any free will on our part. But by using restriction, we can eject the tape, choose a different one from an endless variety, and insert the new tape in place of the old.

On the night of the *Seder* (Meal of Order), we can change our movie for the next year until the following Passover. Every person's initial tape is determined according to acts from his or her previous lifetimes. As long as people do not take action to change this initial movie, their script will remain the same year after year, and their future will be predictable. But on the night of the *Seder*, we are given the opportunity to change the future. The *Zohar* states that every person who connects to the Light revealed on the night of the *Seder* will be transported to a parallel universe and will connect to a tape from which all judgments from past lives have been erased. This is the opportunity that the holiday of *Pesach* offers us, and we should seize it.

On *Pesach*, there is a paradox. *Nissan* can be a negative month if we do not connect to the energy that is transmitted on the evening of the *Seder* and do not reveal it in the world with the right consciousness in the way that Kabbalah teaches us. If we are not in harmony with the universe, then we are subject to the negative aspect of any month. The Torah tells us (*Deuteronomy 30:19*): "And I give you life and death—choose life."

Welcome to the Pesach Haggadah.

If you're reading this *Haggadah* right now, it means you are already well on your way to freedom—freedom from chaos, suffering, ego, death. But this freedom is an offer with a start date and an expiry date; it involves taking advantage of special energy available only at a certain time of year.

Sometimes it may feel as if we're stuck and that there's no way to change. Everyone in the world suffers from something. There are moments when we think our dilemmas cannot be solved, that we have problems so great that they cannot be fixed. But *Pesach* gives us the Light to dissolve and fill every place where we have darkness—in every single aspect of our life: personal, spiritual, physical, financial.

The self-help business is one of the most influential industries today. There's so much talk about depression, anger, low self-esteem. The truth is there's no information that alone will solve our problems. No one has found the winning formula. The missing ingredient is always the Light. Knowing the problem and having a logical, linear solution isn't enough. That's how we operate all year long. We must have the Light to solve the problem. But we can never do enough to warrant a constant connection to the Light.

On *Pesach*, we can receive the Light to solve all our problems. Satan's game with us can be over. We don't have to feel that there are things that can't be solved. Every question has an answer. Every situation has a potential positive outcome. The Light to accomplish this exists for us at *Pesach*.

What's worse than not knowing that these openings exist—not knowing that on *Rosh Hashanah* we get life, not knowing that on *Pesach* we get the Light to remove our problems—is attempting to make a connection to *Pesach* without really understanding the technology, without understanding what's going on during the process of the *Seder*. We make an effort to connect; we take time out from our hectic day for the sake of improving our life, but we don't necessarily do it properly, so we lose our focus, our priorities, and all because we don't make the effort to learn what the process is really about.

We have to go within and figure out what our problems are, what questions we have, and where we want the Light to remove the darkness. We have to identify our darkness so that when *Pesach* comes, we know where to direct the Light.

The Light will not enter into a place where we ourselves are afraid to go.

Many times, we are afraid to admit there's a problem, afraid to go and realize how big the problem is, afraid to feel the emptiness, to feel the essence and the true magnitude of whatever problem or question is plaguing us. What is it that makes us lose sleep, shut down, get depressed, and keeps us from becoming who we want to be? If we don't ask these questions, if we get stuck in that path, then the Light also gets stuck. The Light will only enter where we let it in.

The first step is to internalize the fact that the Light doesn't do anything that we don't do. In Psalms 121, King David wrote *HaShem Tzilcha* (God is your shadow). The Light does what we do. And what we don't want to do, the Light doesn't do. Not because it doesn't want to, but because it can't. Whatever self-imposed limitations we have, we must understand that these limitations also limit the Light. Nothing—not even God, our priest, or our rabbi—can make the Light work for us. We have to go into the darkness, admit it's there, and feel it, for better or worse. We have to take a cold, hard look at ourselves. See the problems, the qualities that lead us to our destructive relationships, and our destructive behavior. Finding the places inside us that are dark is half the battle. And until we do, the Light can't remove them.

The second step is to bring that darkness "to Light" with someone else. When we finally open our eyes and find the things that aren't so good about us, things that we're not proud of, that we're even ashamed of, we must open our darkness to someone else. When we're strong enough to share our iniquities—whatever it is that's not perfect, whatever it is that causes us to be on paths we shouldn't be on, places where we know we shouldn't be—when we find the strength to share those dark places with someone else, then the Light flows. The Light will fill up and illuminate those dark places. There can't be any darkness where the Light is.

So, we have to do those two things: Find the darkness within and then be able to find the courage to share it with someone else. When we have the Light, the obstacles in our life almost don't exist. When we don't have the Light in our life, however, it's like wearing a straightjacket in a maximum security prison. With the Light, everything is within reach. Without the Light, the barriers between us and what we want are infinite.

And when we do make room for the Light and it comes in, there's still work to be done. It's not a cakewalk. When blockages arise—and they will—if we don't have the Light, we lack the technology to overcome our obstacles.

It's simple. With the Light in our lives, anything is possible. Without the Light, no lasting form of fulfillment is possible. We just need to take the first step.

Pesach is very much about slavery; you'll see that in the pages that follow. What makes us a slave? Simply put, a slave has no choice, and therefore no Light, no freedom. In our life, when we shut down from the Light, when we shut off those Light thoughts and we're just there to collect a paycheck, to do our own thing, without trying to inject Light in the day and in the things we do, then we are slaves. It's not just at work either. We are enslaved to what we think our path needs to be: to the doctor's prognosis, to the lawyer's advice. Whenever we relinquish control, whenever we say, "I'm not going to trust the Light," we're locking ourselves inside the prison and throwing away the keys.

We must constantly be asking ourselves, "How can I inject Light into the situation?" When we don't inject Light, it means we are slaves. And when there's no Light, there's no choice. If we don't let the Light in, we shut down our own power.

Each and every one of us is a slave in one aspect of our life or another. Making sure we stop being slaves is what we need to be working on during *Pesach*. It's not that *Pesach* gives us the Light or the power to end the slavery itself. *Pesach* is a time to realize that we're a slave; that we have darkness, and we're not letting the Light in. But when we realize we're a slave and we tell ourselves to stop and let the Light in, that is the true power of *Pesach*: putting the Light in those places where we're slaves.

If we just follow blindly without seeking the opportunity or lesson, how we can share or remove ourselves from the situation to see where our best possible outcome is? Do we really believe that the situation can disappear in five seconds, like those people who are misdiagnosed? Why does something happen to one person and not another? How can we ensure we have the best possible movie?

Inject the Light.

Take a piece of paper and write down the darkness, where you feel you've shut down, become enslaved and empty. What part of your life needs Light? There are many different things in our life that plague us—jealousy, unworthiness, finances, anger, depression—all obviously ego-related. We all have compartments within. Look inside each one and identify the darkness, those places where you want the Light to come in. This exercise brings us to an even bigger kabbalistic concept: If we don't prepare, we can't fully connect.

If a person has surgery, there's pre-op preparation. When you take a test at school, you study. You can't just show up and expect to do the job. The main work happens before every single event. Therefore, the more darkness we identify ahead of time, the more darkness we can remove at *Pesach*.

Life isn't easy. We all go through pain. I know that it's not a simple switch from darkness to Light. There is a process and it takes work. The question is, how much darkness are you willing to let go of?

As long as you're not in the place you want to be, it means there's darkness in your life. We have to figure out who we are and who we want to be, where we are and where we want to be. Make a list detailing where you presently stand and your goals. To become that person and get to that place, we must remove the darkness.

This list that you've composed: Put it away; take it out again tomorrow or the day after, and keep adding to it. And if you're participating in a *Seder*, the main connection at *Pesach*, bring the list with you. You'll be able to use it at the "Burning of the *Chametz*," in the morning of the *Pesach Seder* which you'll read more about shortly.

To be successful on this journey, even if you don't buy fully into Kabbalah or the idea of *Pesach*, you should be prepared to give 100 percent. If you decide that you want to give *Pesach* a try, go all out. Be present. Do the exercises. Do the connections. But don't do it because you've been told you should or it's the right thing to do. At least know what you're getting into.

This book contains the "why" of what we do on *Pesach*. When we know the "why," we feel a connection, and then we can go from being an observer to really contributing and taking part.

The word *Seder* means "order." The way to achieve freedom is through order. The *Seder* is about a planned, structured way to achieve freedom. We first need structure, and then we gain freedom. When freedom comes first, it's a free-for-all, and I'll-do-whatever-I-want—and that leads to chaos. That's selfishness. That's Satan in control.

What you'll find in this *Haggadah* is a detailed, structured plan for escape from the clutches of ego--satan. At times, the actions might seem strange, the explanations unusual. But know that this technology is not a modern-day invention. It's an ancient prescription for true freedom from limitation and darkness.

The path to this freedom is paved with the words, connections, actions, and consciousness found in this *Haggadah*. All of the "why's" of and for these connections are either things I have been taught by my father and teacher Rav Berg, or they are lessons I gathered from many of history's greatest kabbalists. These secrets are not my invention, they are ancient technologies passed down from kabbalist to kabbalist, from teacher to student throughout the ages.

I wish you success in using this guidebook for *Pesach* and in your quest for lasting freedom.

Yehuda Berg

The Purpose of Pesach (Passover)

There is a spiritual significance and code concealed within the story of the Israelites' slavery in Egypt. "Egypt" is a code word for our ego and reactive behavior. "Slavery" refers to Satan's complete domination over humanity. During the Israelites' inhabitation of Egypt, the Game of Life and Satan's role in it had reached a critical point. Satan was in complete control, and there was no way for mankind to beat him.

And that's when something remarkable happened: The Light intervened on our behalf. Suddenly, ten massive jolts of spiritual energy, signified by the code name "Ten Plagues," were thrust into our world. The shockwave sent Satan reeling. His death grip on us was broken, and we found ourselves on an equal footing with our Opponent. And the moment Satan's stranglehold was broken; chaos vanished, as signified by the Exodus of the Israelites from Egypt and the state of immortality that was achieved at Mount Sinai. This is the power of *Pesach*.

The Israelites went out of Egypt during the season of spring, on the 15th of *Nissan* when the astrological sign of Aries influences the universe. Every spring since the creation of the world, the energy of freedom has existed in potential form. Just as all the energy that is held in captivity during the winter months is released in the spring, so, too, do our souls wait to be set free from the bondage of Egypt.

From the Rav

The Israelites went down to Egypt to detach from negativity and to remove Bread of Shame. This removal is achieved by restricting or resisting reactive behavior at the moment when the opportunity presents itself. The Israelites could then control the movies of their lives. They could fast-forward, rewind, or even change the script altogether!

We know that scripts can be rewritten and that other movies exist. We need simply to read the labels on the movies to choose a desirable one from those available. But first we need to know that such an opportunity exists and when it is scheduled to occur. The optimal time to remove negativity is when the *Desire to Receive for the Self Alone* reaches its high point, which happens during the month of *Nissan*, when Mars, the planet of war, influences the world though the sign of Aries. Aries symbolizes the pioneer who leads the way, and Aries is fortified by the power it gets from Mars—the same power that is also responsible for the spring. By controlling the force of Mars, we can control the power of growth and rejuvenation in our lives, just as nature does in spring. Living in chaos with a lack of control is like living in prison. We can crack the walls of the prison cell at *Pesach* and be free because the occasion affords us an opportunity to activate restriction over the *Desire to Receive for the Self Alone*.

Aviv is the Aramaic word for spring. This word can be separated into two syllables: *Av* (father) and *iv* (in Aramaic, the numerical value of 12). Spring is the first of the 12 months and the father of all the months, which is why Aries is the first sign in the zodiac. On the first day of the month of *Nissan*, we witnessed—for the first time in the history of mankind—a whole nation united in the understanding and practice of the Three Column System. The slaughter of the ram by the Israelites represented the activation of the power of restriction over the *Desire to Receive for the Self Alone*, this desire being the essence of Egyptian culture. The Israelites gained the strength they needed for this breakthrough from the positive aspects of the sign of Aries and the planet Mars. This act changed their movie and made possible the Exodus from Egypt. During the holidays of the lunar month of *Tishrei*, we receive a year's life extension. In the month of *Nissan*, we can change our way of life and correct the rest of the year accordingly.

Rav Elimelech taught that he learned how to connect to the Creator from the Kozaks. He had heard a story about a young guard who had fallen asleep during his watch. The Kozaks beat the young soldier to ensure that he did not fall asleep on the job again. Rav Elimelech explained that when it comes to our spiritual work and our connection to the Creator, we cannot fall asleep on the job. We are required to be conscious and present at all times. In Egypt, the Israelites were asleep. Even being enslaved and beaten by the Egyptians did not wake them from their slumber.

They were so steeped in selfishness and the *Desire to Receive for the Self Alone* that had they remained in Egypt for even one more day, they would never have been able to leave. The destiny of the Israelites was to get out of Egypt as part of the natural process of *tikkun* (spiritual correction). But they were so steeped in negativity that they did not have the power to get out on their own. However, they (and even we now) did not actually "earn" the freedom that was given as a gift from the Creator, and this is why the unfortunate truth is that we are still in Egypt. Think about it. Has the world ever truly earned freedom at any point in history? The reason that we are still in Egypt today is because the first time around, we didn't earn the rescue.

Moreover, if we had truly escaped Egypt, would there still be chaos? Would people continue to suffer? This idea is so important that it bears repeating: We are still in Egypt. This is the reason for all the chaos in the world—and in our lives—today. But on *Pesach*, and on the *Seder* night in particular, we have a chance to finally leave for good.

In our connection tonight, it is important to remember that we are not just working to get out of our own personal Egypt—our ego, addictions, and negative behaviors—we are working to get out of the global Egypt that the world has so far failed to earn release from.

The *Seder* night takes us from slavery to freedom. But what does slavery mean for us today? A slave can hold an important position. So if being a slave is not a job description, then what is slavery? Slavery is not having the freedom to make our own choices. Real freedom is the ability to choose. Most of the time, we make choices unconsciously or unwittingly. But *Pesach* awakens us to the awareness that we are making choices at every moment; and ideally, we will carry this awareness with us throughout the whole year.

The motor that fuels miracles—for achieving the Final Redemption—is the telling of the story of the Exodus from Egypt. In just talking about Moses, we are awakened to the reality that we are in Egypt and that we can connect to *Pesach* (freedom from chaos) now. There is an opening for us today. We don't have to connect to the past to connect to this opening; we simply need to read the story.

Pesach takes us from slavery to redemption at any time, but only if we understand and accept that we can be redeemed. In those moments when we feel we've done so many negative things that it would be impossible to change, we can always "go back" to Egypt. Redemption begins with Egypt. Egypt is the recognition that the beginning of bringing on the good is seeing the bad. The Israelites in Egypt had reached the lowest level of humanity, and yet God still took them out and 50 days later gave them immortality.

Galut (exile) is what brings about the *ge'ula* (redemption). This is why Jacob had to go to Egypt in the first place. To achieve greatness, we must willingly face our weaknesses. In other words, understanding the *Galut* means understanding our chaos; understanding our chaos is what brings about the *ge'ula*; understanding the pain is what brings the fulfillment. The *Haggadah* says that the Creator saw our affliction. What do we need to see to have the Creator come into our lives? If we don't see how bad we are, we will never change and never fix ourselves.

From the Rav

The Ari explains that before any form of redemption can occur, it is necessary to go down into the mud of physical difficulty to earn purification. This was the situation of the Israelites at the time of the Exodus—with the significant difference that the Israelites had become addicted to the "mud." Even when Moses promised them the 72 Names of God and the Torah—the tools with which they could connect to wells of cosmic energy and draw endless abundance to themselves and the whole world—they kept complaining about what they had left behind in Egypt. Theirs wasn't a suffering of physical proportions, and neither is ours.

Physical and Spiritual Preparation before Pesach

To maximize our connection to *Pesach* and the Light that we receive, it is valuable to prepare our Vessel so that we can contain and maintain this energy for the whole year. This preparation involves spiritual work that is referred to as spiritual cleansing. We look inward to identify our own specific *Desire to Receive for the Self Alone*, our personal negativity. During this cleansing, we uncover what is real as opposed to illusionary in our life, enabling us to distinguish and acknowledge our true self (our soul) from our masks (our ego).

Because this process occurs in the month of Aries, we are supported by the cosmic energy that exists at this time, which makes evident all those things about ourselves that we don't want to see. In simple terms, we can see how selfish we are, how angry we are, and how very reactive we can be. This awareness comes automatically because this is the nature of Aries. We need not concentrate on a specific brand of personal garbage because all of our negativity will surface. The importance of this insight is clear: If we don't know the negativity is there, we can't get rid of it. So rather than dreading this process, it becomes an exciting, invigorating "spring cleaning" of the soul that we can embrace!

The physical work of *Pesach* is external and straightforward. We have to purge everything in our possession of *chametz* (wheat, barley, oats, rye and spelt—the common grains used in baking bread).

What is so unique about these grains and the baked goods derived from them? Why is bread one of the most common and basic staples in the world when the process of creating it is so involved? After all, we can catch a fish and cook it on pick a fruit and eat it. But to make bread, we have to harvest the wheat, separate it, grind it, make it into flour and then dough, let it rise, and finally bake it. It's a long and laborious process, indeed.

The answer to these questions can be found in the spiritual dimension. Spiritually, bread is the energy of desire. That's why it requires such an extensive and arduous process to create. Bread or baked goods expand and rise in the same way that our ego—our *Desire to Receive*—expands and is pumped up.

The kabbalists tell us to prepare for *Pesach* physically by going through our closets, our cupboards, and our pantries and clean them of any trace of grains—that is, of the *Desire to Receive*. Clean the house. Clean the car. Clean any physical object or space that could house any crumbs of Desire. But for any physical action to have meaning and connection, it requires a spiritual intention. We must clean our physical environment with the consciousness of cleansing our *Desire to Receive*, our selfish agenda. As we search for the crumbs in our couch, we meditate on seeking crumbs of negativity in the crevices of our soul. The crumbs in our soul are our jealousy, hatred, fear, judgment, need for approval, low self-esteem, and sense of entitlement. The physical cleaning is a tool to activate a spiritual process. It's not merely about spring cleaning; it's about using a physical action to stimulate an inner spiritual transformation.

FROM THE RAV

Today, people often confuse searching for the *chametz* with ordinary spring cleaning. This mirrors our confusion between inner spiritual order and external physical tidiness. Searching for the *chametz* is a matter of inner spiritual cleansing, which is needed as preparation for the holiday. Conquering our selfish desire, represented by the *chametz* consciousness, is necessary to ensure that the Light revealed on the night of the *Seder* will promote our correction process and will not be transferred to the Negative Side. We know that it is physically impossible to clean all the physical *chametz* from the house. In the blessing we recite at the time of checking, we declare that any *chametz* we miss is not to be considered. What is important is the cleansing of our inner selfish desire, not the cleaning away of bread crumbs. As we remove the *chametz* the evening before the *Seder* night, we awaken the inner spiritual process of soul-searching. We remember all the times we behaved in hurtful ways toward others. By this inner cleansing, we prepare our spiritual Vessel to download the software that will make it possible for us to connect to the Light and to correct the entire year-to-come from its root level.

CHECKING AND BURNING OF CHAMETZ

After nightfall on the 14th of *Nissan*, when at least three stars are visible in the sky we hide ten pieces of bread in our house; we then turn off the lights and search for these pieces of bread by candlelight. Remember that this search is not just to find and collect the concealed pieces of bread—the true purpose for the search is to find our negativity.

Why ten pieces of bread? Each piece connects us to the ten dimensions of the impure system. The impure system mirrors the structure of *Ten Sefirot* of the Tree of Life. Searching for and finding these ten pieces of bread represent the spiritual and metaphysical purification of our negativity and of our *Desire to Receive for the Self Alone*—the different pieces of *chametz* we find correspond to the different levels of negative energy we are clearing out. This exercise is part of the technology that destroys the precisely constructed system of negative energy replacing it with the perfected structure of positive energy of the *Desire to Share*.

FROM THE RAV

Rabbi Isaac Luria (the Ari) said that he who abstains from even a tiny bit of *chametz* over *Pesach* is ensured of not sinning [unintentionally] throughout the year. The Ari also wrote a special prayer to recite during the ritual of burning the *chametz*: "May it be your will, God, that just as I am destroying *chametz* from my home and my domain, so shall all outside forces and the spirit of impurity be removed from the Earth, and may You remove our Evil Inclination from within us and give us a heart of flesh to serve You in truth, and may all darkness and wickedness be consumed in smoke. Amen."

Before beginning the search, we say the following prayer/meditation:

בָּרוּךְ יהוה ע״ב ורבוע מ״ה אַתָּה יְהוֹוָהדֹיאהדונהי אֱלֹהֵינוּ ילה
מֶלֶךְ הָעוֹלָם אֲשֶׁר קִדְּשָׁנוּ בְּמִצְוֹתָיו וְצִוָּנוּ
עַל בִּעוּר וָחָמֵץ:

*Blessed are You, Lord, our God, King of the world, Who has sanctified
us with His commandments and obliged us to check the Chametz.*

Baruch Ata Adonai Eloheinu Melech Ha'olam Asher Kidshanu Bemitzvotav
Vetzivanu Al Bi'ur Chametz.

The letters making up these words are the instruments that transfer energy from the
impure system to the pure system. This blessing is a spiritual cable for the transfer
of metaphysical energy necessary to transform the metaphysical structure of the
Chametz (*Desire to Receive*) into the *Desire to Share*. The key to a successful transfer
is our consciousness and the internal work we do to remove our negativity and
transform our nature from the *Desire to Receive* to the *Desire to Share*.

We use a candle as a tool because the candle's flame connects us to and is an
embodiment of the *Desire to Share*.

Once the exercise of finding the ten pieces is complete, we recite
the following prayer three times:

כָּל יֹלי וַחֲמִירָא דְּאִיכָּא בִרְשׁוּתִי. דְּלָא וַחֲזִיתֵיהּ וּדְלָא
בִיעַרְתֵּיהּ, לִבְטִיל וְלֶהֱוֵי [הֶפְקֵר Add on the third time]
כְּעַפְרָא דְּאַרְעָא:

*Any Chametz that is in my possession, which I did not see or check will
be canceled and destroyed and be (abandoned) like the soil of the land.*

Kol Chamira De'ika Virshuti. Dela Chazitei Udela Vi'arteih Livtil Velehevei
(add on third time: Hefker) Ke'afra De'ar'a.

כָּל ילי וַחֲמֵץ וּשְׂאוֹר ג' מוֹוֹזין דְּאלֹהים דְּקטנוּת שֶׁיֵּשׁ בִּרְשׁוּתִי,
שֶׁלֹא רְאִיתִיו וְשֶׁלֹא בִיעַרְתִּיו, יִתְבַּטֵּל וְיִהְיֶה יהוה
[הֶפְקֵר Add on the third time] כְּעָפָר הָאָרֶץ אלֹהים דֹההין ע״ה:

This prayer is the tool we use to nullify any remaining *chametz* that we may have overlooked. As we recite the prayer out loud, we concentrate on spiritual purification.

Then the collected pieces of *chametz* are set aside until the morning.

The next morning before 10 o'clock, we burn the pieces of bread that we collected the night before. When we burn the *chametz* we are actually burning the negativity of the *Desire to Receive*. At the time of the burning, we are completely cleansing all the selfish desires that remain in our thoughts.

After we have burnt the *chametz*, we recite the following prayer three times:

כָּל יּ׳ וַחֲמִירָא דְאִיכָּא בִרְשׁוּתִי. דַּחֲזִיתֵיהּ וּדְלָא
וַחֲזִיתֵיהּ. דְּבִעַרְתֵּיהּ וּדְלָא בִיעַרְתֵּיהּ. לִבְטִיל
וּלֶהֱוֵי [הֶפְקֵר Add on the third time] כְּעַפְרָא דְאַרְעָא:

Any Chametz that is in my possession, which I see or did not see, and have checked and burnt or have not checked or burnt will be canceled and destroyed and be (abandoned) like the soil of the land.

Kol Chamira De'ika Virshuti. Dachaziteih Udela Chazitei Devi'arteih Udla Vi'arteih Livtil Velehevei (add third time: Hefker) Ke'afra De'ar'a.

The Hebrew translation:

כָּל יּ׳ וְחָמֵץ וּשְׂאוֹר ג׳ מווזין דאלהים דקטנות שֶׁיֵּשׁ בִּרְשׁוּתִי,
שֶׁרְאִיתִיו וְשֶׁלֹּא רְאִיתִיו, שֶׁבִּעַרְתִּיו וְשֶׁלֹּא בִּעַרְתִּיו
יִתְבַּטֵּל וְיִהְיֶה יּ׳ [הֶפְקֵר Add on the third time] כְּעָפָר
הָאָרֶץ אלהים דההין ע״ה:

This special meditation is to eliminate the negative side, and we scan it from right to left:

וַיֹּאמֶר יְהוָֹ֒אדנ״יאהדונהי

אילופ״ד ההי״י יווד״י ההי״י

אֶל־הַשָּׂטָן יִגְעַר יְהוָֹ֒אדנ״יאהדונהי

אילופ״ד ההי״י יוואד״י ההי״י

בְּךָ הַשָּׂטָן וְיִגְעַר יְהוָֹ֒אדנ״יאהדונהי

אילופ״ד ההא״א יוואד״ו ההא״א

בְּךָ הַבּוֹחֵר בִּירוּשָׁלָ֑ם

אילופ״ד ההה״ה יווד״ו ההה״ה

יֵשָׁהֲטוֹנֵ״ה

הֲלוֹא

אלו״ה

זֶה אוּד

ה׳ צבאות

מֻצָּל מֵאֵשׁ   אלהים דיורין ע״ה:

וְהוּא יְיֹוֹזֹד הַמְסוּגָל לְגֶרַע הַס״א.

And say the following verse three times:

לֹא־יָרֵעוּ וְלֹא־יַשְׁחִיתוּ בְּכָל בּ״ן, לכב, יבמ הַר רבוע אלהים - ה קָדְשִׁי
כִּי־מָלְאָה הָאָרֶץ אלהים דההין ע״ה דֵּעָה אֶת־יְהוָֹ֒אדנ״יאהדונהי כַּמַּיִם
לַיָּם ילי מְכַסִּים:

לאי רעו ולא ישוז יתו בכל הרק דעי כים
לאה האר צדע האת יהו הכם ימל ימם כסי מיה

*They will neither injure nor destroy in all of My sacred mountain, for
the earth will be filled with the knowledge of Hashem as water covering
the sea bed.*

Lo Yarei'u Velo Yashchitu Bechol Har Kadshi Ki Malah Ha'aretz De'a Et
Adonai Kamayim Layam Mechasim.

FROM THE RAV

The checking search for *chametz* takes place on the evening before *Pesach*, and the burning of the *chametz* takes place on the morning of *Pesach*. The checking for *chametz* and its removal is an important piece of kabbalistic technology. The burning of the *chametz* brings an end to our *Desire to Receive for the Self Alone* and removes the Angel of Death from within us.

The searching for and burning of the *chametz* is the foundation on which we install the software for the night of the *Seder*. It serves to resurrect our soul (at the *Neshamah* level) from the prison in which it has been confined—a prison of materialistic consciousness and selfish desire. The burning of the *chametz* erases the negative consciousness of the ego in preparation for the reading of the *Haggadah* and the installation of the software that can produce a new movie of our lives.

INNER ASPECT OF CHAMETZ

The kabbalists teach us that *chametz* refers to even the smallest particle of dust. This is a lesson about the importance of any action or thought, no matter how small or insignificant. If the truth be known, anything and everything we do on *Pesach* is mashu (something)—it is the insignificant speck of dust that becomes significant. Thus, anything negative we do on *Pesach* is that much more dangerous. If a person gets angry or steals during *Pesach*, it is a much more serious transgression. This teaches us that it is the insignificant "dust particle" that ruins relationships.

Because of the nature of the zodiac sign of Aries and the energy of Mars that rules over Aries, everything that happens during the week of *Pesach* is exaggerated. When the cosmic window of *Pesach* is open, our actions are magnified. So we must be extra cautious with our actions and words.

During the seven days of *Pesach*, we don't eat bread. Although the *Seder* meal provides the connection to *Pesach*, if we cannot follow all the kabbalistic technology for the week of *Pesach*, do just this one thing: Don't eat of the five proscribed grains (wheat, barley, oats, rye, and spelt) for the full seven days. This is a prescription for protecting ourselves from the effects of negativity—from wars, and disorder that come from ego, pride, and anger—for the entire year.

The *Zohar* tells us that *chametz* is considered to be like Satan, which is why we are recommended not to eat it during the week of *Pesach*. But if *chametz* compared to Satan's energy, why do we eat it during the rest of the year? What makes *Pesach* different? The answer is found in the Book of Genesis, which describes the existence of two realities: the Tree of Life Reality, and the Tree of Knowledge of Good and Evil Reality. The rest of the year, we live in the Tree of Knowledge Reality where we are influenced by the forces of both good and evil; in this reality, we are unaffected by *chametz*. During *Pesach*, however, we are connected to the Tree of Life Reality. For seven days, we virtually live in this realm. While in the realm of the perfection of the Tree of Life, we do not want to have any connection to Satan. By eating *chametz* on *Pesach*, we are drawn straight back to the Tree of Knowledge Reality, resulting in a huge missed opportunity. Who would not want to live in the Tree of Life Reality for even a day, even a week? The more we experience this reality, the easier it is for us to maintain the Tree of Life consciousness on our own for the rest of the year.

THE SEDER

The night of *Pesach* is known as the *Leil haSeder*, which means "Night of Order." On this night, we speak about miracles, and yet *seder* means "order." This reveals the kabbalistic truth that within the universe of order, miracles are the norm and in the universe of chaos, destruction is the norm. On *Leil haSeder*, we have the opportunity to transfer from the universe of chaos and destruction to the universe of order and miracles.

On *Leil haSeder*, we begin reading the *Haggadah* as slaves, but we leave the night as free men and women. No matter who we are coming in, by the end of the evening's connection, we will be free. All we need to do is just let go.

On *Pesach*, we have the power to change what the kabbalists tell us are the three most difficult destinies to change: children, life, and sustenance. The keys to unlock fate in those areas are given to us at *Pesach*.

FROM THE RAV

During the first night of *Pesach*—and only during the first night—the universe is free from the chains of destiny. Only on this night can we access the cosmic assistance needed to change and replace our movie for a better one without our having to be completely righteous human beings. Anyone can use this opportunity to activate the software in the book of connection—the *Haggadah*—to draw spiritual abundance from the hardware that is available at this time in the universe. Anyone can change his or her movie as if with a magic wand, thereby breaking free from preordained destiny. This is the whole secret of *Pesach*.

Pesach is for the universe. Everything we do on a physical level is also being done by the angels. When we drink the four cups of wine, the angels are doing the meditations. The entire universe participates in the awe and the power of *Pesach*.

The *Seder* night is the one time during the year when night is considered day and darkness is considered Light. The word "Passover" refers to the moment when God came to smite the first-born of the Egyptians and passed over the houses of the Israelites. Instead of judgment that night, the Israelites received mercy. According to Kabbalah night progresses from judgment to mercy, but on *Pesach*, night goes from mercy to judgment—and night becomes day. All of our judgments can be washed away because night is day on *Pesach*.

THE SEDER PLATE

When charged with the energy of *Pesach*, the *Seder Plate* itself and the food items placed on it become a highly sophisticated tool connecting us to the *Ten Sefirot*—the kabbalistic Tree of Life.

SHANK BONE – ZERO'A – CHESED

FROM THE RAV

Specifically, at *Pesach*, we can reveal the positive side of Mars, which is the power of rejuvenation. Mars is the planet of war. The *Desire to Receive for the Self Alone* is always the cause of any war. Mars is the channel for this consciousness, as it is responsible for the illusion of separation that prevents people from seeing the quantum connection between things. This consciousness is responsible for the physical proximity between Mars and the Earth, the realm of *Malchut*.

The ram that appeared to Abraham at Isaac's sacrifice is the ram that is revealed in the spring at Passover—the symbol of selfish desire. For this reason, Abraham the Patriarch made the connection between the sign of Aries and the planet Mars. Both represent the same consciousness—that of the *Desire to Receive for the Self Alone*—and both connect to the energy of judgment.

The world's center of judgment is Egypt. This is the reason the Egyptians chose the ram as one of their gods. The Egyptians understood that spiritual reality determines the events of the physical world. They recognized the power of Aries and knew that Aries consciousness is manifested in the physical world through the ram. They didn't worship the animal itself, but rather the spiritual energy the ram represents. The Egyptians knew how to connect through the ram to the energy of the cosmic sign of Aries, and through Aries, they controlled the revelation of judgment in the world.

The shank bone or burnt chicken neck on the *Seder* Plate is our reminder of the sacrificing of the ram by the Israelites prior to the *Pesach* event. Because the internal energy of the ram is the *Desire to Receive for the Self Alone*, we now have an opportunity to sacrifice our *Desire to Receive for the Self Alone*. To really share, we need to sacrifice our own negative characteristics. Having this consciousness activates the energy of the *Sefira* of Chesed, bringing mercy and sharing into our lives.

Abraham, Isaac's father, told the Creator that he could forsee, according to the stars, that he was not destined to have children, to which the Creator replied, "You are above the charts and the stars." Isaac's birth was the first occasion in history that the laws of the stars did not prevail. From that moment onward, we have the ability to rise above the stars' influence. The birth of Isaac was a milestone — the hold that the stars had on us was broken.

On the night of the *Seder*, the ram gives us control over the zodiac and over our physical world.

EGG – BEITZA – GEVURAH

The longer we boil an egg, the harder it becomes. The hard-boiled egg on the *Seder Plate* awakens us to our own stubbornness. The more people oppose us, the harder we become and the more entrenched in our own ideas. Our nature is to expend as much energy as possible to prove our point—to be right at all costs. We usually sacrifice the good of a situation if it serves to validate and strengthen our own position. Kabbalah teaches that a hard-boiled egg's internal energy is one of judgment, thus connecting us to the *Sefira* of *Gevurah*. The energy of judgment can break the pattern we have of clinging to our own opinions and ideas.

By eating the hard-boiled egg with the consciousness that this connection softens our stubbornness, we receive the ability to really listen to and learn from the people around us, in this way awakening the strength to let go of our own ideas and accept opposing views.

BITTER HERB – MAROR – TIFERET

The *Sefira* of *Tiferet* contains Central Column energy—the balance between Right and Left. *Maror* or raw horseradish is our connection to this energy of balance. When we eat the *Maror* at the *Seder*, we experience a "taste of death" because the *Maror* is so bitter. On the surface, *Maror* seems like a harsh tool of transformation because of its strong smell and unforgiving taste, but the longer we chew it (without swallowing it too quickly), the sweeter it becomes. This change in taste from bitter to sweet teaches us that when we experience challenges and discomfort, we can either shorten or lengthen the process through our thoughts and actions. *Pesach* gives us the opportunity to correct our reactive negative deeds of the past—from our current life and from previous lifetimes. For some of us this process of *tikkun*, or correction, is swift, while for others it takes lifetimes. If we choose to react to the challenges and try to "swallow them too quickly without chewing," we extend the process, encountering the same hardships over and over again until we finally make the correction. On the flip side, when we embrace our *tikkun* and "chew beyond the taste of death," we automatically shorten the process, bringing more spiritual balance into our lives.

FRUIT BLEND – CHAROSET – NETZACH

Our connection on the *Seder Plate* to the *Sefira* of *Netzach* is a unique blend of fruits and spices called *Charoset*. This jam-like substance was formulated by 16th century Kabbalist Rav Isaac Luria (the Ari). The ingredients of *Charoset* are hyacinth root, ginger, cinnamon, grapes, figs, pomegranates, dates, nuts, apples and quince.

Embedded in the word *Charoset*, we find the name Ruth (רות) רות, the great grandmother of King David. Moav, a man born out of an incestuous relationship between a father and daughter, was an ancestor of Ruth. Because of her ancestry Ruth could easily have chosen a path where she had no chance to bring any spiritual Light into the world. Instead, she made choices that made her the ancestor of King David, who is the seed of the Messiah. From Ruth, we learn that no matter how sordid or shameful our past may be, we can still rise to great spiritual heights the moment we make the decision to do so. When we eat the *Charoset*, we are imbued with the strength to make this choice.

PARSLEY – KARPAS – HOD

The *Karpas* (parsley) connects us to the *Sefira* of *Hod*. The letters of the word *Karpas* can be re-arranged to read: פרך ס (*Samech parech*). The word *parech*, loosely translated, means "hard work in captivity." Traditionally, we are told that the slavery and hard work that the Israelites endured involved whips, chains, and Pharaoh, who kept the Israelites enslaved in Egypt. The Torah states, however, that the Israelites had it pretty good in Egypt, so much so that after the Exodus every time things got a little rough in the desert, they begged Moses to take them back to Egypt. The Ari explains that the exile in Egypt was not physical in nature. Instead, it was a spiritual exile. As long as they were slaves in Egypt, the Israelites were victims—not accountable or responsible for their lives. If any chaos fell upon them, they did not have to look in the mirror and accept responsibility. It's much easier to be a victim (a slave) than it is to accept responsibility for life's problems. This victim mindset was the real slavery in Egypt.

The exile of the Israelites led to true freedom and control over their destiny. But with freedom and control comes responsibility—and that was an uncomfortable prospect for the Israelites. This is the spiritual significance behind the Israelites onstant complaints and desire to return to Egypt. The Israelites were trying to bdicate the responsibility. It was much easier for them to be enslaved by their go and to be victims of circumstance while their reactive nature laid all the lame for their chaos on people and events that were "out of their control."

The story of Passover is about freedom from victim-hood. The reality is that no vent is out of our control. Our reactive nature blinds us to the freedom that is ossible. It's much easier to be a slave to ignorance and remain a victim. We'd ather not have to look in the mirror and accept responsibility for every ounce of haos and hardship that befalls us. The irony is that the moment we accept this esponsibility, we hold the power of both freedom and control over the cosmos n the palm of our hand.

Through the *Karpas*, we gain the ability to become masters of our destiny. We ;ain the strength to accept the spiritual truth that we are responsible for both our ;ood fortune and our misfortune. We might ask, "How can a piece of parsley ossibly give us this enormous power of freedom?" Just as a microscopic atom ontains enough energy to vaporize an entire city, the spiritual energy of the arsley, on this one night, has the power to vaporize our reactive nature through he energy contained in the Aramaic letters of the word *Karpas*. Eating the parsley ; simply the physical action required to allow this energy to manifest.

ROMAINE LETTUCE – CHAZERET – YESOD

Chazeret or romaine lettuce on the *Seder* Plate connects us to the *Sefira* of *Yesod*. *Yesod* is a reservoir that collects all the energy from the *Sefirot* above it—the Jpper Worlds—and funnels this energy into our world of *Malchut*. Kabbalah xplains that Joseph is our spiritual connection to the *Sefira* of *Yesod*. While he vas alive, Joseph accumulated all the wealth of the world in Egypt and dispersed : throughout the land. By eating the *Chazeret*, we can access this same power to ollect all our negative traits and all the chaos that appears in our life, group these nto a single target, and wipe them out in one single shot.

SEDER PLATE – HAKE'ARA – MALCHUT

The physical plate is our connection to *Malchut*, our material world. Kabbalah eaches that King David is our link to the *Sefira* of *Malchut*. When King David was orn, he came into the world with no Light of his own and was destined to die at irth. Adam foresaw this situation and gave 70 of his 1000 years of life to King)avid so that King David could live.

The *Seder Plate* itself has no spiritual Light of its own. Its spiritual Light comes rom all the items placed on it. We, too, have no spiritual sustenance of our own n this physical world—our Light comes from the Upper Worlds. It's important o remember that nothing ever happens in this world without an opening first

occurring in the Upper Worlds. On the night of the *Seder*, we receive all ou
spiritual Light from the Upper *Sefirot* through our connection to the items on th
Seder Plate.

THE THREE MATZOT (CHOCHMAH, BINAH, AND DA'AT)

Once the *Seder Plate* is set, three *Matzot* are placed directly under it. These *Matzo*
are our link to the *Sefirot* of *Chochmah*, *Binah*, and *Da'at*. *Da'at* is unique in tha
it is not considered to be part of the *Ten Sefirot* but functions instead like a way
station, collecting the raw energy from *Keter*, *Chochmah*, and *Binah*—the Uppe
Three *Sefirot* and source of all the fulfillment and goodness that appear in ou
lives. *Da'at* then combines this collected energy into one force and transfers it t
the Lower Seven *Sefirot*.

Moses was the only human being ever to attain the level of *Da'at*. The kabbalist
say that Moses was a chariot, appearing to be half man and half angel, and tha
he achieved the status of the greatest prophet that ever lived. And the kabbalist
also teach us that the true greatness of Moses was as a man who cared for ever
single human being. Moses was willing to give of himself and to help everyon
Although he was the leader of an entire nation, he had the heart, soul, and mindse
to consider and care for the needs of each person. No matter how spirituall
elevated we become in life, we can never set ourselves too high to be out of reac
of other people—regardless of what spiritual level we think they are on. In fac
when a person reaches a high level of spirituality, care and consideration fo
others is automatic, these being the qualities that elevated them in the first plac
We can use this knowledge to measure our own spiritual level. If we think tha
we are above or more important than someone else, then we have not achieve
an elevated state of spirituality.

Matzah is made from a simple combination of wheat and water, teaching u
simplicity. Whatever we have, we need to be happy with. Generally, a person wh
has 100 of something wants 200, then wants 300 more—in other words, alway
wants more. *Matzah* is about being okay with what we have, but at the same tim
having a desire for more.

There is a story of a man who came to his teacher with a problem. For si
months, he had been preparing *Matzot*: planting the wheat, grinding it by hand
making sure no water touched the flour, hiring someone to watch the wheat—i
short, following all of the precautions and as well as the precise prescription t
make the *Matzot*. When the *Matzot* were finally ready, he put them on the table
and someone came in and stole them. He told the kabbalist, "I did all this work
and now the *Matzot* are gone." The kabbalist replied, "All the work you did is sti
here. Even though the *Matzot* you made are gone, you can use any *Matzah* now t
make the connection."

The Order of the Seder Plate
According to Rabbi Isaac Luria, (the Ari):

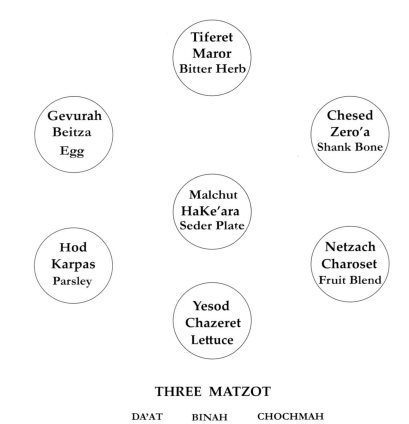

Tiferet
Maror
Bitter Herb

Gevurah
Beitza
Egg

Chesed
Zero'a
Shank Bone

Malchut
HaKe'ara
Seder Plate

Hod
Karpas
Parsley

Netzach
Charoset
Fruit Blend

Yesod
Chazeret
Lettuce

THREE MATZOT

DA'AT   BINAH   CHOCHMAH

ד   ד   ד

The Fifteen Steps Of The Seder

**Kadesh . Urchatz . Karpas . Yachatz . Magid.
Rachtza . Motzi . Matza . Maror . Korech .
Shulchan Orech. Tzafun . Barech . Halel . Nirtza.**

סדר הקערה לדעת רבינו האריז״ל:

תפארת
מרור

גבורה
ביצה

וחסד
זרוע

מלכות
הקערה

הוד
כרפס

נצח
וחרוסת

יסוד
וחזרת

שלוש מצות

דעת   בינה   וחכמה

ה   ה   ה

THE FIFTEEN STEPS OF THE SEDER

קַדֵּשׁ. וּרְחַץ. כַּרְפַּס. יַחַץ. מַגִּיד. רָחְצָה.
מוֹצִיא. מַצָּה. מָרוֹר. כּוֹרֵךְ. שֻׁלְחָן עוֹרֵךְ.
צָפוּן. בָּרֵךְ. הַלֵּל. נִרְצָה.

THE 15 STEPS OF THE SEDER

FROM THE RAV

The keyboard on our *Pesach* computer is the *Haggadah*, the *Pesach* connection book. There are 15 keys on this keyboard. Each one activates another level in the computer program that brings order and redemption to the world. The name of the levels are *Kadesh, Urchatz, Karpas, Yachatz, Magid, Rachtzah, Motzi, Matzah, Maror, Korech, Shulchan Orech, Tzafun, Barech, Halel,* and *Nirtzah.* Through meditation on these stages and the *Ten Sefirot* represented by the *Seder Plate* and the *Matzot,* we can connect to the power of *Pesach*—providing we fulfill two conditions. First, we must recognize the internal cosmic paradox: In order to receive, we must first restrict. Second, as we sit around the *Seder* table, we must understand the wider cosmic meaning of *Pesach.* On the night of the *Seder,* we have an opportunity to make a personal decision that from this moment forward, we will make every possible effort to convert the negative energy inside us to positive energy, using every opportunity to restrict. When we restrict, we transform: The negative energy is removed and we fill ourselves with Light. This is exactly what happens to those of us with the right consciousness on the night of the *Seder.*

The *Seder* gives us the opportunity to change our present situation and create order out of chaos. It allows us to break Satan's grip, end chaos, and even the score. There are 15 unique steps in the course of the *Seder* that capture the Light available to us. Each one activates another level that brings order and redemption to our lives and to the world.

STAGE ONE:

KADESH

LeShem Yichud

For the sake of unifying The Holy One, blessed be He, and His Shechinah, with fear and mercy, and with mercy and fear, to unify the name of Yud Key with Vav Key completely, in the name of all Israel, I am ready and willing to apply the connection of Kiddush and the connection of First Cup out of Four Cups, and may the pleasantness of Hashem, our God, be upon us and establish the action of our hands upon us and establish the action of our hands.

STAGE ONE: KADESH

As with the baking of bread, wine-making, too, requires an arduous process to come to fruition. First, the grapevine must be grown under controlled conditions and tended carefully until the grapes ripen. The grapes are then plucked from the vine and thrown into a press, where they are crushed. The grape's juice is then stored for fermentation. The end result is wine, which is a source of tremendous energy and spiritual power.

THE FIRST CUP OF WINE—EMANATION (ATZILUT)

We drink four cups of wine during the *Seder* to connect us to the four-letter Name of God—the Tetragrammaton—and to the four Upper Worlds of *Atzilut* (Emanation), *Bri'ah* (Creation), *Yetzirah* (Formation), and *Asiyah* (Action). The four Aramaic letters of the Tetragrammaton, יהוה, are transmitters of the spiritual forces of these Upper Worlds and bring their energy into our physical world.

LeShem Yichud

LeShem Yichud unites our thoughts and our actions with the Light and the Upper Worlds. For this reason, it precedes the prayers. Many times, we have a thought to do the right thing, but our actions contradict our original thought and intention. Throughout the *Seder*, we need to make a conscious effort to improve ourselves spiritually. *LeShem Yichud* helps keep us true to our positive thoughts and intentions, especially the day after the *Seder*.

STAGE ONE:

קַדֵּשׁ

קַדֵּשׁ - מווֹ וחכמה מאימא
גדלות א' דאו"א, יוד הי ויו הי, יוד הי ויו הי.
קטנות ב' דאו"א, אכדט"ם, אכדט"ם.
גדלות ב' דאימא, יוד הי ויו הי.

LeShem Yichud

לְשֵׁם יהוה שדי יִחוּד קוּדְשָׁא בְּרִיךְ הוּא וּשְׁכִינְתֵּיהּ (יאהדונהי) בִּדְחִילוּ
וּרְחִימוּ (יאההויהה) וּרְחִימוּ וּדְחִילוּ לְיַחֲדָא שֵׁם יהוה שדי יוד קֵי
בְּואו קֵי בְּיִחוּדָא שְׁלִים (יהוה) בְּשֵׁם יהוה שדי כָּל ילי יִשְׂרָאֵל, הִנְנִי
מוּכָן וּמְזוּמָּן לְקַיֵּים מִצְוַת קִידּוּשׁ וּמִצְוַת כּוֹס מום, אלהים רִאשׁוֹן
שֶׁל אַרְבַּע כּוֹסוֹת, וִיהִי אל נֹעַם ע"ה קס"א אֲדֹנָי כלה אֱלֹהֵינוּ ילה עָלֵינוּ
רבוע ס"ג וּמַעֲשֵׂה יָדֵינוּ יהוה אדני כּוֹנְנָה רבוע מ"ה עָלֵינוּ רבוע ס"ג וּמַעֲשֵׂה יָדֵינוּ
יהוה אדני כּוֹנְנֵהוּ:

The entire order of the *Haggadah* is about us. The first two steps are called *Kadesh* (to make holy) and *Urchatz* (to wash). We are so far off spiritually, but the Creator makes us holy; we are so filthy and dirty, but the Creator washes us. Even though *Kadesh* and *Urchatz* might not have a direct correlation with each other, for us they do, so that we can become holy and clean Vessels for the Light of the Creator.

Kabbalah teaches that when the Creator took Abraham into the land of Israel, only then did the land of Israel become holy. Abraham knew that only after he entered the land of Israel was it considered to have a special energy. Everywhere we go, even on vacation, we could be the person who brings the Light to that place. We need to feel that we are ambassadors of the Light, that we bring Light to wherever we go, and that every one of us can be like Abraham.

In the *Kiddush*, we say that *Pesach* is the time of freedom (*zeman cherutenu*). The concept of time denotes a specific moment, but freedom is about being free with no time constraints. "Time of freedom" seems to be a contradiction, but the universe is set up like that. Sometimes, the universe is set up for miracles and healing, and sometimes for chaos and destruction.

On Shabbat we start here:

(Whispering: *Then there was evening and then there was morning*)
*The sixth day. The heaven and the earth and all their troops were
complete. On the seventh day, God finished the work He did, and
on the seventh day, He ceased from all work which He did.
And God blessed the seventh day and sanctified it,
because in that day He ceased from all Its work, which
God created to act.*

On any other day we start here:

With your permission, my masters: (*everyone answers:* Lechayim)
*Blessed are You, Hashem, our God, King of the universe, Who creates
the fruit of the vine.*

*Blessed are You, Hashem, our God, King of the universe, Who has chosen
us from all nations, exalted us above all tongues, and sanctified us with it.
communications. And You, Hashem, our God, have lovingly given us:*

During the *Kiddush*, the Creator gives us *simcha* (happiness) and *sasson* (joy). We don't have
to do anything to be happy; our resting state should be happy. But unfortunately, our
resting state is usually unhappy. The reason we get depressed is because of the curtains
we have put up from the things we have done.

The Rav Isaac Luria only reached his spiritual level because of happiness. Happiness is
something that actually takes away the influence of Satan. The fact that we are happy is
like a pill that eats away at the darkness.

Both Moses and Einstein understood that time is an illusion. On a deeper level of reality
past, present, and future are really connected as one unified whole. Time is like a revolving
wheel: The same "spoke" of freedom that was at the top of the wheel some 3400 years
ago in Egypt comes around again every year at this time. Events do not pass us by, rather
we move through the wheel of time, revisiting the same opportunities each year. The only

On Shabbat we start here:

בלחש: (וַיְהִי אֶל עֶרֶב רבוע יהוה ורבוע אלהים וַיְהִי אֶל בּוֹקֶר)
יוֹם ע"ה = נגד, זן, מזבח הַשִּׁשִּׁי. וַיְכֻלּוּ ע"ב, ריבוע יהוה הַשָּׁמַיִם
י"פ טל, י"פ כוזו וְהָאָרֶץ אלהים דההין ע"ה וְכָל יל" צְבָאָם: וַיְכַל
אֱלֹהִים מום, אהיה אדני, ילה בַּיּוֹם ע"ה = נגד, זן, מזבח הַשְּׁבִיעִי
מְלַאכְתּוֹ אֲשֶׁר עָשָׂה וַיִּשְׁבֹּת בַּיּוֹם ע"ה = נגד, זן, מזבח הַשְּׁבִיעִי
מִכָּל יל" מְלַאכְתּוֹ אֲשֶׁר עָשָׂה: וַיְבָרֶךְ עסמ"ב אֱלֹהִים מום,
אהיה אדני, ילה אֶת יוֹם ע"ה = נגד, זן, מזבח הַשְּׁבִיעִי וַיְקַדֵּשׁ אֹתוֹ כִּי
בוֹ שָׁבַת מִכָּל יל" מְלַאכְתּוֹ אֲשֶׁר בָּרָא קנ"א ב"ן אֱלֹהִים מום,
אהיה אדני, ילה לַעֲשׂוֹת:

On any other day we start here:

סַבְרִי מָרָנָן: (וכולם עונים: לְחַיִּים)

בָּרוּךְ יהוה ע"ב ורבוע מ"ה אַתָּה יְהוֹוָאהּדונהי אֱלֹהֵינוּ ילה מֶלֶךְ הָעוֹלָם
בּוֹרֵא פְּרִי ע"ה אלהים דאלפין הַגָּפֶן:

בָּרוּךְ יהוה ע"ב ורבוע מ"ה אַתָּה יְהוֹוָאהּדונהי אֱלֹהֵינוּ ילה מֶלֶךְ הָעוֹלָם
אֲשֶׁר בָּחַר בָּנוּ מִכָּל יל" עָם וְרוֹמְמָנוּ מִכָּל יל" לָשׁוֹן אלהים פשוט ויודין

---

things that change are the "set decorations," which give us the illusion of a new year and a new life.

When we hear the phrase "*the time of redemption is now*" during the *Kiddush*, we are connected to the idea that there is no time or space. The word *kiddush* means "holy"—a code for the spiritual realm where all miracles, freedom, and fulfillment originate, the realm known as the *Ein Sof* (the Endless World).

The word "holy" refers to what is whole and complete, and links us to the spiritual realm of the Endless World, which is a realm of wholeness and perfection. In the Endless World, there is no space or time, leaving no room and no moments for chaos to enter. With that understanding, when we participate in the *Kiddush*, we connect to the realm of the Endless World, transcend time and space, and tap the same power of miracles, freedom, and redemption that occurred some 3400 years ago.

(on Saturday we add: *Sabbaths for rest) appointed times for gladness, feasts and times for joy,* (on Saturday we add: *this Shabbat and) this Feast of Matzot, the time of our freedom, with love, holy reading, in memorial of the Exodus from Egypt. For You have chosen and sanctified us above all peoples* (on Saturday we add: *and Sabbaths and) Your holy festivals* (on Saturday we add: *in love and favor) in gladness and joy have You granted us. Blessed are You Hashem, who sanctifies* (on Saturday we add: *the Sabbath and) Israel and the festive times.*

When *Pesach* falls on Saturday night we say Havdallah (in the following box), before we say the blessing of Shehecheyanu.

Blessed are You, Hashem, our God, King of the universe, Who has kept us alive, sustained us, and brought us to this moment.

We drink while leaning to the left.

HAVDALAH

Blessed are You, Hashem, our God, King of the universe, Who creates the illumination of the fire.

Blessed are You, Hashem, our God, King of the universe, Who differentiates between sacred and secular, between light and darkness, between Israel and the nations, and between the seventh day and the six days of action. Between the Holy Shabbat and the Holiday You differentiated.

HAVDALAH (ON SATURDAY NIGHT)

When *Pesach* falls on the Shabbat, we use the technology of *Havdalah* (differentiation) to distinguish between the two powerful forces of Shabbat and *Pesach*. This also gives us the ability to distinguish between the forces of good and evil at play in our day-to-day lives We often fall prey to the illusion that bad things are good for us and that good things are bad for us. The *Havdalah* connection helps us make the distinction between positive and

וְקִדְּשָׁנוּ בְּמִצְוֹתָיו. וַתִּתֶּן לָנוּ יְהֹוָאֲדֹנָי אֱלֹהֵינוּ

בְּאַהֲבָה (בשבת: שַׁבָּתוֹת לִמְנוּחָה וּ) מוֹעֲדִים לְשִׂמְחָה. חַגִּים

וּזְמַנִּים לְשָׂשׂוֹן. אֶת יוֹם (בשבת: הַשַּׁבָּת הַזֶּה וְאֶת יוֹם

וְחַג הַמַּצּוֹת הַזֶּה) וְאֶת יוֹם טוֹב

מִקְרָא קֹדֶשׁ הַזֶּה. זְמַן חֵרוּתֵנוּ. בְּאַהֲבָה מִקְרָא

קֹדֶשׁ. זֵכֶר לִיצִיאַת מִצְרָיִם כִּי בָנוּ בָחַרְתָּ וְאוֹתָנוּ קִדַּשְׁתָּ

מִכָּל הָעַמִּים (בשבת: וְשַׁבָּתוֹת וּ) וּמוֹעֲדֵי קָדְשֶׁךָ

בְּאַהֲבָה וּבְרָצוֹן בְּשִׂמְחָה וּבְשָׂשׂוֹן הִנְחַלְתָּנוּ.

בָּרוּךְ אַתָּה יְהֹוָאֲדֹנָי מְקַדֵּשׁ (בשבת: הַשַּׁבָּת וּ)

יִשְׂרָאֵל וְהַזְּמַנִּים:

When *Pesach* falls on Saturday night we say Havdallah (in the following box),
before we say the blessing of Shehecheyanu.

בָּרוּךְ אַתָּה יְהֹוָאֲדֹנָי אֱלֹהֵינוּ מֶלֶךְ הָעוֹלָם

שֶׁהֶחֱיָנוּ וְקִיְּמָנוּ וְהִגִּיעָנוּ לַזְּמַן הַזֶּה:

We drink while leaning to the left.

HAVDALAH

בָּרוּךְ אַתָּה יְהֹוָאֲדֹנָי אֱלֹהֵינוּ מֶלֶךְ

הָעוֹלָם בּוֹרֵא מְאוֹרֵי הָאֵשׁ:

בָּרוּךְ אַתָּה יְהֹוָאֲדֹנָי אֱלֹהֵינוּ מֶלֶךְ

הָעוֹלָם הַמַּבְדִּיל בֵּין קֹדֶשׁ לְחוֹל וּבֵין אוֹר

לְחֹשֶׁךְ וּבֵין יִשְׂרָאֵל לָעַמִּים וּבֵין

יוֹם הַשְּׁבִיעִי לְשֵׁשֶׁת יְמֵי הַמַּעֲשֶׂה. בֵּין

קְדֻשַּׁת שַׁבָּת לִקְדֻשַּׁת יוֹם טוֹב הִבְדַּלְתָּ.

negative, giving us a deeper insight and greater awareness about what is good and bad for
us in our personal life.

And between the Seventh day from the six days of action You had sanctified. And distinguished and had sanctified Your Nation, Israel, with Your sanctity. Blessed are You, Hashem, differentiating between the holiness of the Shabbat and the holiness of a festival.

STAGE TWO:

URCHATZ

We wash our hands without a blessing.

STAGE TWO: URCHATZ

The letters of *Urchatz*, when re-arranged, form the word *rotze'ach* רוצח, which means "murderer." Our hands contain the energy of judgment and negativity because they carry out our negative deeds. By pouring water over our hands, the spiritual cleansing power inherent in the water helps us destroy or "murder" all forms of negativity from ourselves and from our environment.

וְאֶת יוֹם ע״ה = נגה, זו, מוּזּוּ הַשְּׁבִיעִי מִשֵּׁשֶׁת יְמֵי הַמַּעֲשֶׂה
הִקְדַּשְׁתָּ. וְהִבְדַּלְתָּ וְהִקְדַּשְׁתָּ אֶת עַמְּךָ ה הוויות, נגמ יִשְׂרָאֵל
בִּקְדֻשָּׁתֶךָ: בָּרוּךְ יהוה ע״ב ורבוע מ״ה אַתָּה יְהֹוָאדנ׳׳איאהדונהי
הַמַּבְדִּיל בֵּין קֹדֶשׁ לְקֹדֶשׁ:

STAGE TWO:

יכוין ביוד הי מעם ע״ב.
יכוין שנכנס ג׳׳כ אור וחכמה של אימא שהוא בוחסד עולה,
שיערע הוחכמה בוחסד לעולם, והוא יה במילוי יוד הי,
שהוא שרע עם ע״ב שכבר נכנס, וז׳׳א רוחץ בה ומתמתק.
וכשתכה יוד בהי עולה רוחץ עם האותיות.

We wash our hands without a blessing.

There is an extra letter *Vav* ו in the word *urchatz*, which indicates the importance of physically washing our hands as opposed to just meditating on them. Each time we draw light, we must manifest it through a physical action—good thoughts are not enough; there needs to be a follow-through action. The act of washing our hands destroys the negative forces, whereas merely thinking about doing this will never achieve that same result.'

STAGE THREE:

KARPAS

We take a piece of celery or parsley, dip it in salt water, and bless it as follows:

Blessed are You, Hashem, our God, King of the universe, Who creates t fruit of the earth.

STAGE FOUR:

YACHATZ

STAGE THREE: KARPAS

Although parsley seems to be an insignificant vegetable, if we don't do the *Karp* connection, it's as if we have not done the *Seder.* Even the most insignificant details a important. For example, a flaw in a small seal in the rocket booster of the space shutt *Challenger* caused the whole shuttle to blow up. The most seemingly insignificant detai are often the most important. People whom we think of as insignificant have many tim become the most important ones in our lives. We should never think of anything anyone as insignificant.

According to Kabbalah, the inner essence of salt is a positive force and water embodi the energy of mercy, so when we eat the *Karpas* dipped in salt water, we sweeten a judgments that are due us as a result of our past negative deeds.

STAGE FOUR: YACHATZ

Yachatz means "to split in half." We take the middle *Matzah* of the three *Matzot* fro under the *Seder Plate* and split it in two pieces—one piece bigger than the other. Eac *Matzah* is a unique device for connecting us to the Upper Worlds. The top *Matzah* is tool to connect us to the *Sefira* of *Chochmah*, or Right Column energy. The middle *Matz* connects us to *Binah*, or Left Column energy. The bottom *Matzah* connects us to *Da'at*, Central Column energy. We are now going to use these three spiritual tools called *Matz* to help us cleanse ourselves and reprogram our life.

The smaller of the two pieces of the middle *Matzah* is then placed back between the to and bottom *Matzot.* Traditionally, the larger piece, known as the *Afikoman*, is wrappe carefully and hidden for the children to find and return to the table for the end of th meal after negotiating its value and receiving a prize.

STAGE THREE:

כַּרְפַּס

כרפס - קטנות א' דאימא דוזכמה, ומוישך עמה בינה ודעת,

אלף למד הי יוד מם,

אלף למד הה יוד מם,

אלף למד הא [אל״ף בצורת יו״י] יוד מם,

אלף למד הא [אל״ף בצורת יו״ד] יוד מם.

ונרמז בשם כרפ״ס - כר״פ עולה ע״ב בסוד אלהי״ם דיודי״ן שהוא העיקר,
מוזיצוניות הגּצוה של אימא ונכנס בר״ק דז״א והוא ס, הרי כרפ״ס.

We take a piece of celery or parsley, dip it in salt water, and bless it as follows:

בָּרוּךְ יהוה ע״ב ורבוע מ״ה **אַתָּה יְהֹוָּהֵהּיֵּאֵהֵדוּנהי אֱלֹהֵינוּ** ילה **מֶלֶךְ הָעוֹלָם בּוֹרֵא פְּרִי** ע״ה אלהים דאלפין **הָאֲדָמָה:**

STAGE FOUR:

יַחַץ

יכוין בהארת מווזין דאבא להבריות הוזיצונים. וכיון שנכנסו המווזין של אלהים
של אימא בכרפס שעולה על אלהים, ומכ״ש שיכנסו שאר אלהים פי׳ של ההין
וישל אלפין, אולי יתגבר הדין לזה צריך להאיר ממווזין של אבא, ויכוין שאלו
הם מווזין של קטנות א' פי׳ מנה״י של אימא, ומה שיכוין בהארה של אבא
הוא ה' של אלהים נוזלקת לעניין דלת לבדה והואי לבדה, וזאת ההא היא
מאלהים של בינה של אבא שהיא פנימית הוד שלו, והיא מצה אמצעית.

יחץ - הארת קטנות א' דאבא מבינה שלו,

למתק של אימא, אלהי״ם [ה' בצייור ד״י].

When we split the middle *Matzah*, we meditate to achieve the following:

1) **The ability to separate good from evil,** allowing us to recognize our good tendencies as well as our negative ones.

2) **The ability to break our Left Column** (*Desire to Receive*) **energy,** thereby gaining control over this desire. Without our *Desire to Receive*, however, we cannot receive Light from the Creator, so our aim is not to eliminate or destroy our *Desire to*

STAGE FIVE:

MAGID

Receive, but to control and transform it from a *Desire to Receive for the Self Alone* into the *Desire to Receive for the Sake of Sharing*.

3) **The ability to achieve wholeness and rejuvenation.** According to the Ari, once we have broken the middle *Matzah* into two different-sized pieces, we visualize the smaller of the two pieces to be in the shape of the letter *Dalet* (ד) and the larger piece to be in the shape of the letter *Vav* (ו). The letter *Dalet* has an inner essence of being poor, so the smaller piece of *Matzah* helps us recognize that we are a poor Vessel, that we have nothing of our own, and that everything we have is from the Light. With this consciousness, we can draw the Light of Redemption available on this night into our lives.

Rav Israel of Koznitz says that the *Matzah* is broken in two is to teach us that the only way we can connect to the Creator is if we have a broken heart. A broken heart will fix everything—there is nothing as complete as a broken heart. The bigger piece of *Matzah* (the *Afikoman*) that we hide for the children reminds us that we are all broken inside, that the world is broken, too, and that it will be the children that will bring the world back together. It is the responsibility of our generation to fix what is broken and to help elevate the consciousness of children. It is for us to take care of the children and give to them as we do when we hide the *Afikoman* for them to find.

There is a fine line between sadness and a broken heart: Sadness is the suffering, while a broken heart is the pain. Sadness is no good on its own, but combined with a broken heart; sadness is good and brings us closer to the Creator.

According to Kabbalah, we hide the *Afikoman* because we want to capture and hide the Light of Redemption that the *Matzah* gives us, for the rest of the coming year. We put the *Afikoman* to the side so that later we can have more. *Yachatz* is about the consciousness of keeping this Light for later.

Hiding the *Afikoman* is also to remind us that the revelation that happened in Egypt is only part of it; that the real "going out of Egypt" will happen when the Final Redemption comes.

When we hide the *Afikoman*, we do so with the consciousness that all of our positive actions, including giving charity, should be hidden and concealed like the *Afikoman*. Many people perform positive actions out of concern for what other people will say about them. Real charity occurs when we go outside our comfort zone and there is a true element of sacrifice, where the action is concealed without any reward or recognition for the ego. The highest form of charity is when a person gives without ever knowing

STAGE FIVE:

מַגִּיד

מַגִּיד - מווז בִּינָה מֵאִימָא.
גְּדְלוּת א דְאוּ"א, יוֹד הֵי וָאו הֵי, יוֹד הֵי וָאו הֵי.
קְטַנוּת ב דְאוּ"א, א"ם ג"ל א"ם ג"ל.
גְּדְלוּת ב דְאִימָא, יוֹד הֵי וָאו הֵי.

whom he gave and the recipient does not know who gave to him. This act of giving brings genuine blessing to the giver.

The connection to *Yachatz* helps us forget about our past positive deeds, which might otherwise make us spiritually complacent and focuses us on the next round of positive actions that we can achieve today and in the future.

STAGE FIVE: MAGID

The kabbalists have taught us that Elijah the prophet wrote the *Haggadah*. The word *Haggadah* means "saying." The *Haggadah* tells us that we are supposed to talk about going out of Egypt all the days (including the nights) of our life. The moment a person wants to have Light in his or her life, "going out of Egypt" is a promise that if we want, there is always a way back. This is a promise to even the most negative and evil of people that no matter how dark the night and no matter how low they are, they should not to give up because the "going out of Egypt" also happens at night.

Every story in the *Haggadah* is a code that conceals hidden wisdom. It is for this reason that many stories, when taken literally seem out of touch with our present-day life. When we look beyond the surface level of each story we expose the message and meaning concealed inside.

The word *magid* comes from the word "to tell," signifying the power of speech. The Ari reveals to us that the word *Pesach* is a combination of two words: *peh* and *sach* (respectively, "the mouth" and "speaks"). The Rav explains that when we recite the words of the *Haggadah*, we should meditate on the fact that just as the mouth can deliver ideas from the hidden world of the mind into this physical world, speaking the words of the *Haggadah* on this night enables us to draw all the hidden forces of life and miracles from the Upper Worlds. As we make the ideas physical—as we speak the words of the *Haggadah* with the consciousness of drawing the Light of Redemption from the Upper Worlds—we draw and manifest this energy in our lives and in the lives of the people around us.

We raise the *Seder* Plate and reveal the *Matzot*
LeShem Yichud

For the sake of unifying The Holy One, blessed be He, and His Shechinah
with fear and mercy, and with mercy and fear, to unify the name of Yu
Key with Vav Key completely, in the name of all Israel, I am ready an
willing to apply the connection of telling about the Exodus from Egyp
and may the pleasantness of Hashem, our God, be upon us, and establis
the action of our hands upon us and establish the action of our hands.

The Ari adds that the word *sach* has a numerical value of 68, the same value as the wor *chayim* (life). This shows us that *peh – sach* is also a code for "the life force that is bein revealed through the mouth." The night of the 15th of *Nissan*, the night of the *Seder*, is th one time of the year when the highest energy from the *Sefira* of *Chochmah* is flowing all th way down to *Malchut*, our physical world. This energy is called *chayim*. This is the sam force that killed the first-born of the Egyptians that night of Passover some 3400 year ago. Since the Egyptians were totally and completely connected to the Negative Side giving in to their reactive impulses, the force of life for them manifested as death. So the end of the day, our mouth and our words are the key to removing chaos. What we sa how we say it, and to whom we say it is what either creates or ends all our problems.

Why is it so important to eat, to drink, and to speak—that is, to use our mouths— throughout the *Seder*? The kabbalists teach that everything we connect to has Light withi it, so it is important to inject Light into everything we are doing. In the desert, carrying th Ark of the Covenant made the Israelites stronger. The actual power of the action the did gave them power to do it more.

The *Haggadah* tells us that in every generation, it is important for us to view ourselves and feel as i we personally are going out of Egypt. Having this mindset is what our spiritual transformatio is all about—freedom from our chaos. And when we see ourselves as personally going out o Egypt, to question whether we are the *erev rav* (mixed multitude), who died because they ha no hope, or are we the Israelites who left and actually got out of Egypt.

In every generation, there is a new understanding of the meaning of "going out of Egypt"— new consciousness that develops. The Ari had a certain consciousness; Rav Ashlag had certain consciousness, as did Rabbi Shimon. Things change but still are the same, it's a important. It is just another layer, another understanding relative to that generation.

Revealing the Matzot and the Raising of the Seder Plate

With all of the miracles that happened during *Pesach*, it would be foolish to think that th entire world was created for the reality that exists now. Obviously there is a perfection, fc

We raise the *Seder* Plate and reveal the *Matzot*

LeShem Yichud

לְשֵׁם יהוה שדי יִחוּד קוּדְשָׁא בְּרִיךְ הוּא וּשְׁכִינְתֵּיהּ ‹‹איהה יהוה›› בִּדְחִילוּ ‹‹יאההויהה›› וּרְחִימוּ וּרְחִימוּ וּדְחִילוּ ‹‹איההיוהה›› לְיַחֲדָא שֵׁם יהוה שדי יוּד כֵּ בּוֹאוּ כִּי בְּיְוֹוּדָא שְׁלִים ‹‹יהוה›› בְּשֵׁם יהוה שדי כָּל ‹‹י›› יִשְׂרָאֵל, הַרֵ מוּכָן וּמְזוּמָן לְקַיֵּם הַמִּצְוָה לְסַפֵּר בִּיצִיאַת מִצְרַיִם מצר, וִיהִי אל נֹעַ ע"ה קס"א אֲדֹנָי ללה אֱלֹהֵינוּ ילה עָלֵינוּ יהה רִיבוּע ס"ג וּמַעֲשֵׂה יָדֵינוּ יהוה אדני כּוֹנְנָ רבוע מ"ה עָלֵינוּ יהה רִיבוּע ס"ג וּמַעֲשֵׂה יָדֵינוּ יהוה אדני כּוֹנְנֵהוּ:

rselves and for the world, greater than we can comprehend for all of this to be the way it All our actions during the *Seder*, including the raising of the *Seder Plate*, are tools that tivate powerful metaphysical forces that can dramatically alter our lives for the better. he *Seder Plate* itself is our connection to the *Sefira* of *Malchut*, our physical world. *Malchut* o represents God's presence in this world, a presence known as the *Shechina*. As we raise e *Seder Plate*, we are helping to raise ourselves and the *Shechina* out of exile. The *Shechina* in exile and not in its correct place—the Temple—because of all our negative actions.

ie Rav says that there are two forms of jealousy: one where a person envies and grudges his neighbor for owning the exact same items as he himself does, and the her where a person envies his neighbor for owning what he himself does not. In the st case, the envier feels that no one else should have anything; in the second case, the vier might be motivated to acquire similar possessions, but does not wish any kind of will towards the other person.

ie first form of envy is the one that is the cause for the exile of the *Shechina*. But ienever we perform an action of sharing or restriction, overcoming our selfish nature, d do it not just for ourselves but as part of the greater whole, we open the doors r many others to overcome the same aspect of jealousy within themselves and thus gether help to end the exile.

hen we pray, it's vital to feel the pain of the *galut*—that the Shechina is in exile. The idea feeling pain is not just about *Pesach*; it concerns our daily lives as well. When we are nscious of the distance between us and the Light, our ability to draw on the power of e technology of the *Zohar*, the 72 Names of God, and the *Ana Beko'ach* is enhanced.

LeShem Yichud

LeShem Yichud unifies our thoughts and our actions. Many times we have a thought to do the right thing, but our actions are the complete opposite of our original thought

HaLachma Anya

We pour the second cup of wine.

This is the poor bread that our forefathers ate in the land of Egypt. Let all t hungry people come and eat. Let all the needy come and celebrate the Pesac This year, over here—next year, in the land of Israel. This year, slave— next year, free.

---

and intention. Dieting and exercising are prime examples. This connection unifies our thoughts and actions, and for that important reason, it precedes the prayers. This helps us to make a conscious effort to improve ourselves spiritually. *LeShem Yichud* helps keep us true to our positive thoughts and intentions, especially the day after the *Seder*.

HaLachma Anya

This particular section describes the *Matzah* as *halachma anya* (bread of affliction of tl poor man). Bread is known as a code for sustenance, so why in this case is it described the "bread of affliction?" Most people, when they run after sustenance (*parnasa*), do n elevate the sparks within the sustenance. When we chase after something we desire, v do not have certainty in the Light and in our spiritual process, so the blessings that we a destined to receive cannot be revealed. Sustenance affects the person who has it. For person who connects to and is certain of the Light of the Creator, money comes eas because the sparks of Light inherent in the money want to be elevated, and the way v continue to elevate these sparks is by sharing the Light that we get from them.

The word *lachma* (bread) comes from the word *milchama*, which means "war." During Pesa our bread (the *Matzah*) is poor, so our spiritual war is diminished. The only way to win tl war is from a place of lack. If we are totally full, there is no way we are going to win.

On *Pesach*, we gain freedom even though we don't deserve it. What's more, although v may not have come into this world with sustenance, we also gain sustenance without havil earned it. *Pesach* is the one time of the year when we can connect to and receive tl additional special Light from our personal potential "bank of Light" without earning it.

"Bread" also connects us to our ego and reactive nature. Just as bread has the pow to expand and rise, our ego has the ability to expand and motivate us to rise to gre heights in the material world. *Matzah* is bread that has no yeast and is restricted fro rising, thus making the bread of *Pesach* "poor" in terms of the *Desire to Receive for the Se Alone*. *Matzah* is best described as "bread without ego." By eating the *Matzah* with tl consciousness, we receive the power to shut down our ego so that we can free ourselv

HaLachma Anya

We pour the second cup of wine.

הָא לַחְמָא עַנְיָא דִּי אֲכָלוּ אַבְהָתָנָא בְּאַרְעָא דְמִצְרָיִם מצר. כָּל

דְּכְפִין ייתי יֵיתֵי וְיֵיכוֹל. כָּל ייתי דִּצְרִיךְ יֵיתֵי וְיִפְסַח.

הָשַׁתָּא הָכָא לְשָׁנָה אלהים פשוט ויודין הַבָּאָה בְּאַרְעָא דְיִשְׂרָאֵל

הָשַׁתָּא עַבְדֵי לְשָׁנָה אלהים פשוט ויודין הַבָּאָה בְּנֵי וְזוֹרִין:

---

rom the slavery of reactive behavior. The Creator cannot give us 100 percent fulfillment when we are absorbed by our own egos. We came into this physical world to rid ourselves f our selfish desires. Reciting this verse of *HaLachma Anya* awakens us to all the specific egative traits that we came to correct in this lifetime. "This is the Bread of poverty we te in Egypt" can be translated in spiritual terms to mean: "These are our negative traits bread) that enslave us in our day-to-day lives (Egypt)."

he word *anya* means "poor," and the *Zohar* says that the only prayers accepted into Heaven are those of the poor. Does that exclude the rich from having their prayers nswered? Absolutely not. If a rich man realizes that he could lose all his wealth in a noment and that he is not the source of his own success, he also understands that without he Creator, he is a poor man. Put another way, when we recognize that the Light is the ource of all our good fortune and financial success, Satan cannot manipulate our ego to nake us believe that we are the geniuses behind our achievements.

HaLachma anya has the same numerical value as the words *Kav Yamin* (Right Column). he energy of the Right Column is pure sharing and unconditional caring with no hidden genda, no wanting something in return. The secret to freeing ourselves from bondage is hrough the arousal of this kind of no-strings-attached caring for and sharing with others. By connecting to "bread of affliction," we can also eradicate any and all judgment we night have about our friends and enemies.

THE SECOND CUP OF WINE—CREATION (BRI'AH)

he second cup connects us both to *Hei* (ה), the second letter of the Tetragrammaton the four-letter Name of God) and to the Upper World of *Bri'ah*.

THE FOUR QUESTIONS—MA NISHTANAH

What differentiates this night from all other nights?
All other nights we may eat both bread and Matzah.
Tonight is all Matzah. All other nights we may eat all sorts
of vegetables. Tonight is all horseradish. All other nights we do
not dip even once. Tonight (we dip) twice. All other nights we
may eat either sitting (or reclining) or partying
(on cushioned chairs). Tonight all of us are reclining.

THE FOUR QUESTIONS—MA NISHTANAH

Here we ask four questions about why Passover is different from all other nights. The traditional and literal answer to these questions, as given in the *Haggadah*, is: "We were slaves in Egypt." However, this response does not have any relevance to our lives today. Kabbalah explains that the *Haggadah* is actually raising a deeper question: Why did the sages prescribe the specific actions of the *Pesach Seder* on this very night?

On the *Seder* night—and only on the *Seder* night—there is a unique window of opportunity in the cosmos. It is a time when we can break free and escape the prison of our ego. The freeing of the Israelites from Egypt that occurred some 3400 years ago was for one purpose—to create a reservoir of energy for all future generations so that we could access the power of freedom in our personal lives. Because energy never dissipates, the energy of freedom returns every year on this night. We are given an opportunity to connect to this energy through the technology of the *Haggadah*, the *Seder Plate* and everything on it as well as through the specific actions we perform during the *Seder*.

The words *ma nishtana* mean "what is different," teaching us that a part of connecting to the energy of redemption is in doing things differently. The power of Satan is doing things the same way all the time. Just by waking up at a different time each day, for example, can cause a big spiritual shift to occur, even though the action itself is not something of a spiritual nature. On the night of the *Seder*, if we behave the same way as we do all other nights of the year, this freedom from chaos cannot be achieved. It is essential that we are different during and after the *Seder*, especially when we get back into the real world: We cannot be the same person we were the day before. When we make an effort to be more tolerant and

THE FOUR QUESTIONS—MA NISHTANAH

מַה נִּשְׁתַּנָּה הַלַּיְלָה הַזֶּה מִכָּל הַלֵּילוֹת.

שֶׁבְּכָל הַלֵּילוֹת אָנוּ אוֹכְלִין חָמֵץ וּמַצָּה הַלַּיְלָה הַזֶּה כֻּלּוֹ מַצָּה:

שֶׁבְּכָל הַלֵּילוֹת אָנוּ אוֹכְלִין שְׁאָר יְרָקוֹת הַלַּיְלָה הַזֶּה כֻּלּוֹ מָרוֹר:

שֶׁבְּכָל הַלֵּילוֹת אֵין אָנוּ מַטְבִּילִין אֲפִילוּ פַּעַם אֶחָת הַלַּיְלָה הַזֶּה שְׁתֵּי פְעָמִים:

שֶׁבְּכָל הַלֵּילוֹת אָנוּ אוֹכְלִין בֵּין יוֹשְׁבִין וּבֵין מְסֻבִּין הַלַּיְלָה הַזֶּה כֻּלָּנוּ מְסֻבִּין:

---

ompassionate--not because it is morally correct, but because we know what this kind of ehaviour achieves and the freedom it brings--it gives us genuine and lasting fulfillment.

hroughout the *Haggadah*, especially starting with the *Ma Nishtana*, we are in a question-nd-answer mode because getting out of our chaos starts with asking questions. The roblem is that we are asleep. All of us are enslaved to our ego and our material existence. Ve are captives to our careers, jobs, relationships, fears, and anxieties or we are held in bondage o other people's perceptions of us. On the *Seder* night, however, the actions that we perform ossess the same power and spiritual energy that the Israelites aroused in Egypt so long ago.

t doesn't matter what kind of year we experienced previously or what level we have ttained spiritually, during *Pesach*, we are automatically elevated to a higher spiritual level. nd it's important to be cognizant that whatever positive action we do, we are doing it ot just for ourselves but also as part of the whole. One of the benefits of being in unity vith everyone at the *Seder* is that we automatically attain the level of the highest spiritual erson in the room. Thus it is in our own best interest to surround ourselves with the nost positive spiritual people possible on this particular night of the year.

Avadim Hayinu

We reveal the Matzot and say:

We were enslaved to Pharaoh in Egypt. Then Hashem, our God, took us out from there with a mighty hand and an outstretched arm. Had not The Holy One, blessed be It, taken our fathers out from Egypt, then we, our children, and our grandchildren would have remained enslaved to Pharaoh in Egypt. Even if we were all wise, understanding, experienced, and knowledgeable about the Torah, we would still need to make the connection through telling about the Exodus from Egypt. The more one tells about the Exodus, the better.

The Story of the Five Sages

Once upon a time, Rabbi Eliezer, Rabbi Yehoshua, Rabbi Elazar ben Azaryah, Rabbi Akiva, and Rabbi Tarfon were reclining (at the Seder) in

---

Avadim Hayinu

"We were slaves in Egypt and God took us out of bondage." This verse does not refer just to the Israelites back in ancient Egypt but is also a direct reference to us now. Furthermore, it teaches us that the only way a person can gain real freedom is through the power of *Pesach.*

The Ari says that only after the Israelites attained genuine spiritual freedom were they able to receive the Revelation on Mount Sinai and the state of immortality. How many of us would be willing to endure a little discomfort in order to attain true immortality? When we are willing to free ourselves from the bondage of our ego, however painful that may be for our pride, we attain immortality.

The Story of the Five Sages

Some kabbalists would not sleep the night of the *Seder*, nor throughout the entire week of *Pesach*. This was the case even as they aged and were afraid for health reasons. When they were asked why it was so hard to go to sleep during this time. Their answer was that if you had just won the lottery would you go to sleep, or would you not wait for the morning to arrive so that you could go and collect your winnings. This does not mean that we should be up all night and find it hard to sleep; it is meant for us to be as excited as those kabbalists.

AVADIM HAYINU

We reveal the Matzot and say:

עֲבָדִים הָיִינוּ לְפַרְעֹה בְּמִצְרַיִם מצר וַיּוֹצִיאֵנוּ יְהֹוָה אֱלֹהֵינוּ
מִשָּׁם יהוה שדי בְּיָד חֲזָקָה וּבִזְרֹעַ נְטוּיָה וְאִלּוּ לֹא הוֹצִיא הַקָּדוֹשׁ
בָּרוּךְ יהוה ע"ב ורבוע מ"ה הוּא אֶת אֲבוֹתֵינוּ מִמִּצְרַיִם מצר הֲרֵי אָנוּ
וּבָנֵינוּ וּבְנֵי בָנֵינוּ מְשֻׁעְבָּדִים הָיִינוּ לְפַרְעֹה בְּמִצְרַיִם מצר וַאֲפִילוּ
כֻּלָּנוּ חֲכָמִים כֻּלָּנוּ נְבוֹנִים כֻּלָּנוּ זְקֵנִים כֻּלָּנוּ יוֹדְעִים אֶת הַתּוֹרָה
מִצְוָה עָלֵינוּ ריבוע ס"ג לְסַפֵּר בִּיצִיאַת מִצְרַיִם מצר וְכָל יל הַמַּרְבֶּה
לְסַפֵּר בִּיצִיאַת מִצְרַיִם מצר הֲרֵי זֶה מְשֻׁבָּח:

THE STORY OF THE FIVE SAGES

מַעֲשֶׂה בְּרַבִּי אֱלִיעֶזֶר וְרַבִּי יְהוֹשֻׁעַ וְרַבִּי אֶלְעָזָר בֶּן עֲזַרְיָה
וְרַבִּי עֲקִיבָא וְרַבִּי טַרְפוֹן שֶׁהָיוּ מְסֻבִּין בִּבְנֵי בְרַק וְהָיוּ

When we tell the stories of the kabbalists doing certain things, it is not because we are supposed to act like them, but rather what we can learn and take from them is their excitement and appreciation.

There is a story of five kabbalists who had seen the destruction of the Second Temple with their own eyes. They had personally experienced the pain and suffering, the bloodshed and devastation. However, years after the destruction of the Second Temple they sat together to learn what they could do to end the chaos. They did not fall into the "woe is me" mindset, they simply moved on. What we can learn from them is that when challenges strike, and they will, we should not fall into the consciousness of the situation, rather we can learn from these kabbalists to accept what is or what has happened and look towards what we need to do to change the circumstances. No matter how destroyed we are, we need always look for how we can end the chaos. The destruction these kabbalists saw is like nothing that has ever existed before in the world.

Throughout the evening, they continued to discuss the *Shema* prayer, and how the word *Shema* does not refer to the physical prayer, but rather to *mesirut Nefesh* (surrendering our soul). The kabbalists spent the entire night talking about redemption until they surrendered their souls, accomplishing *mesirut Nefesh*.

Bnei Brak, telling about the Exodus all that night, until their students came and said to them: "Our teachers, it is time to read the morning Shema."

THE STORY OF RAV ELAZAR

Said Rabbi Elazar ben Azaryah: "I am like a seventy-year-old man. And yet was never privileged to have the Exodus from Egypt mentioned at nights, until Ben Zoma expounded it: 'In order that you remember the day you left Egypt all the days of your life.' 'The days of your life' refer to the days alone; while 'all the days. . .' refers also to the nights. And the sages say that 'the days of your life' refers to this world alone, while 'all the days. . .' refers also to the time of Messiah.'"

BARUCH HAMAKOM

Blessed is the Omnipresent, blessed is He. Blessed is the One Who gave the Torah to His people, Israel, blessed is He.

Everyone in this world—both the positive and the negative people we encounter—can serve as our teacher. The *Haggadah* has devoted valuable space to include the story of these five kabbalists, giving them status equal to the great holy sages, thereby teaching us that we can all learn from any and every one. The *Talmud* asks the question: "Who is smart person?" and answers: "The one who learns from every person."

THE STORY OF RAV ELAZAR

When Rav Elazar was 18 years old, he was asked to become the leader of the nation. He had a great fear that no one would respect him because of his youth, so God made him look 70 years old. The spiritual lesson behind this story concerns the power of mind over matter. What we believe, we will achieve—positive or negative.

Rav Elazar gave a discourse concerning why the Exodus story is recounted only at night. Daylight is a time when the energy of mercy permeates our universe, as apposed to the energy of judgment that prevails at night. Rav Elazar teaches us that it is during our time

מְסַפְּרִים בִּיצִיאַת מִצְרַיִם מצר יְלֹי אוֹתוֹ הַלַּיְלָה מלה עַד
שֶׁבָּאוּ תַלְמִידֵיהֶם וְאָמְרוּ לָהֶם רַבּוֹתֵינוּ הִגִּיעַ זְמַן קְרִיאַת
שְׁמַע שֶׁל שַׁחֲרִית:

THE STORY OF RAV ELAZAR

אָמַר רַבִּי אֶלְעָזָר בֶּן עֲזַרְיָה הֲרֵי אֲנִי אני, טדהד כוזו כְּבֶן שִׁבְעִים
שָׁנָה וְלֹא זָכִיתִי שֶׁתֵּאָמֵר יְצִיאַת מִצְרַיִם מצר בַּלֵּילוֹת עַד
שֶׁדְּרָשָׁהּ בֶּן זוֹמָא, שֶׁנֶּאֱמַר, לְמַעַן תִּזְכֹּר אֶת יוֹם עדה = נגד, זך, מזבח
צֵאתְךָ מֵאֶרֶץ אלהים דאלפין מִצְרַיִם מצר כֹּל יְלֹי יְמֵי וַזַּיְיךָ: יְמֵי וַזַּיְיךָ
הַיָּמִים נגד. כֹּל יְלֹי יְמֵי וַזַּיְיךָ הַלֵּילוֹת. וַחֲכָמִים אוֹמְרִים יְמֵי וַזַּיְיךָ
הָעוֹלָם הזה הו. כֹּל יְלֹי יְמֵי וַזַּיְיךָ לְהָבִיא לִימוֹת הַמָּשִׁיחַ:

BARUCH HAMAKOM

בָּרוּךְ יהוה עב ורבוע מה הַמָּקוֹם יהוה ברבוע, רפ אל בָּרוּךְ יהוה עב ורבוע מה הוא בָּרוּךְ
יהוה עב ורבוע מה שֶׁנָּתַן תּוֹרָה לְעַמּוֹ יִשְׂרָאֵל. בָּרוּךְ יהוה עב ורבוע מה הוא.

---

of darkness, when we cannot feel the Light in our lives, that our complete certainty in the Lightforce of the Creator is what will connect us back to the Light, even more so than when things are going well for us.

BARUCH HaMAKOM

With the revelation of the Torah, we were given a physical tool for connecting to the Creator in a practical way. True appreciation of this great gift of the Torah gives us the opportunity to penetrate its inner essence, to reveal the insight and guidance necessary for our spiritual transformation and growth. A student once came to the great sage Hillel and asked him to explain all the secrets of the Torah while standing on one leg. Hillel gave careful consideration to this request and then replied, "Love your neighbor as yourself. All the rest is commentary. Now go and learn."

THE FOUR SONS

There are four paths we can use when connecting to God:

There are four paths we can use when connecting to God: The Torah speak.
about four sons: A wise one, a wicked one, a simple one, and one who doe.
not know enough to raise a question.

THE WISE ONE

What does the wise son say? "What are the testimonies, decrees, an
ordinances which Hashem, our God, has commanded you?" Therefore
explain to him according to the Pesach regulations—that one may not hav
dessert after the final taste of the Pesach offering.

THE WICKED ONE

What does the wicked son say? "Of what purpose is this work to you?
He says "to you," thereby excluding himself. By excluding himself from

---

THE FOUR SONS

There are four paths we can use when connecting to God, and these paths relate to th
story of the four sons.

No matter who you are, you are made up of elements of these four children—the wis
one, the wicked one, the simple one, and the one who doesn't know how to ask. Eac
of the four sons has his own path. The only reason a child will be off his or her path i
because their parents did not believe in them. The only reason that we will be off our pat
is because no one believed in us.

THE WISE ONE

The wise son asks, "Why do we need to repeat the question and continue asking? Wh
are we repeating the answer? We are all learned people here. We know why we were take
out of Egypt; we know how it was done."

To this, the kabbalists reply, "All of this wisdom, all these answers come from the worl
that *Pesach* connects you to, the world of the Tree of Life. You may be smart, you ma

THE FOUR SONS

There are four paths we can use when connecting to God:

כְּנֶגֶד זֶן, מִזְבֵּחַ אַרְבָּעָה בָנִים דִּבְּרָה רְאֵה תוֹרָה: אֶחָד אהבה, דאגה וְזֶן חיים, בינה ע"ה. וְאֶחָד אהבה, דאגה רָשָׁע. וְאֶחָד אהבה, דאגה תָּם י"פ רבוע אהיה וְאֶחָד אהבה, דאגה שֶׁאֵינוֹ יוֹדֵעַ לִשְׁאוֹל:

THE WISE ONE

וְזֶכֶם וחיים, בינה ע"ה מָה מ"ה הוּא אוֹמֵר. מָה מ"ה הָעֵדֹת וְהַחֻקִּים וְהַמִּשְׁפָּטִים אֲשֶׁר צִוָּה פוי יְהֹוָהאדנילאהדונהי אֱלֹהֵינוּ ילה אֶתְכֶם. וְאַף אַתָּה אֱמֹר לוֹ כְּהִלְכוֹת הַפֶּסַח אֵין מַפְטִירִין אַחַר הַפֶּסַח אֲפִיקוֹמָן:

THE WICKED ONE

רָשָׁע מָה מ"ה הוּא אוֹמֵר. מָה מ"ה הָעֲבֹדָה אלהים ע"ה, מום ע"ה הַזֹּאת לָכֶם. לָכֶם וְלֹא לוֹ. וּלְפִי שֶׁהוֹצִיא אֶת עַצְמוֹ מִן הַכְּלָל כָּפַר

---

now the answers intellectually, but are you connected to wisdom? Are you connected to e Tree of Life? This is why we repeat these questions and answers every year."

o be able to connect to wisdom is about being more than a Vessel; it's about being a nannel. A Vessel is someone's genius, but what the person does with the Vessel determines 'hether he is a channel for the Light or not. Is he using his genius to change the world nd to change himself? It's about being a big Vessel versus being a big channel.

THE WICKED ONE

'he wicked son tauntingly asks, "Why do you bother with all these rites and rituals?"

'hat's the difference between this question and the one the wise son asked? The wicked on's question comes from a negative place; it is rooted in uncertainty and skepticism. The idden message in the wicked son's question is: "Nothing we do will work. Why should ny of our actions change anything?"

 great sage once said, "To questions, there are answers; but to answers, there are no nswers." The wicked person already has the negative answer in his mind. He asks his

the congregation, he denies a basic principle. Therefore, blunt his teeth [ta.
away his sharpness]. Tell him: "That is why Hashem did so for me, wh
I went out of Egypt." "For me," but not for him. Had he been there,
would not have been redeemed.

THE SIMPLE ONE

What does the simple son say? "What is this?" Tell him: "With might a
Hashem take us out of Egypt, from the house of bondage."

---

question rhetorically, as a way to put forth his negative opinions. He does not seek tru
He is not really asking a question, but is merely stating his pessimistic viewpoint
influence others and advance his own negative agenda. The underlying motivation of t
wicked person is his unwillingness to take responsibility for any of his negative action

The Ari states that the real exile in Egypt was an exile of the mind. The Egyptia
literally programmed everyone to believe that there was no Law of Cause and Effect
work in our universe. The Egyptians knew how to connect to the Light through negati
paths; their magicians, who were versed in the occult arts, would perform random ac
of black magic to highlight the lack of order in our world, proving that everything w
chance, random, uncontrollable chaos. This perspective relieves us of any responsibil
and accountability for our actions.

The Israelites were so thoroughly programmed that they did not even realize they were
slavery. For this very reason, a wicked person can never really leave Egypt—because
doesn't even realize that he is in Egypt. The wicked person is happy in his ways, ignora
to the truth that a far more fulfilling and happier life exists on a different path.

Our lesson is this: We can gain real freedom and peace of mind in our lives by realizi
that we are slaves to our reactive nature. If we think everything is fine, we will never atta
true freedom. The root of our own negativity is our inability to understand that whatev
happens to us happens for a reason. Bad things occur to awaken us to our reactive wa
The real freedom brought about by the Exodus was our new awareness of the conceal
order and the Universal Laws at work in the universe.

At the *Seder*, we are given the free will to choose how to connect to the Light. For examp.
we can utilize the electrical current in our home to provide warmth and comfort to o
family, or we can connect to this current in destructive ways by sticking our finger into
wall socket.

בְּעִקָּר. וְאַף אַתָּה הַקְהֵה אֶת שִׁנָּיו וֶאֱמוֹר לוֹ. בַּעֲבוּר זֶה עָשָׂה יְהֹוָׄאֲדֹנָׄי לִי בְּצֵאתִי מִמִּצְרַיִם מצר־ לִי וְלֹא לוֹ. אִלּוּ הָיָה שָׁם יהוה עדי לֹא הָיָה יהה נִגְאָל:

THE SIMPLE ONE:

תָּם י"פ רבוע אהיה מַה מ"ה הוּא אוֹמֵר. מַה מ"ה זֹּאת. וְאָמַרְתָּ אֵלָי בְּחֹזֶק יַד הוֹצִיאָנוּ יְהֹוָׄאֲדֹנָׄי מִמִּצְרַיִם מצר מִבֵּית ב"פ רא עֲבָדִים:

's important that when we ask questions concerning spiritual truths, we leave our preconceived notions and personal beliefs behind and open ourselves up to objectively hear the spiritual viewpoint.

THE SIMPLE ONE

The simple son asks, "Why did God have to kill all the Egyptians? Were we brought to his world to suffer? Why was there so much judgment on the Egyptians?"

The traditional answer is that the Egyptians had to pay for all their negative actions and therefore brought the plagues upon themselves. Here again, the entire story of Exodus is a code that contains a deeper spiritual significance. It is we who are the Egyptians. The Egyptians represent our own negative characteristics. When our lives are governed by our selfish impulses, we bring plagues of chaos upon ourselves.

Another frequent question is: "Why must we perform the rituals of *Pesach* every year? Why couldn't a great prophet like Moses accomplish the mission and bring peace forever?"

The answer is that Moses did not have the spiritual force of the people to further empower him. The greatest advantage of our current age is that today there are many people, both young and old, who are learning the wisdom and technology of Kabbalah and are applying it to their own lives. When we achieve a critical mass, the Final Redemption, world peace, and immortality will become the new reality.

THE ONE WHO DOES NOT KNOW HOW TO ASK

As for the one who is unable to ask, initiate the subject for him as state
"And you shall tell your son on that day: 'Because of this, Hashem did
for me, when I went out of Egypt.'"

YACHOL MEROSH CHODESH

One might think that the discussion of the Exodus commences with t
first day of the month of Nissan, but the Torah says: "You shall te
your son on that day." The expression "on that day" may mean mere
"during the daytime"; therefore, the Torah adds: "It is because of this th
Hashem did so for me when I went out of Egypt." The pronoun "this
implies something tangible; thus, "you shall tell your son" applies only whe
Matzah and Maror lie before you—at the Seder.

MITCHILAH

Originally our ancestors were idol worshipers, but now the Omnipresent he
brought us near to its service.

THE ONE WHO DOES NOT KNOW HOW TO ASK

The fourth son who doesn't know how to ask questions is connected to us because w
don't know how to open our hearts. Our inability to open our hearts is why we are i
such personal chaos and why the world looks like it does today. The *Haggadah* says: "Y
shall open for him" for the son who can't ask the question because it is hard to open ou
hearts and to love someone even though they have hurt us, or to trust even though w
have been abandoned.

Often, we ourselves don't know what to do, what to ask, or where to look for answers. Th
Zohar says: "*Open to me the eye of a needle, and I will open to thee the Supernal Gates.*" Each one o
us has a responsibility to help create the opening of the eye of a needle for all those wh
are lost in chaos. We have a responsibility to *help*—but not to preach to or coerce—famil
friends, strangers, and everyone with whom we come into contact to activate the Light o
sharing and to help create this opening. *This* is really our opportunity to share.

THE ONE WHO DOES NOT KNOW HOW TO ASK

וְשֶׁאֵינוֹ יוֹדֵעַ לִשְׁאוֹל אַתְּ פְּתַח לוֹ. שֶׁנֶּאֱמַר, וְהִגַּדְתָּ לְבִנְךָ בַּיּ
ע״ה = נגד, זן, מזבח הַהוּא לֵאמֹר בַּעֲבוּר זֶה עָשָׂה יְהֹוָֽאֲדֹנָ֥יאהדונהי
בְּצֵאתִי מִמִּצְרָיִם מצר:

YACHOL MEROSH CHODESH

יָכוֹל מֵראשׁ רִיבוע אלהים ואלהים ואלהים דיודין ע״ה וֹחֹֹדֶשׁ י״ב הויית תַּלְמוּד לוֹמַ
בַּיּוֹם ע״ה = נגד, זן, מזבח הַהוּא. אִי בַּיּוֹם ע״ה = נגד, זן, מזבח הַהוּא יָכוֹ
מִבְּעוֹד יוֹם ע״ה = נגד, זן, מזבח תַּלְמוּד לוֹמַר בַּעֲבוּר זֶה. בַּעֲבוּר זֶ
לֹא אָמַרְתִּי י״פ אדני ע״ה אֶלָּא בְּשָׁעָה מצר מ״ה שֶׁיֵּשׁ מַצָּה ע״ב ס״ג וּמָרוֹ
מֻנָּחִים לְפָנֶיךָ סמ״ב:

MITCHILAH

מִתְּחִלָּה עוֹבְדֵי עֲבוֹדָה אלהים ע״ה, מום ע״ה זָרָה הָיוּ אֲבוֹתֵינוּ. וְעַכְשָׁ
קֵרְבָנוּ הַמָּקוֹם יהוה ברבוע, ר״פ אל לַעֲבוֹדָתוֹ. שֶׁנֶּאֱמַר, וַיֹּאמֶר יְהוֹשֻׁ

YACHOL MEROSH CHODESH

he *Haggadah* asks why the Exodus did not begin on *Rosh Chodesh Nissan* (Aries), which falls on
e first day of the lunar month and includes the celebration of the New Moon. The first day
the month is the seed of the entire month. Why are we connecting to the Effect and not to
e Cause? The answer is that we need the first 14 days of *Nissan* to prepare and expand our
ernal Vessel to receive the overwhelming energy of freedom we are given at *Pesach*.

he first 12 days of *Nissan* connect us to the 12 tribes of Israel, thus giving us control
er the 12 signs of the zodiac so that no negative astrological influences can disrupt
prevent our freedom from bondage throughout the year to come. Knowledge is the
nnection: By understanding of the purpose of the first 12 days, we can make an effort
be connected to positivity and be unified with everyone participating in the *Seder*.

MITCHILAH

nd I gave Isaac to Abraham." We know from the Bible that Abraham and Sarah could not
ve children—Sarah was barren and Abraham was old. The birth of Isaac was above
ture, above the influence of the stars, and above the influence of this world.

As it is written, Joshua said to all the people: "So says Hashem, God ᵢ Israel: Your fathers always lived beyond the Euphrates River. Terach, tₕ father of Abraham, and the father of Nachor, they served other gods. Thₑ I took your father Abraham from beyond the river and led him throuₓ all the land of Canaan. I multiplied his offspring and gave him Isaac. ᵀ Isaac I gave Jacob and Esau. To Esau I gave Mount Se'ir to inherit, bᵤ Jacob and his children went down to Egypt."

BARUCH SHOMER

Blessed is that which keeps His pledge to Israel; blessed is He. For the Hoₐ One, Blessed is He, calculated the end of bondage in order to do as He saᵢ to our father Abraham at the Covenant between the parts, as it is stateₑ God said to Abraham, "Know with certainty that your offspring will ₑ aliens in a land not their own; They will serve them and they will oppreₑ them for 400 years; but also upon the nation which they shall serve wilₗ execute judgment, and afterwards they shall leave with great possessions.'

There is a story about a couple who had been married for years and yet could not conceiᵥ children of their own. The whole family went to see a kabbalist who told them that eithₑ they needed to get a divorce, as this marriage was not the path for them, or they could deciₒ to stay together without having children. Everyone cried, pleading and begging until tₕ kabbalist could not take it anymore. He left the family and went into another room wheₑ he beseeched the Creator, saying, "You can do anything; You are above nature." When tₕ kabbalist came back to the family, he told the couple that they would now conceive a chiₗ There are two realities: destiny and above destiny, where everything is possible.

The phrase *"Originally, our forefathers were idol worshippers"* is a direct reference to Abrahamₛ father, Terach, who was an idol worshipper and the world's largest idol maker. Abrahaₘ could easily have felt that because he was the son of an idol worshipper, he had no hoₚ of transforming himself. Instead, Abraham realized that he could create a path of hₑ own away from idol worship, thereby becoming not only connected with the Creator bᵤ also our channel for mercy (*Chesed*) in this world. According to Kabbalah, idol worshᵢ is the "worship" of anything outside ourselves that controls our behavior and motivatₑ us. If something or someone determines our degree of happiness or sadness, then ᵥ have surrendered control. Real freedom is about taking control of our own lives aₙ emotions and generating happiness and emotional security from within. It does not mattₑ

אֶל כָּל יכי הָעָם כֹּה הוי אָמַר יְהוָֹה אלהדאאהדונהי אֱלֹהֵי דמב, ילה יִשְׂרָאֵ
בְּעֵבֶר רבוע יהוה ורבוע אלהים הַנָּהָר יָשְׁבוּ אֲבוֹתֵיכֶם מֵעוֹלָם תֶּרַ
אֲבִי אַבְרָהָם רמייז, ווייפ אל וַאֲבִי נָחוֹר וַיַּעַבְדוּ אֱלֹהִים מום, אהיה אדני;
אֲחֵרִים: וָאֶקַּח אֶת אֲבִיכֶם אֶת אַבְרָהָם רמייז אל מֵעֵבֶר י
ורבוע אלהים הַנָּהָר וָאוֹלֵךְ אוֹתוֹ בְּכָל בין, לכב, יבמ אֶרֶץ אלהים דאלפין כְּנַ
וָאַרְבֶּה יצחק, דייפ בין אֶת זַרְעוֹ וָאֶתֶּן לוֹ אֶת יִצְחָק דייפ בין וָאֶתֵּן לְיִצְחָ
דייפ בין אֶת יַעֲקֹב זייפ יהוה, יאהדונהי אידהנויה וְאֶת עֵשָׂו. וָאֶתֵּן לְעֵשָׂו אֶ
הַר שֵׂעִיר לָרֶשֶׁת אוֹתוֹ, וְיַעֲקֹב זייפ יהוה, יאהדונהי אידהנויה וּבָנָיו יָרְ
מִצְרָיְמָה מצר:

BARUCH SHOMER

בָּרוּךְ יהוה עייב ורבוע מייה שׁוֹמֵר הַבְטָחָתוֹ לְיִשְׂרָאֵל, בָּרוּךְ יהוה עייב ור
מייה הוּא, שֶׁהַקָּדוֹשׁ בָּרוּךְ יהוה עייב ורבוע מייה הוּא וִחִשֵּׁב אֶת הַקֵּץ ּ
לַעֲשׂוֹת. כְּמָה מייה שֶׁאָמַר לְאַבְרָהָם רמייז, ווייפ אל אָבִינוּ בִּבְרִית בֵּ
הַבְּתָרִים. שֶׁנֶּאֱמַר, וַיֹּאמֶר לְאַבְרָם יָדֹע בייב מייב תֵּדַע כִּי גֵר
קנייא יִהְיֶה ייי זַרְעֲךָ בְּאֶרֶץ אלהים דאלפין לֹא לָהֶם וַעֲבָדוּם וְעִנּוּ אֹתָ
אַרְבַּע מֵאוֹת שָׁנָה: וְגַם ייל אֶת הַגּוֹי אֲשֶׁר יַעֲבֹדוּ דָן אָנֹכִי ּ
וְאַחֲרֵי כֵן יֵצְאוּ בִּרְכֻשׁ גָּדוֹל להוי, מבה, יזל, אום:

---

at happened yesterday or what our personal situation is; we can decide to make a change
our life.

BARUCH SHOMER

lessed is the One, Who keeps His promises to us" teaches us that the Lightforce of the Creator
ver changes. It is only we who create the illusion of change. When we cover a white
ht bulb with a blue cloth, the light radiates blue. But the light itself never changed; the
ange is only from our perspective—a result of our own actions. Thus, the Light of the
eator is always there to share infinite fulfillment with us. It is up to us to remove our
ious coverings, filters, and curtains. Through this connection, we get the strength to
ver compromise our spiritual growth but to remain consistent in our positive actions
d to not be concerned with other people's perceptions and opinions. We become
powered to look for ways to share and to stop our reactive impulses, regardless of the
stacles people throw in our way.

VEHI SHE'AMDAH

We now cover the Matzah, raise our cup of wine, and say:

It is this that has stood by our fathers and us. For not only one has risen again
us to annihilate us, but in every generation they rise against us to annihila
us; and the Holy One, Blessed be He, rescues us from their hands.

We lower the cup of wine, reveal the Matzah and say:

TZE ULMAD
Go and learn

What Laban the Aramean attempted to do to our father Jacob. F
Pharaoh decreed against only the males and Laban attempted to upro
everything, as it is said: "An Aramean attempted to destroy my fath
Then he descended to Egypt and sojourned there, with few people; and the
he became a nation—great, mighty, and numerous."

VEHI SHE'AMDA

The *Haggadah* talks about pain and suffering throughout history, making it clear th
nothing really changes except the name of the enemy. There is a story about a kabbali
who was constantly under attack by an anti-kabbalist. Some people came to tell t
kabbalist that this man who was always speaking against him was sick. They thought t
kabbalist would be happy, but the kabbalist was upset and told all his students to pr
without stopping for this man to get well. No one understood the kabbalist's fervor f
keeping the anti-kabbalist alive. The kabbalist prayed and fasted until his mother could
take it anymore and asked her son, "Why are you praying and fasting for this man
recovery? He does not love you. He hates you. He has only done things against you
The kabbalist replied, "Obviously, Heaven and the universe have decided I am suppose
to have an enemy. If he dies, I don't know who the new enemy will be." The truth is th
it is not about the enemy—it is about us. We need to make a spiritual change; just getti
rid of the attacker will not get rid of the problem.

Vehi she'amda means "She that stood for us," referring here to the Creator in the feminin
Kabbalah teaches us that when we speak about the female aspect of anything, we a
connecting to our world of *Malchut*, and because *Malchut* has nothing of itself, its importa
to remember that everything we get is a free gift (*matnat chiman*). No matter how much
how hard we work, all that we get is still *matnat chinam*—a free gift from the Creator.

VEHI SHE'AMDAH

We now cover the Matzah, raise our cup of wine, and say:

וְהִיא שֶׁעָמְדָה לַאֲבוֹתֵינוּ וְלָנוּ אהבה, אלהים מום, אלהים שֶׁלֹּא אֶחָד ראגה בִּלְבָד עָמַד עָלֵינוּ רִיבּוּעַ ס"ג לְכַלּוֹתֵנוּ אֶלָּא שֶׁבְּכָל ב"ן, לכבב, יבמ דּוֹר וָדוֹר ר"יו, גבורה עוֹמְדִים עָלֵינוּ רִיבּוּעַ ס"ג לְכַלּוֹתֵנוּ, וְהַקָּדוֹשׁ בָּרוּךְ יהוה ע"ב ורבו מ"ה הוּא מַצִּילֵנוּ מִיָּדָם:

We lower the cup of wine, reveal the Matzah and say:

TZE ULMAD

צֵא וּלְמַד

מַה מ"ה בִּקֵּשׁ לָבָן הָאֲרַמִּי לַעֲשׂוֹת לְיַעֲקֹב ז"פ יהוה, יאהדונהי אידהנוי אָבִינוּ. שֶׁפַּרְעֹה לֹא גָזַר אֶלָּא עַל הַזְּכָרִים וְלָבָן בִּקֵּשׁ לַעֲקוֹר אֶת הַכֹּל יל"י. שֶׁנֶּאֱמַר: אֲרַמִּי אֹבֵד אָבִי וַיֵּרֶד ר"יי מִצְרַיְמָה מ... וַיָּגָר שָׁם יהוה עד"י בִּמְתֵי מְעָט וַיְהִי אל שָׁם יהוה עד"י לְגוֹי גָדוֹל להוו, מבה, יזל, אום עָצוּם וָרָב ע"ב ורבוע מ"ה:

TZE ULMAD

aac, the son of Abraham the Patriarch, had two sons, Esau and Jacob. In the Torah story,
e learn that their uncle Laban had two daughters, Rachel and Leah. Rachel was destined
 marry Jacob, while Leah was destined to marry Esau. According to this marriage plan,
achel would then give birth to the 12 tribes. Laban wanted to uproot everything. He
d Leah marry Jacob in the hopes that the 12 tribes would never be born and that we'd
ver attain control over the 12 signs of the zodiac and would thus remain slaves to the
fluence of the 12 constellations. We learn from this story that no matter how much an
il person schemes, Light always overcomes darkness. Both Rachel and Leah ended up
arrying Jacob, and the 12 tribes were born anyway.

 matter how dark things appear to be, we can change it. Plans may change, but the
tcome will always be positive. We also gain a measure of control over the 12 signs of
e zodiac simply by connecting to this section of *Tze Ulmad*.

Vayered Mitzrayimah

"Then he descended to Egypt—compelled by Divine decree. He sojourne[d] there." This teaches that our father Jacob did not descend to Egypt to settl[e] but only to sojourn temporarily, as it says: "They (the sons of Jacob) said [to] Pharaoh, 'We have come to sojourn in this land because there is no pastu[re] for the flocks of your servants, because the famine is severe in the land o[f] Canaan. And now, please let your servants dwell in the land of Goshen.'"

Bimtei Me'at

They descended with few people, as it is written: "With seventy persons yo[ur] forefathers descended to Egypt, and now Hashem, your God, has made yo[u] as numerous as the stars of heaven."

Veyhisham

There he became a nation. This teaches that the Israelites were distincti[ve] there. Great and mighty was the nation, as it says: "And the children o[f]

Vayered Mitzrayimah

The literal explanation of *Vayered Mitzrayimah* tells us that Jacob traveled down into Egyp[t] as a captive by virtue of an order issued by the word of God. Kabbalist Rav Naftali Ts[vi] of Rupshitz explains the spiritual meaning: "Word of God" is a code for the sacred wor[d] of the Torah. "Egypt" is a code for a person's own negativity. "Jacob" is a code signifyi[ng] all the souls of Israel. Jacob went into "Egypt" to arouse the Light of the Creator so th[at] he could defeat his own reactive nature. His purpose was to set up the spiritual framewo[rk] that would pave the way for the Revelation of the Torah on Mount Sinai some tw[o] and a half centuries later. If Jacob had not embarked on this perilous journey into t[he] negativity, there would have been no way for the Torah to be revealed.

Bimtei Me'at

This section states: *"Seventy people accompanied Jacob into Egypt, but now they are many."* Eac[h] of these 70 people represented one of the 70 nations of the world. These 70 people we[re] responsible for giving their spiritual Light and sustenance to their respective nations. Th[e] phrase *"but now they are many"* is about the transference of responsibility. Each person [a]

VAYERED MITZRAYIMAH

וַיֵּרֶד ר״י מִצְרַיְמָה מ״צר אָנוּס עַל פִּי הַדִּבּוּר ר״ו, גבורה וַיֵּגֶר קס״א ב״ן
שָׁם יהוה שדי, מְלַמֵּד שֶׁלֹּא יָרַד יַעֲקֹב ז״פ יהוה, יאהדונהי אידהנויה אָבִינוּ
לְהִשְׁתַּקֵּעַ בְּמִצְרַיִם מ״צר אֶלָּא לָגוּר ד״פ ב״ן ע״ה שָׁם יהוה שדי שֶׁנֶּאֱמַר,
וַיֹּאמְרוּ אֶל פַּרְעֹה לָגוּר ד״פ ב״ן ע״ה בָּאָרֶץ אלהים דאלפין בָּאנוּ כִּי אֵין
מִרְעֶה רעה לַצֹּאן מלוי אהיה דיודין ע״ה אֲשֶׁר לַעֲבָדֶיךָ כִּי כָבֵד הָרָעָב ע״ה
בָּאָרֶץ אלהים דאלפין כְּנָעַן וְעַתָּה יֵשְׁבוּ נָא עֲבָדֶיךָ בְּאֶרֶץ
גֹּשֶׁן: אלהים דאלפין

BIMTEI ME'AT

בִּמְתֵי מְעָט, כְּמָה מ״ה שֶׁנֶּאֱמַר, בְּשִׁבְעִים נֶפֶשׁ יָרְדוּ אֲבֹתֶיךָ
מִצְרַיְמָה מ״צר וְעַתָּה שָׂמְךָ יְהֹוָאדנילאהדונהי אֱלֹהֶיךָ ילה כְּכוֹכְבֵי
הַשָּׁמַיִם י״פ טל, י״פ כוזו לָרֹב ע״ב ורבוע מ״ה:

VEYHISHAM

וַיְהִי אל שָׁם יהוה שדי לְגוֹי, מְלַמֵּד שֶׁהָיוּ יִשְׂרָאֵל מְצֻיָּנִים שָׁם יהוה
שדי: גָּדוֹל להוו, מבה, יזל, אום עָצוּם, כְּמָה מ״ה שֶׁנֶּאֱמַר, וּבְנֵי יִשְׂרָאֵל

---

he planet would now be responsible for making his or her own connection to the Light. With this personal responsibility comes global responsibility. When the destruction of he Temple occurred, it became necessary for each person to build and place his or her wn "rock" back in the Temple for the Temple to be reconstructed. We can achieve this bjective only through our personal correction and spiritual transformation. If one places heavy rock on top of a weak rock, the weaker rock collapses and the Final Temple will ever be built. What causes this heaviness? Ego. All of us, whether we are a great and oly person or a factory worker, are equal in the eyes of the Creator. If we keep this onsciousness of equality, without any ego, our own rock will stand solid and firm with ll the other rocks on top of it and below it. This will lead to the appearance of the Final emple.

VAYEHI SHAM

Vhen the Israelites built the Temple, there was a crooked stone, all misshapen and nperfect, that was brought to them. They rejected it and threw it to one side. At the

Israel were fruitful, increased greatly, multiplied, and became very, very mighty; and the land was filled with them."

VaRav

As it says, they were numerous: "I made you as numerous as the plants of the field; you grew and developed, and became charming, beautiful of figure and your hair grew long, but you were naked and bare. And I passed over you and saw you rolling in your blood and I said to you: 'Through your blood shall you live.' The Egyptians did evil to us, and afflicted us, and imposed hard labor upon us."

Vayare'u

As it is stated, the Egyptians did evil to us: "Let us deal with them wiser, lest they multiply and, if we happen to be at war, they may join our enemies and fight against us and then leave the country."

---

end when there was a space for only one more stone, nothing seemed to fit. Someone suggested that they try the disgusting stone. They placed it in the space and it fit. It is the imperfect people who will bring about the Final Redemption. It is not up to the spiritual ones; it is up to us—the ones with the garbage—to end chaos.

VaRav

The physical words of the Torah are not to be taken literally; rather, they are a code. The kabbalists reveal that the importance of the Torah is not in the words themselves but in the inner meaning of each word, as revealed by the *Talmud*, the *Midrash*, and the *Zohar*. The *Zohar* deciphers this code. This connection helps us decipher the spiritual secrets of the Torah as well as the spiritual secrets of our own life so that we can see the spiritual laws at work in our life—the order beneath the chaos.

Vayare'u

The word *vayare'u* comes from the word *re'a*, which means "friend." All too often, the Negative Side becomes our friend. Satan makes negative actions appear likable or friendly to us. In the Torah story of Esau coming to Jacob, Esau had intended to bite Jacob in the neck but instead gave him a kiss. Esau's bite was a kiss. Getting kissed by a wicked

פָּרוּ וַיִּשְׁרְצוּ וַיִּרְבּוּ וַיַּעַצְמוּ בִּמְאֹד מ״ה מְאֹד מ״ה וַתִּמָּלֵא הָאָרֶ
אלהים דההין ע״ה אֹתָם:

VaRav

וָרָב ע״ב ורבוע מ״ה, כְּמָה מ״ה שֶׁנֶּאֱמַר, רְבָבָה כְּצֶמַח הַשָּׂדֶה שד
נְתַתִּיךְ וַתִּרְבִּי וַתִּגְדְּלִי וַתָּבֹאִי בַּעֲדִי עֲדָיִים עֲדָיִם שָׁדַיִם נָכֹנוּ וּשְׂעָרֵךְ
צִמֵּחַ וְאַתְּ עֵרֹם וְעֶרְיָה: וָאֶעֱבֹר עָלַיִךְ רבוע מ״ה וָאֶרְאֵךְ מִתְבּוֹסֶסֶת
בְּדָמָיִךְ וָאֹמַר לָךְ בְּדָמַיִךְ חֲיִי וָאֹמַר לָךְ בְּדָמַיִךְ חֲיִי: וַיָּרֵעוּ אֹתָ
הַמִּצְרִים מצר וַיְעַנּוּנוּ וַיִּתְּנוּ עָלֵינוּ ריבוע ס״ג עֲבֹדָה קָשָׁה:

Vayare'u

וַיָּרֵעוּ אֹתָנוּ הַמִּצְרִים מצר, כְּמָה מ״ה שֶׁנֶּאֱמַר, הָבָה נִתְחַכְּמָה
לוֹ פֶּן יִרְבֶּה יהה וְהָיָה כִּי תִקְרֶאנָה מִלְחָמָה וְנוֹסַף גַּם י
הוּא עַל שֹׂנְאֵינוּ וְנִלְחַם בָּנוּ וְעָלָה מִן הָאָרֶץ אלהים דההין ע״ה:

---

erson is getting smitten by them. One of the tricks the Egyptians employed in Egypt
as to try to make the Israelites their friends. There are people we are not supposed to
e friends with. Our power is enhanced when we are able to separate ourselves from the
eople who bring us down.

here is yet another aspect to the word "friend." Every time we begin a new relationship,
's important to ask ourselves, "What do we really want from this relationship? Is it merely
fulfill our own ego and *Desire to Receive*?" It might seem cool to hang out with certain
eople, but all too often Satan has a direct hand in this kind of friendship. Fulfilling
nd lasting relationships are based on a mutual desire to reveal spiritual Light and bring
ositive energy into our world, not in gratification of the ego. Real friends help each other
row spiritually. When we associate with the wrong people, we can end up in trouble. This
ection of *Vayare'u* takes away the power of Satan to influence us to befriend people for
l the wrong reasons.

VAYE'ANUNU

As it is stated, they afflicted us: "They let taskmasters over them in orde
to oppress them with their burdens; and they built Pithom and Ra'amses a
treasure cities for Pharaoh."

VAYITNU

As it is stated, they imposed hard labor upon us: "And the Egyptian
subjugated the children of Israel with hard labor. We cried out to Hashem
our forefathers' God; and Hashem heard our cry and saw our deficienc
our trouble and our oppression."

VANITZAK

We cried out to Hashem, our forefathers' God, as it is stated: "During thos
many days, the king of Egypt died, and the children of Israel sighed because o
the servitude and cried; and the cry because of the servitude rose up to God."

VAYE'ANUNU

This paragraph begins in the plural and ends in the singular. The kabbalists explain tha
the plural refers to the people in Egypt who were in bondage. The singular relates t
the Lightforce of the Creator inside each person, which was also held in bondage. B
remaining in bondage, we imprison the Creator's Light within us, preventing this Ligh
from being revealed in our lives. Once we are become aware of this fact, we receive th
energy to seek our own freedom for the purpose of sharing our Light with others.

VAYITNU

Vayitnu says: "They gave us hard work." We know from the Torah that every time the Israelite
encountered hardships in the desert, they pleaded with Moses to take them back to Egyp
thus prompting the question: "How difficult could it really have been for them in Egypt?"

The *Zohar* explains that "slavery" for the Israelites was a slavery of the soul and mind
Because the Egyptians bombarded the Israelites with black magic and negative thought
and fed their egos, the Israelites lived without any regard for the spiritual consequence
of their behavior. The concept of spiritual Light never entered the equation. Freedor

VAYE'ANUNU

וַיְעַנּוּנוּ, כְּמָה מ״ה שֶׁנֶּאֱמַר, וַיָּשִׂימוּ עָלָיו שָׂרֵי מִסִּים לְמַעַן עַנֹּ
בְּסִבְלֹתָם וַיִּבֶן עָרֵי זחזור, ערי, סנדלפו"ן מִסְכְּנוֹת לְפַרְעֹה אֶת פִּתֹ
וְאֶת רַעַמְסֵס:

VAYITNU

וַיִּתְּנוּ עָלֵינוּ ריבוע ס״ג עֲבוֹדָה קָשָׁה, כְּמָה מ״ה שֶׁנֶּאֱמַר, וַיַּעֲבִ
מִצְרַיִם מצר אֶת בְּנֵי יִשְׂרָאֵל בְּפָרֶךְ: וַנִּצְעַק אֶל יְהֹוָֽאדנילאהדונהי
אֱלֹהֵי דמב, ילה אֲבֹתֵינוּ וַיִּשְׁמַע יְהֹוָֽאדנילאהדונהי אֶת קֹלֵנוּ וַיַּרְא אלף כו
יהוה אֶת עָנְיֵנוּ וְאֶת עֲמָלֵנוּ וְאֶת לַחֲצֵנוּ:

VANITZAK

וַנִּצְעַק אֶל יְהֹוָֽאדנילאהדונהי אֱלֹהֵי דמב, ילה אֲבֹתֵינוּ, כְּמָה מ״ה שֶׁנֶּאֱמ
וַיְהִי אל בַּיָּמִים נלך הָרַבִּים הָהֵם וַיָּמָת מֶלֶךְ מִצְרַיִם מצר וַיֵּאָנְחוּ בְ
יִשְׂרָאֵל מִן הָעֲבֹדָה וַיִּזְעָקוּ וַתַּעַל שַׁוְעָתָם אֶל הָאֱלֹהִים מום, אה
אדני; ילה מִן הָעֲבֹדָה:

---

eans liberation from negative thoughts and limited consciousness that confine us to
ch a narrow view of life and hide all that life can offer us.

VANITSAK

Ve screamed to God and He listened." From this statement, it seems that God listens only to
ose who scream. Must we suffer to the point of screaming aloud before we finally receive
 answer? Does God listen to some screams but not to others? The word "scream" refers
 a scream of recognition that occurs within each one of us. God can help us only if we
nuinely ask for help, and before we can ask for God's help, we first have to see that our
vn negativity has led us into chaos. And second admit to ourselves that we, on our own,
nnot achieve any control or positive change without the Light of the Creator.

anitsak is talking about our desire. There are different spiritual levels to reach God.
:ople who feel they are far away from the Creator can pray. There are those, however,
ho feel that they can't even talk to the Creator at all, that they are so far away from the
reator that they don't even think they can pray. But they need to know that they can.
ne way to get away from Satan is to ask the Creator for help.

Vayishma

And Hashem heard our cry as it is stated:

"God heard their sigh, and God recalled its covenant with Abraham, wi *Isaac, and with Jacob."*

Vayar

Hashem saw our deficiency—that is, the disruption of family life. As it stated: "God saw the children of Israel and God knew."

Ve'et Amaleinu

And our trouble, which refers to the children. As it is stated: "Every son th. is born, you shall cast into the river, but every daughter you shall let live."

Vayishma

"And God listened." The reason most of us feel that our prayers go unanswered is becau we do not know how to ignite them. Most prayers are switched on through the energ of Abraham, Isaac, and Jacob. The forces of energy concealed within the letters of th patriarchs' names serve as the ignition keys necessary to power our prayers. Throug Abraham, Isaac, and Jacob, we are able to thrust our prayers into the Upper Worlds.

It is said that the Baal Shem Tov, a great 18th century kabbalist, had a secret place in th forest where he would go each day to pray. This location was quite powerful, providir the Baal Shem Tov with a direct connection to the Creator. One of the students of th Baal Shem Tov came to pray to the Creator and said, "I do not know the secret locatic where my holy master prays each day, but I do know the secret words, and I know th forest in which he prays. Therefore, please accept my prayer." His prayers were accepte Another student came to pray to God and said, "I do not know the secret words of n master, nor do I know the location of his prayers, but I do know a man who knows th forest in which my master prays. Please accept my prayer on their merit." His praye were answered.

By mentioning the names of Abraham, Isaac, and Jacob in our prayers, we are asking th Creator to accept our prayers on the merit of these great patriarchs.

Vayishma

וַיִּשְׁמַע יְהֹוָ֙הֱאֱהֱהֹיֵאהדונהי אֶת קֹלֵנוּ, כְּמָה מ"ה שֶׁנֶּאֱמַר,
וַיִּשְׁמַע אֱלֹהִים מום, אהיה אֶת נַאֲקָתָם וַיִּזְכֹּר אֱלֹהִים מום, אהיה
אֲדֹנִי; ילה אֶת בְּרִיתוֹ אֶת אַבְרָהָם רמ"ח, וז"פ אל אֶת יִצְחָק ד"פ בן וְאֶת
יַעֲקֹב ד"פ יהוה, יאהדונהי אידהנויה:

Vayar

וַיַּרְא אלף למד יהוה אֶת עָנְיֵנוּ, זוֹ פְּרִישׁוּת דֶּרֶךְ ב"פ יב"ק אֶרֶץ אלהים
דאלפין· כְּמָה מ"ה שֶׁנֶּאֱמַר, וַיַּרְא אלף למד יהוה אֱלֹהִים מום, אהיה אדני; ילה אֶת
בְּנֵי יִשְׂרָאֵל וַיֵּדַע ב"פ מ"ב אֱלֹהִים מום, אהיה אדני; ילה:

Ve'et amaleinu

וְאֶת עֲמָלֵנוּ, אֵלּוּ הַבָּנִים· כְּמָה מ"ה שֶׁנֶּאֱמַר, וַיְצַו פַּרְעֹה
לְכָל יה אדני עַמּוֹ לֵאמֹר כָּל ילי הַבֵּן הַיִּלּוֹד הַיְאֹרָה
תַּשְׁלִיכֻהוּ וְכָל ילי הַבַּת תְּחַיּוּן:

Vayar

"And the Creator saw our affliction" refers to a spiritual consciousness of feeling the pain of others. When the Creator sees the pain of the people, it is as if the Creator is experiencing the same amount of pain in the same way that a parent feels the pain of a child.

If a friend or acquaintance of ours broke an arm, would we really feel the same pain in our arm? This is the spiritual level we are striving for. According to Kabbalah, all the souls of humanity descended from one unified soul, so when we strive to feel the pain of others, it's not because it is a nice, spiritual thing to do. The real reason we are doing so is because every person is actually a part of each one of us on a deeper level of reality. When we have a cut on our arm, our entire body reacts and tries to heal it. The same principle is at work here.

Ve'et Amaleinu

It is important to teach our children the spiritual lessons of life because whether we know it or not, they will follow the path we set for them. Even while they sleep, our children are

Ve'et Lachatzenu

And our oppression, which refers to verbal pressure, as it is stated: "And I have seen how the Egyptians are oppressing them." "Hashem brought us out of Egypt with a mighty hand and with an outstretched arm, with great awe, with signs and wonders."

Vayotzi'enu

And God took us out of Egypt—not through an angel, not through a seraph, and not through a messenger. But the Holy One, Blessed be He, in Its glory and by Itself, As it says: "I will pass through the land of Egypt on that night; I will slay all the firstborn in the land of Egypt from man to beast; and upon all the gods of Egypt I will execute judgment; I, God."

Ve'avarti

"I will pass through the land of Egypt on that night," not "I and an angel." "I will slay all the firstborn in the land of Egypt," not "I and a

---

affected by our spiritual actions. The Ari, in the *Gate of Reincarnation*, explains that part of a person's soul comes from the mother and part comes from the father, thereby creating an unseen spiritual link between both parents and the child. As parents striving to teach our children these life lessons, it's not about "do-as-I-say-but-not-as-I-do"—it's through our actions and our example that we will be successful.

Ve'et Lachatzenu

The sages explain that *Ve'et Lachatzenu* is about "our pressure"—the force to motivate spiritual transformation. Such pressure can be self-imposed, such as when we choose to shut down our reactive impulses, or it can come from difficult external circumstances. Being held in bondage in Egypt was reactive pressure designed to provoke change through pain. Rav Ashlag teaches that these two paths are always available to us. *Ve'et Lachatzenu* gives us the strength and awareness to always recognize and choose the proactive path and to avoid the path of torment and suffering.

Vayotzi'enu

"The Creator freed us in Egypt." This opportunity for freedom from slavery occurs only once a year—at *Pesach*. Since our slavery is the root of all the chaos in our life, we can't afford

Ve'et Lachatzenu

וְאֶת לַחֲצֵנוּ, זוֹ הַדְּחַק. כְּמָה מ״ה שֶׁנֶּאֱמַר, וְגַם יג״ל רָאִיתִי אֶת
הַלַּחַץ אֲשֶׁר מִצְרַיִם מצר לֹחֲצִים אֹתָם: וַיּוֹצִאֵנוּ יְהוָֹה
מִמִּצְרַיִם מצר בְּיָד חֲזָקָה וּבִזְרֹעַ נְטוּיָה וּבְמֹרָא גָּדֹל לְהוּ, מבה, יזל, או
וּבְאֹתוֹת וּבְמֹפְתִים:

Vayotzi'enu

וַיּוֹצִאֵנוּ יְהוָֹה אלהינו מִמִּצְרַיִם מצר, לֹא עַל יְדֵי מַלְאָךְ יאהדונהי
וְלֹא עַל יְדֵי שָׂרָף וְלֹא עַל יְדֵי שָׁלִיחַ. אֶלָּא הַקָּדוֹשׁ בָּרוּךְ יהו
ע״ב ורבוע מ״ה הוּא בִּכְבוֹדוֹ וּבְעַצְמוֹ. שֶׁנֶּאֱמַר, וְעָבַרְתִּי בָאָרֶץ אלהי
דאלפין מִצְרַיִם מצר בַּלַּיְלָה מלה הַזֶּה והו וְהִכֵּיתִי כָל ילי בְּכוֹר בְּאֶרֶץ
אלהים דאלפין מִצְרַיִם מצר מֵאָדָם מ״ה וְעַד בְּהֵמָה ב״ן, לכב, יבמ וּבְכָל ב
לכב, יבמ אֱלֹהֵי דמב, ילה מִצְרַיִם מצר אֶעֱשֶׂה שְׁפָטִים אֲנִי אני, טדה״ד כוז
יְהוָֹה:

Ve'avarti

וְעָבַרְתִּי בָאָרֶץ אלהים דאלפין מִצְרַיִם מצר בַּלַּיְלָה מלה הַזֶּה והו, אֲנִי
אני, טדה״ד כוז״ו וְלֹא מַלְאָךְ יאהדונהי. וְהִכֵּיתִי כָל ילי בְּכוֹר בְּאֶרֶץ

---

o waste this opportunity. Normally, the Lightforce works through intermediaries such
s Abraham, Isaac, and Jacob, or the angels, but on *Pesach*, we have a direct connection.
Awakening an appreciation for this direct connection to the Creator helps to preserve it.
While it's human nature to appreciate something only after we have lost it, this section
helps prevent that from happening.

Ve'avarti

"*The Angel of Death passed through Egypt during this night and killed all the first-born males.*" Taken
literally, this seems cruel, but the spiritual meaning hidden inside this verse concerns the
Universal Law of Cause and Effect. When a person plugs a lamp into a wall socket
and turns it on, light from the bulb fills the room. The electricity from the socket is

seraph"; "And upon all the gods of Egypt will I execute judgments," no
"I and the messenger." "I, Hashem," not any other.

BeYad Chazakah

With a mighty hand which refers to the pestilence, as it is stated: "Behold
the hand of Hashem shall strike your cattle which are in the field, th
horses, the donkeys, the camels, and the sheep"—a very severe pestilence.

Uvizro'a

And with an outstretched arm, which refers to the sword, as it is stated
"His drawn sword in his hand, outstretched over Jerusalem."

Uvmora

And with great awe: This is the revelation of the Shechinah. As it n
stated, "Has God ever attempted to take unto Itself a nation from th

---

considered to be a positive and productive force. If the same person sticks his finger into the same socket and gets electrocuted, should we say that the electrical current punished the individual? Of course not. Did the nature of the electricity change in the second scenario? No. What changed was the way the person connected to the energy.

The Light of the Creator works in the same manner. If we behave proactively, with love and concern for others, this force generates Light in our lives. If we abuse others and are reactive, we receive a jolt and a shock. Because of the Law of Cause and Effect, the cosmos works like a mirror, so when the Egyptians swore to massacre the first-born of the Israelites, their intention rebounded on them and they received the same back. The purpose of the Law of Cause and Effect is to allow us the free will to change.

BeYad Chazaka

Kabbalistically, there are three "hands," or energy forces, at work in the cosmos. One is called the Big Hand (*Yad haGedola*), which is Right Column energy. We connect to the Big Hand through the Splitting of the Red Sea. The second hand is called the Strong Hand (*Yad haChazaka*), which is Left Column energy and connects to immortality. We connect to the Left Column throughout the *Haggadah*. The third hand is called the Uplifted Hand

אלהים דאלפין **מִצְרַיִם** מצר **אֲנִי** אני, טדה״ד כוז״ו **וְלֹא שָׂרָף. וּבְכָל** ב״ן, לב

יבם **אֱלֹהֵי** דמב, ילה **מִצְרַיִם** מצר **אֶעֱשֶׂה שְׁפָטִים אֲנִי** אני, טדה״ד כו

וְלֹא הַשָּׁלִיחַ. אֲנִי אני, טדה״ד כוז״ו **יְהֹוָה**אדנ״י **אֲנִי** אני, טדה״ד כוז״ו **הוּ**

וְלֹא אַחֵר:

BeYad Chazakah

בְּיָד וְחֲזָקָה, זוֹ הַדֶּבֶר ראה**. כְּמָה שֶׁנֶּאֱמַר, הִנֵּה** מ״ה יה **יַד יְהֹוָה**אדני

הוֹיָה יהוה **בְּמִקְנְךָ אֲשֶׁר בַּשָּׂדֶה בַּסּוּסִים בַּחֲמֹרִים בַּגְּמַלִּים בַּבָּקָר**

וּבַצֹּאן דֶּבֶר ראה **כָּבֵד מְאֹד** מ״ה**:**

Uvizro'a

וּבִזְרֹעַ נְטוּיָה, זוֹ הַחֶרֶב רבוע ס״ג ורבוע אהיה**. כְּמָה שֶׁנֶּאֱמַר, וְחַרְבּוֹ**

רי״ו, גבורה **שְׁלוּפָה בְּיָדוֹ נְטוּיָה עַל יְרוּשָׁלָיִם.**

Uvmora

וּבְמוֹרָא גָּדוֹל להו, מבה, יזל, אום, **זוֹ גִּלּוּי שְׁכִינָה, א** כְּמָה שֶׁנֶּאֱמַר, **אוֹ**

הֲנִסָּה אֱלֹהִים מום, אהיה אדנ״י; ילה **לָבוֹא לָקַחַת לוֹ גוֹי מִקֶּרֶב גּוֹי בְּמַסֹּ**

Yad Rama), which is Central Column energy. The Exodus from Egypt occurred through
energy of Central Column, the Uplifted Hand.

Uvizro'a

The phrase "*Satan's sword is outstretched over Jerusalem to destroy it*" teaches us that on the
original night of *Pesach* some 3400 years ago, we did not completely finish our spiritual
work. When we think our spiritual work is done, Satan only gets stronger. The force
of Satan is real, and our ego and reactive behavior is at the root of all chaos. With this
awareness, we can access the power of *Pesach*, to help us go the extra mile and not think
that our work is done.

Uvmora

The *Haggadah* explains that "*and with great awe*" is about the manifestation of the *Shechina*,
the presence of God in our physical realm. While in Egypt, the Israelites did not have a

midst of other nation by trials, miraculous signs and wonders, by war, wit
a mighty hand, with outstretched arm, and with awesome revelations, as a
that your God did for you in Egypt, before your eyes?"

UVE'OTOT

And with signs, which refers to the miracles performed with the staff: A
it is stated, "Take this staff in your hand, that you may perform th
miraculous signs with it."

UVMOFTIM

And with wonders, which alludes to the blood. As it is stated: "I will shov
wonders in the heavens and on the Earth."

While we recite the next four words, we pour wine from our cup

Blood (Dam) *and fire* (Va'Esh) *and columns of smoke* (VeTimrot Ashan)

---

strong enough connection to the *Shechina* because they were deep in their own negativit
There are 50 Gates or levels of negativity, and they actually reached the 49th Gate o
Impurity. Once a person reaches the 50th Gate, there is no turning back—his opportunit
for change and transformation in his present lifetime has vanished. Because the Israelite
did not really merit the Exodus from Egypt, they had an opportunity during the 49 day
after *Pesach* (the *Omer*) to work on themselves spiritually and to cleanse each Gate o
Negativity in preparation for receiving immortality at Mount Sinai.

UVE'OTOT

From the time of Creation, the staff of Moses was charged with the power of th
Lightforce of the Creator. Engraved on the staff were the 72 Names of God plus th
42-Letter Name of God (the *Ana Beko'ach*)—the technology Moses used to achieve a
the miracles in Egypt as well as the Splitting of the Red Sea. The 72 Names of Go
and the *Ana Beko'ach* are kabbalistic tools that assist us rise above the influence of th
laws of nature and to overpower them. According to legend, the staff was lodged in th
ground inside Jethro's home. Jethro, the Priest of Midian, knew that the staff possesse
tremendous spiritual powers and offered a lot of money, along with the hand of his daughte

בְּאֹתֹת וּבְמוֹפְתִים וּבְמִלְוֹזָמָה וּבְיָד וְזָקָה וְזָקָה וּבִזְרוֹעַ נְטוּיָה וּבְמוֹרָאִים
גְּדֹלִים ג"פ אל כְּכֹל אֲשֶׁר עָשָׂה לָכֶם יְהֹוָ(אדני אהדונהי) אֱלֹהֵיכֶם יל
בְּמִצְרַיִם מצר לְעֵינֶיךָ ע"ה קס"א:

UVE'OTOT

וּבְאֹתֹת, זֶה הַמַּטֶּה. כְּמָה שֶׁנֶּאֱמַר, וְאֶת הַמַּטֶּה הַזֶּה וּ
תִּקַּח רבוע אהיה ד אלפין בְּיָדְךָ בוכ"ו אֲשֶׁר תַּעֲשֶׂה בּוֹ אֶת הָאֹתֹת:

UVMOFTIM

וּבְמוֹפְתִים זֶה הַדָּם רבוע אהיה. כְּמָה שֶׁנֶּאֱמַר. וְנָתַתִּי מוֹפְתִים
בַּשָּׁמַיִם י"פ טל, י"פ כוזו וּבָאָרֶץ אלהים דאלפין.

While we recite the next four words, we pour wine from our cup

דָּם רבוע אהיה וָאֵשׁ אלהים דיודין ע"ה וְתִימְרוֹת עָשָׁן:

---

n marriage, to anyone who could dislodge it from the ground. When Moses came to the
house of Jethro, he pulled the staff out of the ground, releasing it to its rightful owner.

This connection gives us the ability to transcend the limitations and obstacles of our
physical world. With this consciousness, we inject order into chaos and remove Satan's
influence from our lives.

UVMOFTIM

Of all the Ten Plagues, it was the Plague of Blood that first demonstrated the distinction
between the gods of the Egyptians and the God of the Israelites (the Creator). When an
Israelite drank water, it was a clear and refreshing liquid, while the water in the cup of an
Egyptian would transform into blood. When we connect to the Light of the Creator, we
are given the power of protection against any onslaught of chaos.

thing [another explanation of the preceding verse is that each phrase represents two plagues]. The mighty hand represents two plagues, the outstretched arm another two, the great awe another two, the signs another two, and the wonders another two.

THE TEN PLAGUES

These are the ten plagues that the Holy One, Blessed be He, brought upon the Egyptians in Egypt:

THE TEN PLAGUES

The world was created though ten statements uttered by God, showing us that the connection to the Creator was hidden. Sometimes, we see there is a God; sometimes, we don't see. The Ten Plagues in Egypt removed the curtain of concealment as well as the separation between the Israelites and the Creator, making it possible for the Ten Utterances to be revealed at Mount Sinai.

The Ten Plagues seemed like ephemeral things. The blood only lasted for a month, the frogs died after a while, the boils went away—yet these plagues were supposed to make Pharaoh relent.

The lesson here is that the plagues really had nothing to do with blood or frogs or boils or any of the other seven manifestations. These plagues were the route to destroy the power of Satan. The Ten Plagues are the ten levels of Satan that needed to be destroyed so that the Light of Redemption could enter Egypt and free the Israelites from their bondage. With this understanding, we are given the awareness that when we experience hardship and challenges in our lives, it is the Light giving us these challenges so that we can overcome them and remove Satan's influence in our lives, thereby gaining freedom from chaos.

דָּבָר רְאֵה אַ‏זֵר, בְּיָד וַחֲזָקָה שְׁתַּיִם. וּבִזְרֹעַ נְטוּיָה שְׁתַּיִם וּבְמֹרָא גָּדוֹל לַהוֹ, מכה, יד, אם שְׁתַּיִם. וּבְאֹתוֹת שְׁתַּיִם. וּבְמֹפְתִים שְׁתַּיִם.

THE TEN PLAGUES

סוֹד הָעֶשֶׂר מַכּוֹת שֶׁהֵבִיא הקב״ה עַל הַמִּצְרִים בְּמִצְרִים הָיוּ לְהוֹצִיא כוֹ הָע״ס דִּקְלִיפָה, וְזֶה הַסֵּדֶר:

דָם
א׳ אָה׳ אֲהִ״ה, מַכָּה זוּ נִצְאָה מִמַּלְכוּת דְּמַלְכוּת דִּקְדוּשָׁה וְהֻכְּתָה לְכֶתֶר דְּנוּק׳ דִּקְלִיפָה.

צְפַרְדֵּעַ
עִ״ך דִּינִים, וָא׳ אַד׳ אֲדנ״י, מִיסוֹד דְּמַלְכוּת דִּקְדוּשָׁה לְדַעַת דִּקְלִיפָה.

כִּנִּים
מֵהוֹד דְּמַלְכוּת דִּקְדוּשָׁה לְקַרְקַפְתָּא דִּקְלִיפָה, וְעַטֶרֶת הַזָּכָר דִּקְלִיפָה.

עָרוֹב
יָ׳ יָה׳ יְהוָ׳ יְהֹו״ה, אֵ׳ אֵל׳ אֵלָה׳ אֱלֹהָ׳ אֱלֹהִ״ם, מִנִּצְחוּ דְּנוּק׳ דִּקְדוּשָׁה לִיסוֹד וּת״א דִּקְלִיפָה.

דֶּבֶר
בֵּ׳ אֱלֹהִ״ם, וְל״ד אוֹתִיּוֹת דְּמִילוּי הַמִּילוּי דַּאֲדנ״י, מִת״ת נוּק׳ דִּקְדוּשָׁה לְהוֹד דִּקְלִיפָה.

שְׁחִין
מִגְּבוּרָה דְּנוּק׳ דִּקְדוּשָׁה לְנֶצְחוּ דִּקְלִיפָה.

בָּרָד
מֵחֶסֶד דְּנוּק׳ לְת״ת דִּקְלִיפָה.

אַרְבֶּה
מִבִּינָה דְּנוּק׳ לִגְבוּרָה דִּקְלִיפָה.

וְחֹשֶׁךְ
מֵחָכְמָה דְּנוּק׳ דִּקְדוּשָׁה לְחֶסֶד דִּקְלִיפָה.

מַכַּת בְּכוֹרוֹת
מִכֶּתֶר דְּנוּק׳ [דִּקְדוּשָׁה] לְג״ר דו״א דִּקְלִיפָה.

אֵלּוּ עֶשֶׂר מַכּוֹת שֶׁהֵבִיא הַקָּדוֹשׁ בָּרוּךְ יהוה ע״ב ורבוע מ״ה הוּא עַל הַמִּצְרִים מצר בְּמִצְרַיִם מצר וְאֵלּוּ הֵן:

As we recite each verse, we dip our finger into the wine cup and place a drop onto a napkin or spare saucer.

Blood (Dam)*; Frogs* (Tsfarde'a)*; Vermin* (Kinim)*; Wild Beasts* (Arov)*; Pestilence* (Dever)*; Boils* (Shechin)*; Hail* (Barad)*; Locusts* (Arbe)*; Darkness* (Choshech)*; Deaths of the Firstborn* (Makat Bechorot).

Rav Yehuda

Rav Yehuda abbreviated them by their Hebrew initials:

While we recite the next three words, we dip our finger into the wine cup and place three drops onto a napkin or spare saucer.

DeTSaKH, ADaSH, Be'ACHaB

Rav Yehuda

When we recite or pray from the *Haggadah*, angels—acting as our transportation system—take our words to the Upper Worlds. However, there are certain times when we don't want an intermediary—we want to go straight to the Source. Because the Negative Side also has angels that can influence and sabotage our connections, we employ the Aramaic language and acronyms to bypass them and their negative "transportation routes." The Aramaic language is a communication system that all angels cannot understand, and the acronyms we use are sequences of Aramaic letters that are also beyond the comprehension of the angels. Acronyms and the Aramaic language are our most powerful weapons in the battle against evil and the negative forces.

After the Ten Plagues are recited, we use an acronym given to us by the great sage Rav Yehuda to connect directly with the Creator.

As we recite each verse, we dip our finger into the wine cup and place a drop onto a napkin or spare saucer.

דָּ"ם רבוע אהיה. צְפַרְדֵּעַ ש"ך ע"ה כוק ע"ה. כִּנִּים ק"ך צרופים.

עָרוֹב ע"ב ורבוע אלהים. דֶּבֶר ראה. שְׁחִין. בָּרָד ראה.

אַרְבֶּה יצחק, ד"פ ב"ן. וֹשֶׁךְ ש"ך גיצוצות על ו' מלכים. מַכַּת בְּכוֹרוֹת:

RAV YEHUDA

רַבִּי יְהוּדָה הָיָה נוֹתֵן יהה אבגית"ץ, ושר, אהבת חנם בָּהֶם סִמָּנִים:

While we recite the next three words, we dip our finger into the wine cup and place three drops onto a napkin or spare saucer.

דְּצַ"ךְ עֲדַ"שׁ בְּאַחַ"ב:

RAV YOSSI, RAV ELIEZER, RAV AKIVA

here is an interesting debate concerning how many plagues actually struck Egypt. Rav ossi says there were 10 plagues, with another 50 plagues at the parting of the Red Sea. av Eliezer says there were 40 plagues in Egypt and 200 at the Red Sea. Rav Akiva says ere were 50 plagues in Egypt and 250 at the Red Sea.

n a deeper level, all these great sages are correct. The kabbalists explain that when you ld all the letters of the Ten Plagues together, you get 3280. This equals the number of egative angels residing in our universe. Each of these three kabbalists, using the Holy ame that connected to their soul, connected to a different path to destroy this angelic egativity. All of our souls connect to one or all of these paths. Thankfully, our path to estroy Satan has already been paved by these three great giants.

RAV YOSSI

Rav Yossi the Galilean said, "How does one derive that the Egyptian were struck with ten plagues in Egypt, but with 50 plagues at the sea Concerning the plagues in Egypt, the Torah states: 'The magicians sai to Pharaoh, "It is the finger of God." ' However, of those at the se the Torah says: 'And Israel saw the great hand which Hashem laid upo the Egyptians, the people feared Hashem and believed in Hashem and i Moses, his servant.' How many plagues did they receive with the finger o God? Ten. From now on say, in Egypt they received ten plagues and on th sea they received fifty plagues."

RAV ELIEZER

Rav Eliezer says: "How does one derive that every plague that the Ho One, Blessed be He, inflicted upon the Egyptians in Egypt was equal t four plagues? For it is written: 'It sent upon them Its fierce anger: wrath fury, and trouble and a band of emissaries of evil.' [Since each plagu in Egypt consists of] (1) wrath, (2) fury, (3) trouble, and (4) a band o emissaries of evil, in Egypt they were struck by 40 plagues, and on the se they were struck by 200 plagues."

RAV YOSSI

The kabbalists teach us that Rav Yossi is a spark of the soul of King David and that th name "David, son of Yishai" has the numerical value of 386, which is the same value a Rav Yossi's name. Because the numerical value of the Holy Name *Shin, Pei, Vav* שפו is als 386, we meditate on *Shin, Pei, Vav* before we recite Rav Yossi's words.

RAV YOSSI

רַבִּי יוֹסֵי שפ״ו ע״ה = דוד בן ישי הַגְּלִילִי אוֹמֵר: מִנַּיִן אַתָּה אוֹמֵר שֶׁלָּקוּ הַמִּצְרִים מצר בְּמִצְרַיִם מצר עֶשֶׂר מַכּוֹת וְעַל הַיָּם ילי לָקוּ וַחֲמִשִׁים מַכּוֹת. בְּמִצְרַיִם מצר מַה מ״ה הוּא אוֹמֵר, וַיֹּאמְרוּ הַחַרְטֻמִּים אֶל פַּרְעֹה אֶצְבַּע אֱלֹהִים מוה, אהיה אדני; ילה הִיא. וְעַל הַיָּם ילי מ מ״ה הוּא אוֹמֵר, וַיַּרְא אלף למד יהוה יִשְׂרָאֵל אֶת הַיָּד הַגְּדֹלָה אֲשֶׁ עָשָׂה יְהֹוָהאהדונהי בְּמִצְרַיִם מצר וַיִּירְאוּ הָעָם אֶת יְהֹוָהאהדונהי וַיַּאֲמִינוּ בַּיהֹוָהאהדונהי וּבְמֹשֶׁה מהש, אל שדי עַבְדּוֹ. כַּמָּה מ״ה לָק בָּאֶצְבַּע קס״ג עֶשֶׂר מַכּוֹת. אֱמוֹר מֵעַתָּה, בְּמִצְרַיִם מצר לָקוּ עֶשֶׂ מַכּוֹת וְעַל הַיָּם ילי לָקוּ וַחֲמִשִׁים מַכּוֹת:

RAV ELIEZER

רַבִּי אֱלִיעֶזֶר תקל אוֹמֵר: מִנַּיִן שֶׁכָּל ילי מַכָּה היי וּמַכָּה היי שֶׁהֵבִי הַקָּדוֹשׁ בָּרוּךְ יהוה ע״ב ורבוע מ״ה הוּא עַל הַמִּצְרִים מצר בְּמִצְרַים מצ הָיְתָה שֶׁל אַרְבַּע מַכּוֹת. שֶׁנֶּאֱמַר, יְשַׁלַּח בָּם מ״ה וְחֲרוֹן אַפּוֹ עֶבְר וָזַעַם וְצָרָה אלהים דההין מִשְׁלַחַת מַלְאֲכֵי רָעִים: עֶבְרָה אַוֹת. וָזַע שְׁתַּיִם. וְצָרָה אלהים דההין שָׁלֹשׁ. מִשְׁלַחַת מַלְאֲכֵי רָעִים אַרְבַּ אֱמוֹר מֵעַתָּה, בְּמִצְרַיִם מצר לָקוּ אַרְבָּעִים מַכּוֹת וְעַל הַיָּם י לָקוּ מָאתַיִם מַכּוֹת:

RAV ELIEZER

av Eliezer's name has the numerical value of 530, which is the same value as the Holy
ame *Tav, Kaf, Lamed* תקל. Before we recite Rav Eliezer's discourse, we meditate on the
tters *Tav, Kaf, Lamed*.

Rav Akiva

Rav Akiva said: "How does one derive that every plague that the Holy One, Blessed be He, inflicted upon the Egyptians in Egypt was equal to five plagues? For it is written: 'It sent upon them Its fierce anger, wrath, fury, and trouble and a band of emissaries of evil.' [Since each plague in Egypt consists of] (1) fierce anger, (2) wrath, (3) fury, (4) trouble, and (5) a band of emissaries of evil, in Egypt they were struck by fifty plagues, and on the sea they were struck by 250 plagues."

Dayenu

The Omnipresent has bestowed so many favors upon us!

Had He brought us out of Egypt, but not executed judgments against the Egyptians, it would have sufficed us.

Had He executed judgments against the Egyptians, but not upon their gods, it would have sufficed us.

Had He executed judgments against their gods, but not slain their firstborn, it would have sufficed us.

Had He slain their firstborn, but not given us their wealth, it would have sufficed us.

Had He given us their wealth, but not split the sea for us, it would have sufficed us.

Had He split the sea for us, but not led us through it on dry land, it would have sufficed us.

Rav Akiva

The numerical value of "Rav Akiva" equals 395, which is the same value as the Holy Name *Shin, Tzadi, Hei* שצה. Before we recite Rav Akiva's words, we meditate on the letters *Shin, Tzadi, Hei.*

Rav Akiva

רַבִּי עֲקִיבָא אֹיֶה אוֹמֵר: מִנַּיִן שֶׁכָּל יֶּי מַכָּה וּמַכָּה שֶׁהֵבִיא הַקָּדוֹשׁ בָּרוּךְ יהוה ע״ב ורבוע מ״ה הוּא עַל הַמִּצְרִים מצר בְּמִצְרַיִם מצר הָיְתָה שֶׁל וָחֶמֵשׁ מַכּוֹת. שֶׁנֶּאֱמַר, יְשַׁלַּח בָּם מ״ב וַחֲרוֹן אַפּוֹ עֶבְרָה וָזַעַם וְצָרָה אלהים דההין מִשְׁלַחַת מַלְאֲכֵי רָעִים: וַחֲרוֹן אַפּוֹ אַחַת. עֶבְרָד שְׁתַּיִם. וָזַעַם שָׁלֹשׁ. וְצָרָה אלהים דההין אַרְבַּע. מִשְׁלַחַת מַלְאֲכֵי רָעִים וָחֲמֵשׁ. אֱמוֹר מֵעַתָּה בְּמִצְרַיִם מצר לָקוּ וַחֲמִשִּׁים מַכּוֹת וְעַ הַיָּם יֶּי לָקוּ וַחֲמִשִּׁים וּמָאתַיִם מַכּוֹת:

Dayenu

כַּמָּה מ״ה מַעֲלוֹת טוֹבוֹת לַמָּקוֹם יהוה ברבוע, ר״פ אל עָלֵינוּ ריבוע ס״ג:

אִלּוּ הוֹצִיאָנוּ מִמִּצְרַיִם מצר, וְלֹא עָשָׂה בָהֶם שְׁפָטִים   דַּיֵּנוּ:

אִלּוּ עָשָׂה בָהֶם שְׁפָטִים, וְלֹא עָשָׂה בֵאלֹהֵיהֶם יֶּה   דַּיֵּנוּ:

אִלּוּ עָשָׂה בֵאלֹהֵיהֶם יֶּה, וְלֹא הָרַג אֶת בְּכוֹרֵיהֶם   דַּיֵּנוּ:

אִלּוּ הָרַג אֶת בְּכוֹרֵיהֶם, וְלֹא נָתַן לָנוּ מום, אלהים אֶת מָמוֹנָם   דַּיֵּנוּ:

אִלּוּ נָתַן לָנוּ מום, אלהים אֶת מָמוֹנָם, וְלֹא קָרַע ב״פ אלף למד לָנוּ מום, אלהים אֶת הַיָּם יֶּי   דַּיֵּנוּ:

אִלּוּ קָרַע ב״פ אלף למד לָנוּ מום, אלהים אֶת הַיָּם יֶּי, וְלֹא

Dayenu

Dayenu means "It would have sufficed," and in this song, we thank the Creator for bringing us to Mount Sinai. According to Kabbalah, all of our souls were present during the Revelation at Mount Sinai. The great kabbalist Rav Elimelech said, "Not only do I remember Mount Sinai, but I also remember who was standing next to me there." When our consciousness during this song is one of appreciation for all we have received, this ensures that we never lose it.

Had He led us through it on dry land, but not drowned our oppressors in it, it would have sufficed us.

Had He drowned our oppressors in it, but not provided for our needs in the desert for forty years, it would have sufficed us.

Had He provided for our needs in the desert for forty years, but not fed us the Manna, it would have sufficed us.

Had He fed us the Manna, but not given us the Shabbat, it would have sufficed us.

Had He given us the Shabbat, but not brought us before Mount Sinai, it would have sufficed us.

Had He brought us before Mount Sinai, but not given us the Torah, it would have sufficed us.

Had He given us the Torah, but not brought us into the land of Israel, it would have sufficed us.

Had He brought us into the land of Israel, but not built the temple for us, it would have sufficed us.

AL ACHAT

Thus, how much more should we be grateful to the Omnipresent for all the numerous favors He showered upon us: brought us out of Egypt, executed judgments against the Egyptians and against their gods, slew their firstborn, gave us their wealth, split the sea for us, let us through it on dry land, drowned our oppressors in it, provided for our needs in the desert for forty years, fed us

---

AL ACHAT

"*God has given everything to us.*" The gratitude expressed here is for all that is still coming to us. This is a direct reference to the coming of the Final Temple, when all chaos, death and destruction will come to an end.

הֶעֱבִירָנוּ בְתוֹכוֹ בֶּחָרָבָה דַּיֵּנוּ:

אִלּוּ הֶעֱבִירָנוּ בְתוֹכוֹ בֶּחָרָבָה,

וְלֹא שִׁקַּע צָרֵינוּ בְתוֹכוֹ דַּיֵּנוּ:

אִלּוּ שִׁקַּע צָרֵינוּ בְתוֹכוֹ, וְלֹא סִפֵּק צָרְכֵּנוּ

בַּמִּדְבָּר אברהם, רמ"ח, וז"ז אל אַרְבָּעִים שָׁנָה דַּיֵּנוּ:

אִלּוּ סִפֵּק צָרְכֵּנוּ בַּמִּדְבָּר אברהם, רמ"ח, וז"ז אל

אַרְבָּעִים שָׁנָה, וְלֹא הֶאֱכִילָנוּ אֶת הַמָּן דַּיֵּנוּ:

אִלּוּ הֶאֱכִילָנוּ אֶת הַמָּן, וְלֹא נָתַן לָנוּ מום, אלהים

אֶת הַשַּׁבָּת דַּיֵּנוּ:

אִלּוּ נָתַן לָנוּ מום, אלהים אֶת הַשַּׁבָּת, וְלֹא

קֵרְבָנוּ לִפְנֵי וחכמה בינה הַר רבוע אלהים ה סִינַי נמם, ה"פ יהוה דַּיֵּנוּ:

אִלּוּ קֵרְבָנוּ לִפְנֵי וחכמה בינה הַר רבוע אלהים ה

סִינַי נמם, ה"פ יהוה, וְלֹא נָתַן לָנוּ מום, אלהים אֶת הַתּוֹרָה דַּיֵּנוּ:

אִלּוּ נָתַן לָנוּ מום, אלהים אֶת הַתּוֹרָה, וְלֹא הִכְנִיסָנוּ

לָאָרֶץ אלהים דאלפין יִשְׂרָאֵל דַּיֵּנוּ:

אִלּוּ הִכְנִיסָנוּ לָאָרֶץ אלהים דאלפין יִשְׂרָאֵל, וְלֹא

בָּנָה לָנוּ מום, אלהים אֶת בֵּית ב"פ ראה הַבְּחִירָה דַּיֵּנוּ:

AL ACHAT

עַל אַחַת כַּמָּה מ"ה וְכַמָּה מ"ה טוֹבָה אבא כְּפוּלָה וּמְכֻפֶּלֶת לַמָּקוֹם

יהוה ברבוע, ר"פ אל עָלֵינוּ ריבוע ס"ג. שֶׁהוֹצִיאָנוּ מִמִּצְרַיִם מצר. וְעָשָׂה בָהֶ

שְׁפָטִים. וְעָשָׂה בֵאלֹהֵיהֶם ילה. וְהָרַג אֶת בְּכוֹרֵיהֶם. וְנָתַן לָנוּ מו

אלהים אֶת מָמוֹנָם. וְקָרַע ב"פ אלף למד, ע"ע לָנוּ מום, אלהים אֶת הַיָּם יפ

וְהֶעֱבִירָנוּ בְתוֹכוֹ בֶּחָרָבָה. וְשִׁקַּע צָרֵינוּ בְתוֹכוֹ. וְסִפֵּק צָרְכ

the Manna, gave us the Shabbat, brought us before Mount Sinai, gave us the Torah, brought us to the land of Israel, and built us the temple— to atone for our sins.

RABAN GAMLIEL

Raban Gamliel used to say: "Whoever has not mentioned the following three things on Pesach, has not done his job, namely:

Pesach—*the Pesach offering.* **Matza**—*unleavened bread. And* **Maror**—*bitter herb.*

PESACH

The Pesach meal that our fathers ate the offering during the time of the Temple was because the Holy One, Blessed be He, passed over the houses of our fathers in Egypt, as it is says: "You shall say, 'It is a Pesach offering for Hashem, which passed over the houses of the children of Israel in Egypt when He struck the Egyptians and spared our houses'—and the people bowed down and prostrated themselves."

RABAN GAMLIEL

According to Kabbalah, there is no coercion or obligation to appease God. Everything we do is for our own benefit—to benefit our own soul and achieve lasting fulfillment.

There are three conditions that apply for a person to do his or her spiritual work. At *Rosh Hashanah* during the *Shofar* blowings, we connect to the three patriarchs: Abraham (cleansing idolatry), Isaac (cleansing adultery), and Jacob (cleansing bloodshed), and then the fourth and final set of *Shofar* blowings are for King David (cleansing evil speech).

Raban Gamleil tells us that if we do not say the three words *Pesach*, *Matzah*, and *Maror* we have not properly connected to the *Seder*, as these three conditions that apply to our spiritual work at *Pesach*. In the *Haggadah*, *Pesach* is about the sacrificing (korban) of the ram by the Israelites in Egypt. They were slaughtering the internal energy of the ram—the

בַּמִּדְבָּר אברהם, רמ״ח, ח״פ אל אַרְבָּעִים שָׁנָה. וְהָאֱכִילָנוּ אֶת הַמָּן. וְנָתַ

לָנוּ מום, אלהים אֶת הַשַּׁבָּת. וְקֵרְבָנוּ לְפָנֵי וchochma בינה הַר רבוע אלהים ה סִינַ

נמם, ה״פ יהוה. וְנָתַן לָנוּ מום, אלהים אֶת הַתּוֹרָה. וְהִכְנִיסָנוּ לָאָרֶץ אלהי

דאלפין יִשְׂרָאֵל. וּבָנָה לָנוּ מום, אלהים אֶת בֵּית ב״פ ראה הַבְּחִירָה לְכַפּ

מצפ״ץ עַל כָּל יל״י עֲוֹנוֹתֵינוּ:

RABAN GAMLIEL

רַבָּן גַּמְלִיאֵל הָיָה יהה אוֹמֵר: כָּל יל״י שֶׁלֹּא אָמַר שְׁלֹשָׁ

דְּבָרִים ראה אֵלּוּ בַּפֶּסַח לֹא יָצָא יְדֵי חוֹבָתוֹ, וְאֵלּוּ הֵן:

פֶּסַח. מַצָּה ע״ב ס״ג. וּמָרוֹר:

PESACH

פֶּסַח שֶׁהָיוּ אֲבוֹתֵינוּ אוֹכְלִים בִּזְמַן שֶׁבֵּית ב״פ ראה הַמִּקְדָּשׁ הָיָ

יהה קַיָּם עַל שׁוּם מָה. מ״ה. עַל שׁוּם שֶׁפָּסַח הַקָּדוֹשׁ בָּרוּךְ יהוה ע

ורבוע מ״ה הוּא עַל בָּתֵּי אֲבוֹתֵינוּ בְּמִצְרַיִם מצר. שֶׁנֶּאֱמַר, וַאֲמַרְתֶּ

זֶבַח פֶּסַח הוּא לַיהֹוָהאההיאהרונהי אֲשֶׁר פָּסַח עַל בָּתֵּי בְּנֵי יִשְׂרָאֵ

בְּמִצְרַיִם מצר בְּנָגְפּוֹ אֶת מִצְרַיִם מצר וְאֶת בָּתֵּינוּ הִצִּיל וַיִּקֹּד הָעָ

וַיִּשְׁתַּחֲווּ:

Desire to Receive for the Self Alone—in themselves. What we are sacrificing at the *Seder* is our idol worship. *Matzah* cleanses adultery and *Maror* has the numerical value of the word death to killing." The actual speaking of the story of *Pesach* is to cleanse lashon hara evil speech).

PESACH

Pesach means we can "pass over" our past. We don't have to pay for everything that we have done; there are certain actions we can do that cleanse in a way that is disproportionate to their original negativity. One action can wipe out 50 years of negativity. We have to know that we can clean the slate no matter how many years or lifetimes we go through. Even if we are not ready or worthy, we can perform the action that can clean the negativity, either right now or at any point in the future.

Matzah

We show the *Matzah* to everyone:

Matzah. Why do we eat this unleavened bread? Because the dough of our fathers did not have time to become leavened before the King of Kings, the Holy One, Blessed be He, revealed Itself to them and redeemed them, as it is written: "They baked the dough which they had brought out of Egypt into unleavened bread, for it had not fermented, because they were driven out of Egypt and could not delay, nor had they prepared any provisions for the way."

Maror

We show the *Maror* to everyone:

Maror. Why do we eat this bitter herb? Because the Egyptians embittered the lives of our fathers in Egypt, as it says: "They embittered their lives with hard labor, with mortar and bricks, and with all manner of labor in the field; whatever service which they performed with hard labor."

Matzah

It says that the reason *Matzah* is so thin and flat is because the Israelites were thrown out of Egypt and could not wait for their dough to rise. The reason they were thrown out of Egypt is because the moment the Light turns on, the darkness disappears.

Matzah limits our *Desire to Receive* . This does not mean we don't eat anything, but rather that we do without excess. There is no problem in having; there is a problem, however, with having too much. There is no problem with having a winter house and summer house. Nor is there a problem having money and enjoying it. But there is a problem in losing appreciation because there is so much excess.

We know that with the actual *Matzah*, there are many, many things that cannot be done to it, including prohibitions and rules regarding how to make it. The kabbalists ask, "Why not just avoid the whole thing and eat only vegetables for these seven days? Why do you need to connect to something to have *Pesach* be perfect?" The answer is that there will always be a test, and we cannot run away from these tests. We can never be without the tests. We need to be tested, and we have to do it—be tested and pass.

MATZAH

We show the *Matzah* to everyone:

מַצָּה ע״ב ס״ג זוֹ שֶׁאָנוּ אוֹכְלִים עַל שׁוּם מָה מ״ה. עַל שׁוּם שֶׁלֹּא
הִסְפִּיק בְּצֵקָם שֶׁל אֲבוֹתֵינוּ לְהַחֲמִיץ עַד שֶׁנִּגְלָה עֲלֵיהֶם מֶלֶךְ
מַלְכֵי הַמְּלָכִים הַקָּדוֹשׁ בָּרוּךְ יהוה ע״ב ורבוע מ״ה הוּא וּגְאָלָם. שֶׁנֶּאֱמַר
וַיֹּאפוּ אֶת הַבָּצֵק אֲשֶׁר הוֹצִיאוּ מִמִּצְרַיִם מצר עֻגֹת מַצּוֹת כִּי לֹא
חָמֵץ כִּי גֹרְשׁוּ מִמִּצְרַיִם מצר וְלֹא יָכְלוּ לְהִתְמַהְמֵהַּ וְגַם יג״ל צֵדָה
לֹא עָשׂוּ לָהֶם:

MAROR

We show the *Maror* to everyone:

מָרוֹר זֶה שֶׁאָנוּ אוֹכְלִים עַל שׁוּם מָה מ״ה. עַל שׁוּם שֶׁמֵּרְרוּ
הַמִּצְרִים מצר אֶת וַזֵּ״י אֲבוֹתֵינוּ בְּמִצְרַיִם מצר. שֶׁנֶּאֱמַר, וַיְמָרְרוּ
אֶת וַזֵּ״ה חַיֵּיהֶם בַּעֲבֹדָה קָשָׁה בְּחֹמֶר וּבִלְבֵנִים וּבְכָל ב״ן, לכב, יבמ עֲבֹדָ
בַּשָּׂדֶה אֵת כָּל יל״י עֲבֹדָתָם אֲשֶׁר עָבְדוּ בָהֶם בְּפָרֶךְ:

MAROR

Maror connects us to the spiritual work and the idea that we need to struggle to do the work.
Why, if *Matzah* connects us to freedom and *Maror* is about the struggle in Egypt, do we
connect to *Matzah* before *Maror*? Shouldn't the struggle in Egypt precede the going out from
Egypt? The reason we connect to *Matzah* before *Maror* is because we don't want to connect to
Egypt and suffering first, lest we get used to our separation from the Light of the Creator.

There is a story of a king and his child. The child did terrible things, and the king sent
him away. After a few months, the king felt bad that he had sent his child away, so he
dispatched someone to find the boy. The minister found the child freezing with no shoes
on. The child asked the man for boots and a blanket saying, "I would be the happiest
person if I had boots and blankets." We get used to our suffering, to being far from
the Creator. We need to first connect to freedom and not to suffering because we don't
always feel that freedom is possible. We don't always want freedom; sometimes, we just
want to not be depressed or not be angry.

Bechol Dor VaDor

In every generation, one must regard himself as if he personally had gon
out of Egypt, as it is says: "And you shall tell your son on that day: 'It wa
because of this that Hashem did for me when I went out of Egypt.'" It wa
not only our fathers whom the Holy One redeemed from slavery; we, too, wer
redeemed with them, as it is written: "It brought us out of there in order t
take us to and give us the land which He had promised to our forefathers."

Lefichach

We cover the *Matzah* and lift the cup while the following is recited:

Therefore, we must thank, praise, pay tribute, glorify, exalt, honor, bless, exto.
and acclaim It which performed all these miracles for our fathers and for u
all those miracles. Brought us forth from slavery to freedom, from grief to jo
from mourning to festivity, from darkness to great light, and from servitude t
redemption. Let us, therefore, recite a new song before Him—Halleluyah!

The numerical value of the word *Maror* (447) is the same as for the word mavet (death
For us to reach the state of immortality that we can achieve on Shavuot, we must firs
taste death. By slowly chewing the *Maror* and embracing the intense pain and discomfo
it generates, we can remove the force of death from our lives.

Bechol Dor VaDor

"In every generation, one should regard himself as if he personally had gone out of Egypt."

It says that going out of Egypt was more difficult than splitting the Red Sea. With th
going out of Egypt, the Israelites were birthed. Like a fetus, while in Egypt they had zer
responsibility. We, too, have to be birthed; we have to go from a state of nothingness–
from someone else taking care of everything—to being our own person.

The reason the Torah was not given in a valley is to show that to be a valley and not hav
ego is no challenge. To be a mountain and not have ego, now that is the challenge.
It says that everything the Israelites did in Egypt, they had to do the same for the Light. I
a person had issues with his foot, he needed to use that for *kedusha* (holiness). It is abo
finding a way to use everything, even the most commonplace things, for the Light.

BECHOL DOR VADOR

בְּכָל בֵּין, לכב, יבם דּוֹר וָדוֹר ריי, גבורה וְחַיָּב אָדָם מ"ה לִרְאוֹת אֶת עַצְ
כְּאִלּוּ הוּא יָצָא מִמִּצְרַיִם מצר. שֶׁנֶּאֱמַר, וְהִגַּדְתָּ לְבִנְךָ בַּיּוֹם ע"ה
נגד, זן, מזבח הַהוּא לֵאמֹר בַּעֲבוּר זֶה עָשָׂה יְהוָֹאדנ"ילאהדונהי לִי בְּצֵאתִ
מִמִּצְרַיִם מצר. שֶׁלֹא אֶת אֲבוֹתֵינוּ בִּלְבָד גָּאַל ע"ה אלה הַקָּדוֹ
בָּרוּךְ יהוה ע"ב ורביע מ"ה הוּא, אֶלָּא אַף אוֹתָנוּ גָּאַל ע"ה אלה עִמָּהֶ
שֶׁנֶּאֱמַר, וְאוֹתָנוּ הוֹצִיא מִשָּׁם יהוה שדי לְמַעַן הָבִיא אֹתָנוּ לָתֶת כ
מוֹם, אלהים אֶת הָאָרֶץ אלהים דההין ע"ה אֲשֶׁר נִשְׁבַּע לַאֲבֹתֵינוּ:

LEFICHACH

We cover the *Matzah* and lift the cup while the following is recited:

לְפִיכָךְ אֲנַחְנוּ וְחַיָּבִים לְהוֹדוֹת לְהַלֵּל לללל, אדני לְשַׁבֵּחַ לְפָאֵר לְרוֹמֵ
לְהַדֵּר לְנַצֵּחַ לְבָרֵךְ לְעַלֵּה וּלְקַלֵּס לְמִי שֶׁעָשָׂה לַאֲבוֹתֵינוּ וְכ
מוֹם, אלהים אֶת כָּל ילי הַנִּסִּים הָאֵלוּ. הוֹצִיאָנוּ מֵעַבְדוּת לְחֵרוּ
מִיָּגוֹן לְשִׂמְחָה, וּמֵאֵבֶל לְיוֹם ע"ה = נגד, זן, מזבח טוֹב והו, וּמֵאֲפֵלָה לְאוֹ
רז, אין סוף גָּדוֹל לללה, מבה, יזל, אום וּמִשִּׁעְבּוּד לִגְאֻלָּה מ"ה. וְנֹאמַר לְפָ
שִׁירָה וְחֲדָשָׁה הַלְלוּיָהּ מוֹם, אלהים; ילה; לללה:

---

hen the Red Sea split, the *erev rav* said, "Oh, Moses can split the sea, but can he take
e of the little puddles?"

hen the Light comes and we change, do we really transform or is it that it is just the big things
t we don't do anymore? The Light has the power to clean up the little pieces of the puzzle.

hen the Israelites left Egypt, they borrowed everything from the Egyptians. They did
t take these things, they borrowed them. This teaches us that our time is borrowed and
t nothing actually belongs to us—today, it is ours, tomorrow, somebody else's.

LEFICHACH

herefore we must thank God." God does not need our thanks. To give "thanks" to God is
give our support and care to others in need. The words "thank God" refer to the spark
God within everyone, not to the Creator. When we appreciate others and take the time
look after others, God looks after us.

HALLELUYAH (FIRST TWO SEFIROT OF THE HALEL)
CHESED

We lower the cup and uncover the *Matzah*:

Halleluyah! Praise, you servants of Hashem, praise the Name of Hasher Blessed be the Name of Hashem from now to eternity. From sunrise i sunset, Hashem's name is praised. High above all nations is Hashe Its glory is all over the heavens. Who is like Hashem, our God, high enthroned, yet looks down upon the heaven and the earth? He raises t destitute from the dust, from the trash heaps He lifts the needy—to se them with nobles, with nobles of His people. He settles down the barr housewife (the Shechinah), and turns Her into a happy mother of sor Halleluyah!

BETSET ISRAEL
GEVURAH

When Israel went forth from Egypt, Jacob's household (went forth) from people of alien tongue (Egypt), Judah became sanctuary, and Israel becau governing. The sea saw and fled, the Jordan (river) turned backward. T mountains skipped like rams and the hills like young lambs. What ails ye

---

HALLELUYAH (FIRST TWO SEFIROT OF THE HALEL SEE PAGE.....)

"*God lifts me up from dust.*" Connecting with and reciting this psalm awakens us to t awareness that no matter how difficult a situation may be or what bind we find oursel in, the Lightforce of the Creator can fix it. Tuning out the whispers of our ego t constantly tell us we are in control helps us to maintain total certainty that the Light c alter our situation at any given moment.

BETSET ISRAEL

The Splitting of the Red Sea resulted in a complete separation from the Egyptian darkne There was no more darkness after that—there was a total separation.

The Zohar says that it is more difficult for the Creator to give a person sustenance tha was to split the Red Sea. When the Israelites reached the Red Sea and saw the Egyptia

HALLELUYAH (FIRST TWO SEFIROT OF THE HALEL)
CHESED

We lower the cup and uncover the *Matzah*:

הַלְלוּיָה מוּם, אלהים; ילה; ללה הַלְלוּ עַבְדֵי יְהֹוָאדניאהדונהי הַלְלוּ אֶת שֵׁ
יְהֹוָאדניאהדונהי יהוה שדי יְהִי שֵׁם יְהֹוָאדניאהדונהי מְבֹרָךְ מֵעַתָּ
וְעַד עוֹלָם: מִמִּזְרַח שֶׁמֶשׁ ב"פ ע"ך עַד מְבוֹאוֹ מְהֻלָּל אדני, ללה שֵׁ
יְהֹוָאדניאהדונהי רָם עַל כָּל גּוֹיִם יְלי יְהֹוָאדניאהדונהי עַל הַשָּׁמַיִם
י"פ טל, י"פ כוזו כְּבוֹדוֹ: מִי יְלי כַּיהֹוָאדניאהדונהי אֱלֹהֵינוּ ילה הַמַּגְבִּיהִי
לָשָׁבֶת: הַמַּשְׁפִּילִי לִרְאוֹת בַּשָּׁמַיִם י"פ טל, י"פ כוזו וּבָאָרֶץ אלהים דאלפין
מְקִימִי מֵעָפָר דָּל מֵאַשְׁפֹּת יָרִים אֶבְיוֹן: לְהוֹשִׁיבִי עִם נְדִיבִים עִ
נְדִיבֵי עַמּוֹ: מוֹשִׁיבִי עֲקֶרֶת הַבַּיִת ב"פ ראה אֵם יוהך הַבָּנִים שְׂמֵחָ
הַלְלוּיָה מוּם, אלהים; ילה; ללה:

BETSET ISRAEL
GEVURAH

בְּצֵאת יִשְׂרָאֵל מִמִּצְרַיִם מצר בֵּית ב"פ ראה יַעֲקֹב ז"פ יהוה, יאהדונהי אידהנו
מֵעַם לֹעֵז: הָיְתָה יְהוּדָה לְקָדְשׁוֹ יִשְׂרָאֵל מַמְשְׁלוֹתָיו: הַיָּם
רָאָה ראה וַיָּנֹס הַיַּרְדֵּן ז"פ יהוה ור' אותיות יִסֹּב לְאָחוֹר: הֶהָרִים י' הויו
רָקְדוּ כְאֵילִים גְּבָעוֹת כִּבְנֵי צֹאן מלוי אהיה דיודין ע"ה: מַה מ"ה כן

---

ght behind them, they feared they were trapped and thought that maybe God would smite
e Egyptians with some kind of plague and kill them all. In our pursuit of sustenance,
e often find ourselves unable to imagine where the money or support will come from.
nd more often than not, we're misguided by exciting clients or opportunities, forgetting
along that our sustenance really comes from the Lightforce of the Creator.

here is a discussion about the splitting of the sea and how the waters separated to reveal
y land in just one second, showing us that we, too, can change in a second.

he Zohar says that the bringing together of souls is like the splitting of the Red Sea.
arriages that work require two people who are willing to change for each other. Like
e land and the sea, they are willing to make sacrifices for each other. It's important

O sea, that you flee? O Jordan, that you turn backward? O mountains, that you skip like rams? O hills, like young lambs? Before the Lord tremble, O earth, before the God of Jacob, which turns the rock into a lake of water, flint into a flowing fountain.

REDEEMER OF ISRAEL

We cover the *Matzah* and raise our cup of wine.

Blessed is Hashem, our God, King of the universe, which redeemed us and redeemed our fathers from Egypt and brought us to this night to eat Matzah and horseradish. In a similar manner, Hashem, our God and the God of our fathers, will enable us to reach in the future other festivals and holidays—in peace, gladdened in the rebuilding of Your city (Jerusalem), joyful at Your

---

to be ready to be whatever we need to be for another person. Sometimes, it's to listen; sometimes, it's to offer a shoulder to cry on; and sometimes, it's to yell at them. We need to be like putty—something that can transform into literally anything that we need to be—to support another person. One second we could be crying; the next, we are screaming. This is what it means to be really there for the other person, like the land and the sea.

The splitting of the Red Sea did not take place just for Moses and the *tzadikim*, but the sea split for each and every person there. Each and every person was worthy of having the sea split for him or her. The sun came up for us today, yet what did we do for it? It's not just that the sun came up, but that the sun came up today for us without our doing anything to deserve it.

When Moses stretched out his arms and his staff to part the Red Sea, the waters didn't move because the Israelites needed to activate their own miracle of nature. A man named Nachshon was the first person to demonstrate complete certainty. He waded into the water until it reached his nostrils and began choking him. At that moment, Satan bombarded him with feelings of fear and uncertainty, but Nachshon didn't waver, and a second later he was breathing fresh air as the waters of the Red Sea parted and climbed toward the heavens. This one person, with his total certainty and with the technology of the 72 Names, achieved mind over matter for an entire nation.

One of the major lessons we learn from the splitting of the Red Sea is that the Israelites found themselves in a place where there was no path—not even a road not taken or one less traveled by. They went where there was no road at all. This is exactly how the Red

הַיָּם יְלֹי כִּי תָנוּס הַיַּרְדֵּן יֽ״פ יהוה וד׳ אותיות תִּסֹּב לְאָחוֹר׃ הֶהָרִים ׳ היוי

תִּרְקְדוּ כְאֵילִים גְּבָעוֹת כִּבְנֵי צֹאן מלוי אהיה דיודין ע״ה׃ מִלִּפְנֵי וחכמה בינ

אָדוֹן אני וְחוּלִי אָרֶץ אלהים דאלפין מִלִּפְנֵי וחכמה בינה אֱלוֹהַּ מ״ב יַעֲקֹב ז״פ יהו

יאהדונהי אידהנויה׃ הַהֹפְכִי הַצּוּר אלהים דההין ע״ה אֲגַם מָיִם וְחַלָּמִישׁ לְמַעְיְנוֹ

ריבוע מ״ה מָיִם׃

REDEEMER OF ISRAEL

We cover the *Matzah* and raise our cup of wine

בָּרוּךְ יהוה ע״ב ורבוע מ״ה אַתָּה יְהֹוָ‏ה‏אדני‏אהדונהי אֱלֹהֵינוּ ילה מֶלֶךְ הָעוֹלָם

אֲשֶׁר גְּאָלָנוּ וְגָאַל ע״ה אלד אֶת אֲבוֹתֵינוּ מִמִּצְרַיִם מצר וְהִגִּיעָנוּ הַלַּיְלָה

מלה הַזֶּה והו לֶאֱכָל בּוֹ מַצָּה ע״ב ס״ג וּמָרוֹר מות׃ כֵּן יְהֹוָ‏ה‏אדני‏אהדונהי

אֱלֹהֵינוּ ילה וֵאלֹהֵי לכב, רמב, ילה אֲבוֹתֵינוּ יַגִּיעֵנוּ לְמוֹעֲדִים וְלִרְגָלִים

אֲחֵרִים הַבָּאִים לִקְרָאתֵנוּ לְשָׁלוֹם, שְׂמֵחִים בְּבִנְיַן עִירֶךָ, וְשָׂשִׂים

בַּעֲבוֹדָתֶךָ, וְנֹאכַל שָׁם יהוה עדי מִן הַזְּבָחִים וּמִן הַפְּסָחִים (במוצ׳

---

d Karen started out almost 40 years ago when they decided to spread the wisdom of
abbalah to everyone throughout the world. This was a time when it was unheard of
at Kabbalah could be made available to all of humanity—this was the road that wasn't
ere.

REDEEMER OF ISRAEL

ith AtBash, an ancient cipher used in Gematria (kabbalistic numerology), the word
a'al spells Keter (crown), which is the seed level of everything. Keter is the first Sefira
d the source of all the thoughts, imagination, feelings, knowledge, and creativity that
e found in our physical world. We are given the ability to seek out the root Cause and
ed level of all the negative events that transpire in our lives so that we can address and
x the seed and remove *their* Effects.

he *Seder* is not only about *Pesach*; it is about *Rosh hashanah*. The kabbalists teach that the
atzah that we eat on *Pesach* activates *Rosh hashanah* to work properly.

*service. There we shall eat of the offerings and Pesach sacrifices (on Shabba
we say: of the Pesach sacrifices and offerings) whose blood will gain the sides of
Your altar for gracious acceptance. We shall then thank You by singing a new
song of praise, for our redemption and for the liberation of our soul. Blessed
are You, Hashem, which has redeemed Israel.*

LeShem Yichud – Second Cup of Wine – Creation (Bri'ah)

*For the sake of unifying The Holy One, blessed be He, and His Shechinah
with fear and mercy, and with mercy and fear, to unify the name of Yud
Key with Vav Key completely, in the name of all Israel, I am ready and
willing to apply the connection of Second Cup out of Four Cups, and
may the pleasantness of Hashem, our God, be upon us, and establish
the action of our hands upon us and establish the action of our hands.*

*Blessed are You, Hashem, our God, King of the universe, Who creates the
fruit of the vine.*

We drink while leaning to the left.

LeShem Yichud – Second Cup of Wine – Creation (Bri'ah)

As mentioned previously, the four cups of wine poured during the *Seder* connect
us to the four-letter Name of God—the Tetragrammaton— יהוה. When we scan the
Tetragrammaton from right to left, the second cup of wine is our connection to the first
letter *Hei* ה.

אוֹמְרִים: מִן הַפְּסָחִים וּמִן הַזְּבָחִים) אֲשֶׁר יַגִּיעַ דָּמָם עַל קִיר מִזְבַּחֲךָ

לְרָצוֹן מהע ע"ה, אל עדי ע"ה וְנוֹדֶה לְךָ שִׁיר וְחָדָשׁ י"ב הויות עַל גְּאֻלָּתֵנוּ וְעַל

פְּדוּת נַפְשֵׁנוּ: בָּרוּךְ יהוה ע"ב ורבוע מ"ה אַתָּה יְהֹוָ‏ה(אהדונהיאהדונהי גָּאַל ע"ה אל

יִשְׂרָאֵל:

LeShem Yichud – Second Cup of Wine – Creation (Bri'ah)

לְשֵׁם יהוה עדי יִחוּד קוּדְשָׁא בְּרִיךְ הוּא וּשְׁכִינְתֵּיהּ (אהדונהי בִּדְחִ‏ילוּ

וּרְחִ‏ימוּ (יאההויהה וּרְחִ‏ימוּ וּדְחִ‏ילוּ (איההויהה לְיַחֲדָא שֵׁם יהוה עדי יוֹד קֵ

בְּ‏וָאו קֵי בְּיִחוּדָא שְׁלִים (יהוה בְּשֵׁם יהוה עדי כָּל ילי יִשְׂרָאֵל, הִנֵּ

מוּכָן וּמְזוּמָּן לְקַיֵּם מִצְוַת כּוֹס מום, אלהים שֵׁנִי שֶׁל אַרְבַּע כּוֹסוֹ

וִיהִי אל נֹעַם ע"ה קס"א אֲדֹנָי כלה אֱלֹהֵינוּ ילה עָלֵינוּ ריבוע ס"ג וּמַעֲשֵׂה יָדֵי

יהוה אדני כּוֹנְנָה רבוע מ"ה עָלֵינוּ ריבוע ס"ג וּמַעֲשֵׂה יָדֵינוּ יהוה אדני כּוֹנְנֵהוּ:

בָּרוּךְ יהוה ע"ב ורבוע מ"ה אַתָּה יְהֹוָ‏ה(אהדי‏אהדונהי אֱלֹהֵינוּ ילה מֶלֶךְ הָעוֹלָ‏ם

בּוֹרֵא פְּרִי ע"ה אלהים דאלפין הַגָּפֶן:

בכוס שני יכוין באלה"ים דההין (אלף למד הה יוד מם) בחיצוניות הוד דאימא
ובפנימיותו ס"ג (יוד הי ואו הי).

We drink while leaning to the left.

LeShem Yichud unites our thoughts and our actions with the Light and the Upper Worlds. For this reason, it precedes the prayers. Many times, we have a thought to do the right thing, but our actions contradict our original thought and intention. Throughout the *Seder*, we need to make a conscious effort to improve ourselves spiritually. *LeShem Yichud* helps keep us true to our positive thoughts and intentions, especially the day after the *Seder*.

STAGE SIX:

RACHTZA

Before we recite the blessing we pour a cup of water over our right
hand twice and then over the left hand twice

Blessed are you, Hashem, our God, King of the universe, which has sanctified
us by His connections and connected us by the washing of the hands.

STAGE SEVEN:

MOTZI

STAGE SIX: RACHTZA

As mentioned previously, our hands are like magnets that attract negative forces because
they manifest the negative thoughts that reside in our hearts and minds. By washing our
hands, we wash away all negative forces that cling to them.

We receive yet another important benefit when we say this blessing. The last three words
of the blessing are Al Netilat Yadayim, and the first letter from each of these three words
(Alef, Nun, Yud) spells ani עני, meaning "a poor person." When you take the last letter
of the same three words, Lamed ל, Tav ת, and Mem מ, they have the same numerical value
as the word ashir עשיר which means "a rich person." By washing our hands and meditating
to inject positive energy into our actions, we begin to uproot ourselves from the level of
ani (poor) and elevate ourselves to the energy of ashir (rich). "Rich" refers not only to
financial well-being, but also to living a life filled with a wealth of meaning. The blessing
will be directed wherever we need this energy.

STAGE SEVEN: MOTZI

The numerical value of Hamotzi Lechem Min HaAretz (the blessing over the *Matzah*)
is the same as that of three kabbalistic meditations—*Pei*, Alef, Yud פאי; Samech, Alef

STAGE SIX:

רָחְצָה

יוד פעמים ה"י דס"ג, האָרה מבינה דו"א לגבורה עלה, וז"א רוחץ בה.

Before we recite the blessing we pour a cup of water over our right
hand twice and then over the left hand

י"ג תיבות כנגד י"ג מידות.

ר"ת עני = ריבוע דמ"ה (יוד יוד הא יוד הא ואו יוד הא ואו הא) ; שתי האותיות האחרונות במלים
עַל נטילַת יָדַים עולות למנין עשיר, שמי שנזהר בנטילת ידים זוכה לעושר

STAGE SEVEN:

מוֹצִיא

מוציא - מווח הווכמה מאבא.
קטנות א' דאבא, אלהי"ם [ה' בציור ד"י].
גדלות ב' עלו, יוד ה' ויו ה'.

---

amed סאל; and Chet, *Tav*, final *Kaf* חתך—for creating sustenance and prosperity in our
ves. Before we eat the *Matzah* and the *Pesach* meal, we pray for sustenance with the
onsciousness that nothing is ours. This awareness that all good fortune emanates from
e Light helps intensify our prayers.

STAGE EIGHT:

MATZAH

LESHEM YICHUD

We raise all three Matzot on the *Seder* Plate while we recite the following:

For the sake of unifying The Holy One, blessed be He, and His Shechinah with fear and mercy, and with mercy and fear, to unify the name of Yu Key with Vav Key completely, in the name of all Israel, I am ready an willing to apply the connection of eating Matzah, and may the pleasantnes of Hashem, our God, be upon us, and establish the action of our hand upon us and establish the action of our hands.

Blessed are You, Hashem, our God, King of the universe, Who brings forth bread from the earth.

We put down the bottom Matzah, break a piece from each of the other two Matzah, and recite the following blessing:

Blessed are You, Hashem, our God, King of the universe, Who ha sanctified us by His connections, and connected us to eat Matzah.

STAGE EIGHT: MATZAH

Matzah requires a special blessing in addition to the blessing over bread. Bread is the on food with a dual nature. We eat bread during the year, tapping all of its positive energy But during Passover, we cannot eat bread or even have one crumb in our homes becaus of the overwhelming infusion of ego-energy that bread transmits.

According to the Zohar, *Matzah* is the medication and antidote against our ego—th Opponent within. Eating *Matzah* also supports us physically, as *Matzah* contains the secre of a healthy immune system and the fountain of youth. To get younger, we need the Ligh The secret to this is a balanced immune system. When we are in the embryonic state pri to our birth, there is no separation, no identity of "self:" there are only undifferentiate cells. Eating *Matzah* takes us back to this embryonic state—where we are willing to los what we are, not wanting thanks or recognition, and doing something because we kno it's right.

For the next seven days after the *Seder* night, we don't eat any bread or food that ca expand. We use *Matzah* as a tool to control and shrink our *Desire to Receive for the Se Alone.* Because bread expands—like our ego—it has the same force of the *Desire to Recei*

STAGE EIGHT:

מַצָּה

מצה – מווז בינה מאבא

קטנות א' דאבא – אֱלֹהִי"ם [ה' בציור ד"ו].

גדלות ב' עלו, יוד הי ואו הי.

LESHEM YICHUD

We raise all three Matzot on the *Seder* Plate while we recite the following:

לְשֵׁם יהוה שדי יְוזוד קוּדְשָׁא בְּרִיךְ הוּא וּשְׁכִינְתֵּיהּ (יאהדונהי) בִּדְוזִיל
וּרְווזִימו (יאההויהה) וּרְווזִימו וּדְווזִילוּ (איההויההה) לְיַווזֵדָא שֵׁם יהוה שדי יוד קְ
בּוֹאוּ קְ בְּיווּדָא שְׁלִים (יהוה) בְּשֵׁם יהוה שדי כָּל ילי יִשְׂרָאֵל, הִנֵּ
מוּכָן וּמְזוּמָן לְקַיֵּם מִצְוַת אֲכִילַת מַצָּה ע"ב ס"ג וִיהִי אל נעם ע"ה קס
אֲדֹנָי כללה אֱלֹהֵינוּ ילה עָלֵינוּ ריבוע ס"ג וּמַעֲשֵׂה יָדֵינוּ יהוה אדני כּוֹנְנָה ריבוע מ
עָלֵינוּ ריבוע ס"ג וּמַעֲשֵׂה יָדֵינוּ יהוה אדני כּוֹנְנֵהוּ:

בָּרוּךְ יהוה ע"ב ורבוע מ"ה אַתָּה יְהֹוָֹאֲהדֹונְהִיאהדונהי אֱלֹהֵינוּ ילה מֶלֶךְ הָעוֹלָם
הַמּוֹצִיא לֶווֶם ג"פ יהוה מִן הָאָרֶץ אלהים דההין ע"ה:

We put down the bottom Matzah, break a piece from each of the other two Matzah, and recite the following blessing:

בָּרוּךְ יהוה ע"ב ורבוע מ"ה אַתָּה יְהֹוָֹאֲהדֹונְהִיאהדונהי אֱלֹהֵינוּ ילה מֶלֶךְ הָעוֹלָם
אֲשֶׁר קִדְּשָׁנוּ בְּמִצְוֹתָיו וְצִוָּנוּ עַל אֲכִילַת מַצָּה ע"ב ס"ג:

Matzah, on the other hand, is unleavened bread that is not given the opportunity to expand. When we eat *Matzah*, our *Desire to Receive* is restricted from expanding.

LeShem Yichud unites our thoughts and our actions with the Light and the Upper Worlds. For this reason, it precedes the prayers. Many times, we have a thought to do the right thing, but our actions contradict our original thought and intention. Throughout the *Seder*, we need to make a conscious effort to improve ourselves spiritually. *LeShem Yichud* helps keep us true to our positive thoughts and intentions, especially the day after the *Seder*.

STAGE NINE:

MAROR

For the sake of unifying The Holy One, blessed be It, and Its Shechina, with fear and mercy, and with mercy and fear, to unify the name of Yu Key with Vav Key completely, in the name of all Israel, I am ready an willing to apply the connection of eating Maror, and may the pleasantne of Hashem, our God, be upon us, and establish the action of our hand upon us and establish the action of our hands.

We take the *Maror*, dip it in the fruit blend, say the blessing, and eat it without leaning.

Blessed are You, Hashem, our God, King of the universe, Who has sanctified us by His connections, and connected us to eat horseradish.

STAGE NINE: MAROR

Why do we eat the *Maror* (bitter herb), which is the "taste of death" on the night o freedom? Why do we want to connect to the energy of death? If you swallow th *Maror* too soon without really chewing it, you need to taste it again. This "tastin death" until it becomes sweet is connected to what we are going through right no in our lives. It is not about what our father did to us when were three—it is abou what is happening right now! If we are shut down, if we don't see our challenges o chaos as a problem or an issue, we are swallowing the *Maror* without chewing it. W have to feel the bitterness of the "taste of death;" we have to go through the pai and discomfort of it completely the first time, or we will have to go through it agai

The more we give up, the more things are concealed from us. To the degree a person give up and feels that he cannot overcome, things are concealed from him or her. There is a dire correlation between how far we feel from the Light and how far we are from the Light.

STAGE NINE:

מָרוֹר

ד' אלפין דארבעה אהיה עלוקות לאה.

מיתוק דיני לאה במווזין.

וזרוס"ת וז"ס הם סוד המווזין:

אהי"ה יהו"ה אהיה

שממתיקים רו"ת עהיא לאה.

והוא זכר לטיט בסוד ב' י"ט - מילוי מ"ה

וד א או א,

הניתנים לב' נוקבין לאה ורזל.

לְשֵׁם יהוה עד״י יְחוּד קוּדְשָׁא בְּרִיךְ הוּא וּשְׁכִינְתֵּיהּ (יאהדונהי) בִּדְחִילוּ וּרְחִימוּ (יאההויהה) וּרְחִימוּ וּדְחִילוּ (איההויהה) לְיַחֲדָא שֵׁם יהוה עד״י יוּד קֵ״ה בְּוָאוּ קֵי בְּיִחוּדָא שְׁלִים (יהוה) בְּשֵׁם יהוה עד״י כָּל יל״י יִשְׂרָאֵל, הִנְנִי מוּכָן וּמְזוּמָּן לְקַיֵּם מִצְוַת אֲכִילַת מָרוֹר וִיהִי אל נעם עה״ה קס״א אֲדֹנָי כלה אֱלֹהֵינוּ יל״ה עָלֵינוּ ריבוע ס״ג וּמַעֲשֵׂה יָדֵינוּ יהוה אדני כּוֹנְנָה ריבוע מ״ה עָלֵינוּ ריבוע ס״ג וּמַעֲשֵׂה יָדֵינוּ יהוה אדני כּוֹנְנֵהוּ:

We take the *Maror*, dip it in the fruit blend, say the blessing, and eat it without leaning.

בָּרוּךְ יהוה ע״ב ורבוע מ״ה אַתָּה יְהֹוָ‎[אדניאהדונהי] אֱלֹהֵינוּ יל״ה מֶלֶךְ הָעוֹלָם אֲשֶׁר קִדְּשָׁנוּ בְּמִצְוֹתָיו וְצִוָּנוּ עַל אֲכִילַת מָרוֹר:

LeShem Yichud unites our thoughts and our actions with the Light and the Upper Worlds. For this reason, it precedes the prayers. Many times, we have a thought to do the right thing, but our actions contradict our original thought and intention. Throughout the *Seder*, we need to make a conscious effort to improve ourselves spiritually. *LeShem Yichud* helps keep us true to our positive thoughts and intentions, especially the day after the *Seder*.

STAGE TEN:

KORECH

We take the Maror, spread it on a Matzah, and eat them together, leaning to the left, without a blessing. Prior to this, we recite the following:

In remembrance of the temple, we do as Hillel did in temple times: I would make a sandwich of Pesach offering and horseradish in a Matza bread and eat them together in order to fulfill what is written in the Torah "They shall eat it with Matzah and bitter herbs."

STAGE TEN: KORECH

The process of *Korech* elevates us above the stars and the signs of the zodiac. Aries the first sign—the seed, where all the control lies.This is one reason that Aries (the ram was chosen for the sacrifice at the Temple on Passover. Aries is also one of the mos problematic signs, with more *Desire to Receive for the Self Alone* than any other sign. I we can rise above the influence of Aries, we can overcome all obstacles and negativit Therefore, the great sage Hillel used the power of *Korech* (putting *Matzah* and *Maro* together) to rise above the negative influences of the 12 signs of the zodiac.

Matzah is about our spiritual connection to the Light and *Maror*, our lack. We need t see our lack and our Light together. Some people just see their Light and have ego; othe see only their darkness and are depressed. A successful person is one who can see an function with both Light and lack.

It says that the difference between Jacob and Esau was very minimal. The kabbalists sai that the difference between Heaven and Hell is splitting a hair so close but so far. There i a wonderful story about a man who leaves this world and arrives at the pearly gates, wher he is given a preview of Heaven and Hell. Both scenarios have the exact same setting people sitting around a huge pot of stew, each holding a wooden spoon with a very lon handle, longer than the length of their arms. In Hell, he sees emaciated people trying t feed themselves, and try as they might they are not able to get the food into their ow

STAGE TEN:

כּוֹרֵךְ

כורך ~ מווז וחסדים מאבא.

קְטַנּוּת א' דאבא,

אלהי"ם

[ה' בּצּיּוּר וו"ו] וּגדלות הב' שׁלו,

יוֹד הא ואו הא יוד הה וו הה,

וזה מפני שׁהחזו"ג נכללים זה מזה על כן יש שׁם גם הגבורות.

יכוין עתה להאיר אל לאה ג"כ ממ"ה וב"ן דאבא

We take the Maror, spread it on a Matzah, and eat them together, leaning to the left, without a blessing. Prior to this, we recite the following:

זֵכֶר לְמִקְדָּשׁ כְּהִלֵּל אדני, ללה. כֵּן עָשָׂה הִלֵּל אדני, ללה. בִּזְמַן שֶׁבֵּית ב"פ ראה הַמִּקְדָּשׁ הָיָה יהה קַיָּם הָיָה יהה כּוֹרֵךְ פֶּסַח מַצָּה ע"ב ס וּמָרוֹר וְאוֹכֵל בְּיַחַד לְקַיֵּם מַה מ"ה שֶׁנֶּאֱמַר עַל מַצּוֹת וּמְרֹרִים יֹאכְלֻהוּ:

---

mouths using the long cumbersome spoons. In Heaven, on the other hand, the people ook healthy, and satiated. The difference is that in Heaven, they were feeding one another sing their long spoons to reach to the mouth of a person who sat opposite them. They ere sharing, because they understood that the only way they can eat—have the real ulfillment and sustenance that they need—is by taking care of one another. So, what is Iell? Hell is not having the ability to share with others.

or us to change from Hell to Heaven, we may have to switch only one thing.

STAGE ELEVEN:

SHULCHAN ORECH

It is customary to eat an egg as part of our meal in honor of the holiday.

STAGE TWELVE:

TZAFUN

We take the *Matza* kept for the *Afikoman,* in remembrance of the Passover offering, to be eaten after one is full. We eat while leaning to the left and recite the following:

LeShem Yichud

For the sake of unifying The Holy One, blessed be He, and His Shechinah with fear and mercy, and with mercy and fear, to unify the name of Yud Key with Vav Key completely, in the name of all Israel, I am ready and willing to apply the connection of eating Afikoman, and may the pleasantness of Hashem, our God, be upon us, and establish the action of our hands upon us and establish the action of our hands.

STAGE ELEVEN: SHULCHAN ORECH

Shulchan Orech means "the table where we eat." Any time we have a meal during the year, we elevate the sparks of Light within the food we eat, but there is an additional spiritual ingredient at the *Seder*—the table where we eat at the *Seder* is a *mizbe'ach* (an altar). Everything we did on the altar in the Temple, we are doing on the table at *Pesach*. This means we have to feel that we are in the Temple, that we have the miracle of the Temple and that we have to prepare everything as if we are in the Temple.

During the *Seder*, the meal is smack in the middle of our connections; we have connections before and after it. It is not that we take a break for a meal, the meal is part of the Light that we connect to on *Pesach*—even the food is part of the system. When we are aware that everything is part of the system, everywhere they go and everything they do become an opportunity for Light to be revealed there for us. However, a person can go to the holiest of places and not be connected at all. In the case of the *Seder*, we are not just eating for physical gratification. We partake of the meal to gain strength to continue with our spiritual work.

STAGE ELEVEN:

שֻׁלְחָן עוֹרֵךְ

שֻׁלְחָן עוֹרֵךְ - בְּסוֹד הַזִּיוּוּג.

STAGE TWELVE:

צָפוּן

צָפוּן - מוֹחַ גְּבוּרוֹת דְּאַבָּא.

קְטַנּוּת א' דְּאַבָּא,

אֱלֹהִ"ם

[ה' בְּצִיּוּר וֹ"וֹ] וְגַדְלוּת ב' שֶׁלוֹ,

יוֹד הֵה וֹ הֵה יוֹד הֵא וָאו הֵא,

כִּי הַגְּבוּרוֹת נִכְלָלוֹת מִן הַחֲסָדִים, אֲבָל שֵׁם ב"ן קוֹדֵם כִּי הוּא בִּמְקוֹמוֹ.

We take the *Matza* kept for the *Afikoman,* in remembrance of the Passover offering, to be
eaten after one is full. We eat while leaning to the left and recite the following:

LeShem Yichud

לְשֵׁם יהוה שדי יְוֹזוֹד קוּדְשָׁא בְּרִיךְ הוּא וּשְׁכִינְתֵּיה (אהדונהי) בִּדְחִיל
וּרְחִימוּ (יאההויהה) וּרְחִימוּ וּדְחִילוּ (איההויהה) לְיַחֲדָא שֵׁם יהוה שדי יוֹד כֵ
בְּוָאו קֵי בְּיוֹזוֹדָא שְׁלִים (יהוה) בְּשֵׁם יהוה שדי כָּל ילי יִשְׂרָאֵל, הִנֵ
מוּכָן וּמְזוּמָן לְקַיֵּם מִצְוַת אֲכִילַת אֲפִיקוֹמֶן. וִיהִי אל נֹעַם ע"ה קס
אֲדֹנָי ללה אֱלֹהֵינוּ ילה עָלֵינוּ ריבוע ס"ג וּמַעֲשֵׂה יָדֵינוּ יהוה אדני כּוֹנְנָה רב
מ"ה עָלֵינוּ ריבוע ס"ג וּמַעֲשֵׂה יָדֵינוּ יהוה אדני כּוֹנְנֵהוּ:

STAGE TWELVE: TZAFUN

zafun means "whatever is hidden." When Jacob went to his father, Isaac, to receive a blessing,
e brought a sacrifice with him, and afterwards Jacob received the blessing from his father.

Stage Thirteen:

BARECH

We pour the third cup and recite the following blessing over the food:

LeShem Yichud

*For the sake of unifying The Holy One, blessed be He, and His Shechinah, with fe
and mercy, and with mercy and fear, to unify the name of Yud Key with Vav K
completely, in the name of all Israel, I am ready and willing to apply the connection (
blessing over the food, as it is written in the Torah: "And you shall eat and you sh
be satisfied and you shall bless Hashem, your God, for the good land which It ga
you," and may the pleasantness of Hashem, our God, be upon us, and establish i
action of our hands upon us and establish the action of our hands.*

How does this story relate to our life? We know that the power of the *Afikoman* is equ
to the sacrifices that occurred in ancient times. The numerical value of *Afikoman* (287)
the same value for *bemirma*, the word for "with deception." This connects to Jacob, wl
used deception against his brother, Esau. Isaac originally wanted to give his blessing
Esau, but Jacob wore his brother's clothes, fooled his father, and received the blessi
instead. This gives us a clue to the significance behind the hiding of the *Afikoman*. Hidi
the *Afikoman* connects us to Jacob's sacrifice and his deception so that we can decei
Satan and remove him from our life. When Jacob walked into his father's tent, the Tor;
tells us that Isaac could smell the Garden of Eden, but when Esau came in, Isaac shiver
because the energy felt like Hell. According to the *Zohar*, when we do the connection (
Tzafun with this understanding, we taste from the Garden of Eden as opposed to tasti
from the fires of Hell.

LeShem Yichud unites our thoughts and our actions with the Light and the Upper
Worlds. For this reason, it precedes the prayers. Many times, we have a thought to
do the right thing, but our actions contradict our original thought and intention.
Throughout the *Seder*, we need to make a conscious effort to improve ourselves
spiritually. *LeShem Yichud* helps keep us true to our positive thoughts and intentions,
especially the day after the *Seder*.

Stage Thirteen: Barech

Birkat haMazon (prayer after the meal) elevates the sparks of Light concealed inside tl
food we just ate. It removes the physical aspect of the meal (temporary energy), leavi
us with the spiritual nourishment.

STAGE THIRTEEN:

בָּרֵךְ:

We pour the third cup and recite the following blessing over the food:

בּרך – מוזו וחסדים מאימא.
גדלות א' דאו"א,

יוד הא ואו הא, יוד הה וו הה,

יוד הא ואו הא, יוד הה וו הה.

קטנות ב' דאו"א, ע"ה ע"ד, ע"ה ע"ד.

גדלות ב' דאימא,

יוד הא ואו הא. יוד הה וו הה.

LeShem Yichud

לְשֵׁם יהוה שדי יְוֹזֹוד קוּדְשָׁא בְּרִיךְ הוּא וּשְׁכִינְתֵּיהּ (אהדונהי) בִּדְזֹוִיק
וּרְוֹזִימוּ (אהדויהה) וּרְוֹזִימוּ וּדְוֹזִילוּ (איהדויההה) לְיַוֹזְדָא שֵׁם יהוה שדי יוד קֶ
בְּיֹאוּ קֵי בִּיֹוֹזְדָא שְׁלִים (יהוה) בְּשֵׁם יהוה שדי כָּל יל' יִשְׂרָאֵל, הִנֵּ
מוּכָן וּמְזוּמָּן לְקַיֵּים מִצְוַת עֲשֵׂה שֶׁל בִּרְכַּת הַמָּזֹון מלוי ע"ב אל יהו
שֶׁנֶּאֱמַר וְאָכַלְתָּ וְשָׂבָעְתָּ וּבֵרַכְתָּ אֶת יְהֹוָֽאֲדֹנָי־אהדונהי אֱלֹהֶיךָ ילה ע
הָאָרֶץ אלהים דההן ע"ה הַטֹּבָה אכא אֲשֶׁר נָתַן לָךְ, וִיהִי אל נֹעַם ע"ה קס
אֲדֹנָי כלה אֱלֹהֵינוּ ילה עָלֵינוּ יל' ריבוע ס"ג וּמַעֲשֵׂה יָדֵינוּ יהוה אדני כּוֹנְנָה רבו
מ"ה עָלֵינוּ ריבוע ס"ג וּמַעֲשֵׂה יָדֵינוּ יהוה אדני כּוֹנְנֵהוּ:

n the beginning of the *Birkat HaMazon* we sing: *"Who nourishes the entire world in His goodness."* The key is the word "entire" (*kulo*): The world can only achieve perfection if ere is unity; if there is a quantum spiritual consciousness. As long as we are living in ur own little bubble, the world will never achieve its perfection. There are no separate ountries or cities—we are all one.

says that the Israelites are like the stars and that each star has light, each one is a channel, ach person has a job to do. Not only do we affect ourselves, we affect others as well as e place we are in. Our actions have much more effect than we think, like a pebble that reates ever-expanding waves when it is thrown into a still lake.

SHIR HAMA'ALOT

A song of elevation When Hashem will return the captivity of Zion, we wi be like dreamers. Then our mouth will be filled with laughter and our tong with glad song. Then they will declare among the nations, "Hashem has dor greatly with these." Hashem has done greatly with us; we were gladdened. (Hashem, return our captivity like brooks in the desert. Those who tearful sow, will reap in glad song. He who bears the measure of seeds walks alor weeping, but will return in exultation, a bearer of his sheaves.

Leader

Gentlemen, let us bless.

Others

Blessed be the name of Hashem from this time and forever.

Leader repeats

Blessed be the name of Hashem from this time and forever.

On Shabbat we add:

With the permission of Shabbat, the queen, with the permission of my teachers, and with the permission of the distinguished people present.

With the permission of my teachers and with the permission of distinguished people present (If ten men join in the blessing we add our God.) Let us bless that of Who we have eaten.

SHIR HAMA'ALOT

שִׁיר הַמַּעֲלוֹת בְּשׁוּב יְהֹוָה (אדני אהדונהי) אֶת שִׁיבַת צִיּוֹן יוסף, ו"פ יהוה, ה' הָיִינוּ כְּחֹלְמִים: אָז יִמָּלֵא שְׂחוֹק פִּינוּ וּלְשׁוֹנֵנוּ רִנָּה אָז יֹאמְרוּ אל בַגּוֹיִם הִגְדִּיל יְהֹוָה (אדני אהדונהי) לַעֲשׂוֹת עִם אֵלֶּה: הִגְדִּיל יְהֹוָה (אדני אהדונהי) לַעֲשׂוֹת עִמָּנוּ ריבוע ס"ג הָיִינוּ שְׂמֵחִים: שׁוּבָה החזק יְהֹוָה (אדני אהדונהי) אֶת שְׁבִיתֵנוּ כַּאֲפִיקִים בַּנֶּגֶב: הַזֹּרְעִים בְּדִמְעָה בְּרִנָּה יִקְצֹרוּ: הָלוֹךְ יֵלֵךְ כלי וּבָכֹה נֹשֵׂא מֶשֶׁךְ הַזָּרַע בֹּא יָבֹא בְרִנָּה נֹשֵׂא אֲלֻמֹּתָיו

Leader

הַב לָן וּנְבָרֵךְ ר"ת ע"ה מ"ב; ס"ת ע"ב

Others

יְהִי שֵׁם יהוה שדי יְהֹוָה (אדני אהדונהי) מְבֹרָךְ רפ"ח מֵעַתָּה וְעַד עוֹלָם:

Leader repeats

יְהִי שֵׁם יהוה שדי יְהֹוָה (אדני אהדונהי) מְבֹרָךְ רפ"ח מֵעַתָּה וְעַד עוֹלָם:

On Shabbat we add:

> וּבִרְשׁוּת שקו צית שַׁבָּת מַלְכְּתָא
>
> וּבִרְשׁוּת שקו צית יוֹמָא טָבָא אוּשְׁפִּיזָא קַדִּישָׁא

בִּרְשׁוּת שקו צית הָרַב רִבִּי מוֹרִי וְהָרַבָּנִית מוֹרָתִי

מָרָנָן וְרַבּוֹתַי

נְבָרֵךְ (המזמן בעשרה אֱלֹהֵינוּ יכלה)

שֶׁאָכַלְנוּ מִשֶּׁלּוֹ:

Others

*Let us bless (If ten men join in the blessing we add our God.) That ([?]
Who we have eaten, and through Whose goodness we live.*

Leader repeats

*Let us bless (If ten men are present, we add: "our God.") That of Who w[?]
have eaten, and through Whose goodness we live.
Blessed is He, and blessed is His name.*

THE FIRST BLESSING—THE WORLD OF EMANATION (ATZILUT)

*Blessed are you, Lord, our God, King of the universe, Who nourishes t[?]
entire world in His goodness—with grace, with kindness, and with merc[?]
He gives nourishment to all flesh, for His kindness is eternal. And throu[?]
His great goodness, we have never lacked and shall never lack nourishmen[?]
for all eternity. For the sake of His great Name, because He is a G[?]
which nourishes and sustains all and benefits all, and He prepares food f[?]
all of Its creatures which He created. As it is said:*

THE FIRST BLESSING—THE WORLD OF EMANATION (ATZILUT)

The Creator gives sustenance to the whole world. Connecting to the first blessing we dra[?]
the power of sustenance and prosperity into our lives. But there is one requirement: I[?]
important to understand that whatever we own is merely on loan to us, that all sustenan[?]
originates with the Creator. This awareness ensures that we keep our sustenan[?]
throughout our entire life. However, if we believe that we are the cause and creators [?]
our own wealth, we open ourselves up to Satan and to the potential for ups and dow[?]
and to a loss of sustenance.

The Baal Shem Tov woke up one Friday morning and realized that he had no food f[?]
Shabbat. So he went and knocked on a neighbor's window, said that he had nothing f[?]
Shabbat, and then turned to go back home to study. The neighbor didn't realize that th[?]

Others

בָּרוּךְ יהוה ע״ב ורבוע מ״ה (בעשרה מ״ה) אֱלֹהֵינוּ ילה שֶׁאָכַלְנוּ מִשֶּׁלוֹ וּבְטוּבוֹ חָיִּינוּ:

Leader repeats

בָּרוּךְ יהוה ע״ב ורבוע מ״ה (בעשרה מ״ה) אֱלֹהֵינוּ ילה שֶׁאָכַלְנוּ מִשֶּׁלוֹ וּבְטוּבוֹ חָיִּינוּ:

בָּרוּךְ יהוה ע״ב ורבוע מ״ה הוּא וּבָרוּךְ יהוה ע״ב ורבוע מ״ה שְׁמוֹ מהש ע״ה, אל שדי ע״ה

THE FIRST BLESSING - THE WORLD OF EMANATION (ATZILUT)

בָּרוּךְ יהוה ע״ב ורבוע מ״ה אַתָּה יְהֹוָוָאהּדונהי אֱלֹהֵינוּ ילה מֶלֶךְ הָעוֹלָם הַזָּן נגד, מזבח אֶת הָעוֹלָם כֻּלּוֹ, בְּטוּבוֹ בְּחֵן מוזי בְּחֶסֶד ע״ב, ריבוע יהו וּבְרַחֲמִים אלהים דיודין, מצפצ, י״פ יי, הוּא נֹתֵן אבגית״ץ, ועֶר, אהבת חנם לֶחֶם ג״פ יהוה לְכָל יה אדני בָּשָׂר כִּי לְעוֹלָם וְחַסְדּוֹ ג״פ יהוה: וּבְטוּבוֹ הַגָּדוֹל לההו, מבה, אום תָּמִיד ע״ה נתה, קס״א קנ״א קמ״ג לֹא וְחָסֵר לָנוּ מום, אלהים, וְאַל יֶחְסַר לָנוּ מום, אלהים מָזוֹן מלוי ע״ב אל יהוה לְעוֹלָם וָעֶד, בַּעֲבוּר שְׁמ מהש ע״ה, אל שדי ע״ה הַגָּדוֹל לההו, מבה, אום כִּי הוּא אֵל ייא״י זָן נגד, מזבח וּמְפַרְנֵס לַכֹּל יה אדני וּמֵטִיב לַכֹּל יה אדני וּמֵכִין מָזוֹן מלוי ע״ב אל יהוה לְכָ יה אדני בְּרִיּוֹתָיו אֲשֶׁר בָּרָא קנ״א ב״ן כָּאָמוּר.

---

erson who knocked on his window was the Baal Shem Tov, but he ran after the sage nyway to give him money to buy what he needed for Shabbat. The Baal Shem Tov says at we are born with our sustenance. Some people expend only a little effort for a lot of ustenance, while others must expend a great deal of effort to get a little. This is because f the curtain between us and the Light. We were destined to have the appropriate mount of sustenance for our needs.

POTEACH ET YADECHA

You open your hands

פֿאִי סאָל וֹזתך

Sustenance through tithing

And satisfy the needs of every living thing.
Blessed are You, Hashem, Who nourishes all.

THE SECOND BLESSING—THE WORLD OF CREATION (BRI'AH)

We thank You, Hashem, our God, because You have given to our forefather
as a heritage a desirable, good, and spacious land; because You removed us
Hashem, our God, from the land of Egypt and You redeemed us from th
house of bondage; for Your covenant which You sealed in our flesh; for You
Torah which You taught us and for Your statutes which You made know
to us; for life, grace, and loving kindness which You granted us; and fo
the provision of food with which You nourish and sustain us constantly, i
every day, in every season, and in every hour. For all, Hashem, our God, w
thank You and bless You. May Your Name be blessed by the mouth of a
living, continuously for all eternity. As it is written: "And you shall eat, and yo
shall be satisfied, and you shall bless Hashem, your God, for the good land tha
It gave you." Blessed are You, Hashem, for the land and for the nourishment.

POTE'ACH ET YADECHA

When we open our hands saying, "*Pote'ach Et Yadecha*," besides requesting sustenance, we ar
asking the Light to enter every chamber of our heart. There are levels of our soul that w
don't know exist or that we have forgotten about, so we don't let people in. When we open ou
hands here, we are saying, "God, please have the Light go into all the chambers of our hear
and all the parts of our soul so that we can open our hearts even more and more and more."

THE SECOND BLESSING—THE WORLD OF CREATION (BRI'AH)

This verse states that we are thanking God. But the Creator does not need our thank
or recognition. In reality, when we recite this verse, we are awakening appreciation i

POTEACH ET YADECHA

פּוֹתֵחַ אֶת יָ֫דֶ֒ךָ ר"ת פאי, ס"ת וזתך (יוֹזְהָתוֹכְהָ)

You open your hands

פאי סאל וזתך

Sustenance through tithing

וּמַשְׂבִּיעַ וזתך לְכָל יה אדני וָ֫י רָצוֹן מהשע ע"ה, אל שדי ע"ה, ר"ת רחל: בָּרוּךְ יהו
ע"ב ורבוע מ"ה אַתָּה יְהֹוָֽאֲהִֽאֱדִֽהֹנֹהִי הַזָּ֫ן נגד, מזבח אֶת הַכֹּל ילי:

THE SECOND BLESSING – THE WORLD OF CREATION (BRI'AH)

נוֹדֶה לְּךָ יְהֹוָֽאֲהִֽאֱדִֽהֹנֹהִי אֱלֹהֵ֫ינוּ ילה עַל שֶׁהִנְחַלְתָּ לַאֲבוֹתֵ֫ינוּ, אֶרֶ
אלהים דאלפין וְחֶמְדָּה ךְ טוֹבָה אכא וּרְחָבָה, וְעַל שֶׁהוֹצֵאתָ֫נוּ יְהֹוָֽאֲהֽדֹנֹ
אֱלֹהֵ֫ינוּ ילה מֵאֶ֫רֶץ אלהים דאלפין מִצְרַ֫יִם מצר, וּפְדִיתָ֫נוּ מִבֵּ֫ית ב"פ רא
עֲבָדִים, וְעַל בְּרִיתְךָ שֶׁחָתַ֫מְתָּ בִּבְשָׂרֵ֫נוּ, וְעַל תּוֹרָתְךָ שֶׁלִּמַּדְתָּ֫נוּ
וְעַל חֻקֶּ֫יךָ שֶׁהוֹדַעְתָּ֫נוּ, וְעַל חַיִּים בינה ע"ה וְחֵן מוזי וָזָ֫ן מוזי וָחֶ֫סֶד ע"ב, ריבוע יהו
שֶׁחוֹנַנְתָּ֫נוּ, וְעַל אֲכִילַת מָזוֹן מלוי ע"ב = אל יהוה שָׁאַתָּה זָן נגד, מזבח וּמְפַרְנֵ
אוֹתָ֫נוּ תָּמִיד ע"ה נתה, קס"א קנ"א קמ"ג בְּכָל ב"ן = נגד, זן, מזב
וּבְכָל ב"ן, לכבם עֵת יי"פ אהיה י' הויות וּבְכָל ב"ן, לכבם שָׁעָה מצר מ"ה
וְעַל הַכֹּל ילי יְהֹוָֽאֲהִֽאֱדִֽהֹנֹהִי אֱלֹהֵ֫ינוּ ילה אֲנַ֫חְנוּ מוֹדִים לָךְ, וּמְבָרְכִים
אוֹתָךְ, יִתְבָּרַךְ שִׁמְךָ בְּפִי כָל ילי וָי תָּמִיד ע"ה נתה, קס"א קנ"א קמ
לְעוֹלָם וָעֶד. כַּכָּתוּב: וְאָכַלְתָּ וְשָׂבָ֫עְתָּ וּבֵרַכְתָּ אֶת יְהֹוָֽאֲהֽדֹנֹ
אֱלֹהֶ֫יךָ ילה עַל הָאָ֫רֶץ אלהים דההין ע"ה הַטֹּבָה אכא אֲשֶׁר נָתַן לָךְ: בָּרוּ
יהוה ע"ב ורבוע מ"ה אַתָּה יְהֹוָֽאֲהִֽאֱדִֽהֹנֹהִי עַל הָאָ֫רֶץ אלהים דההין ע"
וְעַל הַמָּזוֹן מלוי ע"ב = אל יהוה:

ourselves because it is the energy of appreciation that works like a shield to protect our
ood fortune.

The third blessing—The world of Formation (Yetzirah)

Have mercy, please, Hashem, our God, on Israel Your people; on Jerusalem Your city; on Zion, the resting place of Your glory; on the monarchy of the house of David, Your anointed; And on the great and holy house upon which Your Name is called. Our God, our father, tend us, nourish us, sustain us, support us, relieve us, Hashem, our God, and grant us speedy relief from all our troubles. And please, Hashem, our God, do not make us needful of gifts of human hands, nor of their loans, but only of Your Hand that is full, open, holy, and generous, so that we shall gain no shame nor insult for ever and ever.

SHABBAT

If Passover falls on Shabbat, we recite this additional blessing which correlates to the realm of Zeir Anpin, the dimension and source for all the spiritual Light that flows into our world.

May Your energy, Hashem, our God, come for our rescue through Your connections and the seventh day connection, this great and holy Shabbat. For this day is great and holy before You to rest and relax on it in love, to connect and be one with Your energy. And with Your will, Hashem, our God, relieve us from distress, grief, and lament on

---

It says that in the *Birkat HaMazon* we pray a lot for life. The kabbalists ask why is that people pray for life when they are close to death. Why does a person say, "Oh God, let me live." The answer is that most people have a fear of death, but this fear is much stronger when they are facing their imminent demise. When they are facing death, only then do they come to the realization that they have not really started to live, and this realization is so painful that they are afraid to die.

The Third Blessing—The World of Formation (Yetzirah)

"*Have mercy on Israel.*" The word *rachem* (mercy) has a numerical value of 248, the same value as the name *Avraham* (Abraham), who was known for his mercy and sharing. Th

THE THIRD BLESSING – THE WORLD OF FORMATION (YETZIRAH)

רַחֵם אברהם, רמ"ח, ח"פ אל נָא יְהֹוָאַדְהִיאֱהָדונהי אֱלֹהֵינוּ ילה, עַל יִשְׂרָאֵל עַמֶּךְ
ה' הויות, נמם, וְעַל יְרוּשָׁלַיִם עִירֶךָ, וְעַל צִיּוֹן יוסף, ו"פ יהוה, ה"פ אל מִשְׁכַּן כְּ
(רבוע אלהים + ה') כְּבוֹדֶךָ ב' הויות, וְעַל מַלְכוּת בֵּית דָּוִד מְשִׁיחֶךָ ב"פ ראה
וְעַל הַבַּיִת ב"פ ראה הַגָּדוֹל לההו, מבה, יזל, אום וְהַקָּדוֹשׁ שֶׁנִּקְרָא שִׁמְךָ
עָלָיו. אֱלֹהֵינוּ ילה, אָבִינוּ, רְעֵנוּ, זוּנֵנוּ פַּרְנְסֵנוּ וְכַלְכְּלֵנוּ, וְהַרְוִיחֵנוּ
וְהַרְוַח מלוי אלהים דיודין לָנוּ מום, אלהים יְהֹוָאַדְהִיאֱהָדונהי אֱלֹהֵינוּ ילה מְהֵרָ
מִכָּל ילי צָרוֹתֵינוּ. וְנָא, אַל תַּצְרִיכֵנוּ יְהֹוָאַדְהִיאֱהָדונהי אֱלֹהֵינוּ ילה ל
לִידֵי מַתְּנַת בָּשָׂר וָדָם רבוע אהיה וְלֹא לִידֵי הַלְוָאָתָם. כִּי אִם יוה
ע"ה מ"ב לְיָדְךָ בוכ"י הַמְּלֵאָה, הַפְּתוּחָה, הַקְּדוֹשָׁה וְהָרְחָבָה, שֶׁלֹּ
נֵבוֹשׁ וְלֹא נִכָּלֵם לְעוֹלָם וָעֶד:

SHABBAT

If Passover falls on Shabbat, we recite this additional blessing which correlates to the realm of Zeir Anpin, the dimension and source for all the spiritual Light that flows into our world.

רְצֵה אלהים דההין וְהַחֲלִיצֵנוּ יְהֹוָאַדְהִיאֱהָדונהי אֱלֹהֵינוּ ילה בְּמִצְוֹתֶיךָ
וּבְמִצְוַת יוֹם ע"ה = נגד, זן, מזבח הַשְּׁבִיעִי, הַשַּׁבָּת הַגָּדוֹל
לההו, מבה, יזל, אום וְהַקָּדוֹשׁ הַזֶּה וההו. כִּי יוֹם ע"ה = נגד, זן, מזבח זֶה גָּדוֹל
לההו, מבה, יזל, אום וְקָדוֹשׁ הוּא לְפָנֶיךָ סמ"ב, לִשְׁבָּת בּוֹ וְלָנוּחַ בּוֹ
בְּאַהֲבָה יי כְּמִצְוַת רְצוֹנֶךָ. וּבִרְצוֹנְךָ הָנִיחַ לָנוּ מום, אלהים

---

umber 248 is also the number of body parts, both spiritual and physical, that an individual ossesses. By behaving with mercy towards others, as Abraham did, we generate healing nergy to all the 248 parts of our body. With this consciousness we can connect to the pper Worlds, bringing the healing Light to each of our body parts.

ccording to Kabbalah, mercy means "time." We inject time into our emotions so that we on't react impulsively. Waiting and restricting our reaction creates a space for the Light to l, helping us to respond in the spiritual manner that is appropriate for the situation.

the day of our rest. And show us, Hashem, our God, the consolation of Zion, Your city, and the rebuilding of Jerusalem, city of Your holiness, for You are the Master of salvations and Master of consolations.

PESACH

Our God and the God of our forefathers, may they rise, come, reach, be noted be favored, be heard, be considered, and be remembered the remembrance of our forefathers; the remembrance of Messiah, son of David, Your servant the remembrance of Jerusalem, the city of Your holiness; the remembrance of Your entire people, the house of Israel—before You; for deliverance, for goodness, for grace, for kindness, and for compassion, for good life and for peace, on this Day of Matzot Festival. Remember us on it, Hashem, our God, for goodness; consider us on it for blessing; and help us on it for good life. And in the matter of salvation and compassion, pity, pardon us, have mercy upon us, and save us; for our eyes are turned to You, because—You are God, gracious and compassionate King.

UVNEH YERUSHALAYIM

And rebuild Jerusalem, the holy city, soon in our days. Blessed are You, Hashem, Which rebuilds Jerusalem in His mercy. Amen.

It says the Creator helps the fallen (*somech noflim*). In other words, the Creator makes it so we never have to crash. We may fall just enough to fall, but never to crash so hard that we can't get back up.

An eagle carries its young on its wings, so that if someone shoots at them, the mother bird will take the shot. How many of us are eagles, willing to take the shot for someone else, so that they may connect to the Creator?

UVNEH YERUSHALAYIM

It says that in each and every generation, the Temple is being rebuilt. With every positive action we do, another stone is laid on the metaphysical Temple. It is not just that one day

יְהֹוָׁאֲדֹנָי אֱלֹהֵינוּ, שֶׁלֹּא תְהֵא צָרָה וְיָגוֹן
וַאֲנָחָה בְּיוֹם מְנוּחָתֵנוּ. וְהַרְאֵנוּ יְהֹוָׁאֲדֹנָי
אֱלֹהֵינוּ בְּנֶחָמַת צִיּוֹן עִירֶךָ, וּבְבִנְיַן
יְרוּשָׁלַיִם עִיר קָדְשֶׁךָ, כִּי אַתָּה הוּא בַּעַל
הַיְשׁוּעוֹת וּבַעַל הַנֶּחָמוֹת:

PESACH

אֱלֹהֵינוּ וֵאלֹהֵי אֲבוֹתֵינוּ, יַעֲלֶה וְיָבֹא וְיַגִּיעַ, וְיֵרָאֶה
וְיֵרָצֶה וְיִשָּׁמַע, וְיִפָּקֵד וְיִזָּכֵר זִכְרוֹנֵנוּ וּפִקְדוֹנֵנוּ, וְזִכְרוֹן
אֲבוֹתֵינוּ, וְזִכְרוֹן מָשִׁיחַ בֶּן דָּוִד עַבְדֶּךָ
וְזִכְרוֹן יְרוּשָׁלַיִם עִיר קָדְשֶׁךָ, וְזִכְרוֹן
כָּל עַמְּךָ בֵּית יִשְׂרָאֵל לְפָנֶיךָ
לִפְלֵיטָה לְטוֹבָה לְחֵן וּלְחֶסֶד וּלְרַחֲמִים
לְחַיִּים טוֹבִים וּלְשָׁלוֹם. בְּיוֹם חַג הַמַּצּוֹת
הַזֶּה. זָכְרֵנוּ יְהֹוָׁאֲדֹנָי אֱלֹהֵינוּ בּוֹ לְטוֹבָה. וּפָקְדֵנוּ
לִבְרָכָה. וְהוֹשִׁיעֵנוּ בּוֹ לְחַיִּים טוֹבִים. וּבִדְבַר יְשׁוּעָה
וְרַחֲמִים. חוּס וְחָנֵּנוּ, וַחֲמֹל וְרַחֵם עָלֵינוּ
וְהוֹשִׁיעֵנוּ, כִּי אֵלֶיךָ עֵינֵינוּ. כִּי אֵל מֶלֶךְ חַנּוּן
וְרַחוּם אָתָּה:

UVNEH YERUSHALAYIM

וּבְנֵה יְרוּשָׁלַיִם עִיר הַקֹּדֶשׁ בִּמְהֵרָה בְיָמֵינוּ. בָּרוּךְ
אַתָּה יְהֹוָׁאֲדֹנָי בּוֹנֵה בְרַחֲמָיו יְרוּשָׁלָיִם. אָמֵן:

ometime in the future, the Temple will be built; it is being built right now. We need to now it is being built and that it is our actions that are building it.

Conversely, in every generation that the Temple is not being built, it is being destroyed, nd it is our actions that are destroying the Temple.

THE FOURTH BLESSING—THE WORLD OF ACTION (ASIYAH)

Blessed are You, Hashem, our God, King of the universe, the Almighty, our Father, our King, our Sovereign, our Former, our Redeemer, our Creator, our Holy One, the Holy One of Jacob, our Shepherd, the Shepherd of Israel, for every single day It did good, It does good, It will do good to us. The King Who is good and Who does good for all. It was bountiful with us, It is bountiful with us, It will forever be bountiful with us—with grace and with kindness and with mercy, with relief, salvation, success, blessing, help, consolation, sustenance, support, mercy, life, peace, and all good; and of all good things, may It never deprive us.

The leader puts down the cup.

HARACHAMAN

The compassionate One! May He reign over us forever. The compassiona *One! May He be blessed in heaven and on earth. The compassionate On* *May He be praised throughout all generations, may It be glorified throug*

THE FOURTH BLESSING—THE WORLD OF ACTION (ASIYAH)

This blessing means that whatever God gives us is what we need, although it may no necessarily be what we want. If we are missing anything in our life, it may mean we ar not supposed to have it. Although we try to receive everything that life can offer u it's important not to allow ourselves to be controlled by the outcome of our efforts t receive. It's about learning to appreciate fully and be completely happy with all that w have in the present, and not to focus our efforts on attaining the next level of success a a precondition for happiness.

In *Entrance to the Zohar*, Rav Ashlag reveals a powerful lesson about desire: When w restrict our *Desire to Receive for the Self Alone* and transform it into one of sharing, w become completely fulfilled by the Light. Rav Ashlag explains that a person begins lif with a desire to receive 100 units of any commodity. When he attains this 100, Satan the expands his desire so that he now wants 200. When he attains 200 units, Satan expand the desire to 400. When he attains 400 units, Satan expands his Vessel so that he nov desires 800. This expansion continues until the day the man dies. He then leaves thi world, sad and frustrated at having fulfilled only half his desires.

THE FOURTH BLESSING – THE WORLD OF ACTION (ASIYAH)

בָּרוּךְ אַתָּה יְהֹוָה אֱלֹהֵינוּ מֶלֶךְ הָעוֹלָם הָאֵל אָבִינוּ, מַלְכֵּנוּ, אַדִּירֵנוּ, בּוֹרְאֵנוּ, גּוֹאֲלֵנוּ, יוֹצְרֵנוּ קְדוֹשֵׁנוּ קְדוֹשׁ יַעֲקֹב, רוֹעֵנוּ רוֹעֵה יִשְׂרָאֵל הַמֶּלֶךְ הַטּוֹב וְהַמֵּטִיב לַכֹּל שֶׁבְּכָל יוֹם וָיוֹם הוּא הֵטִיב, הוּא מֵטִיב, הוּא יֵיטִיב לָנוּ הוּא גְמָלָנוּ, הוּא גוֹמְלֵנוּ, הוּא יִגְמְלֵנוּ לָעַד לְחֵן וּלְחֶסֶד וּלְרַחֲמִים וּלְרֶוַח הַצָּלָה וְהַצְלָחָה, בְּרָכָה וִישׁוּעָה, נֶחָמָה, פַּרְנָסָה וְכַלְכָּלָה, וְרַחֲמִים וְחַיִּים וְשָׁלוֹם, וְכָל טוֹב, וּמִכָּל טוֹב לְעוֹלָם אַל יְחַסְּרֵנוּ.

The leader puts down the cup.

HARACHAMAN

הָרַחֲמָן, הוּא יִמְלֹךְ עָלֵינוּ לְעוֹלָם וָעֶד.

הָרַחֲמָן, הוּא יִתְבָּרֵךְ בַּשָּׁמַיִם וּבָאָרֶץ

הָרַחֲמָן, הוּא יִשְׁתַּבַּח לְדוֹר דּוֹרִים, וְיִתְפָּאַר בָּנוּ לָעַד

---

he phrase: *"The King Who is good and Who does good for all"* means that the Creator does nly good for us. There is a story about a kabbalist, Rav Chanoch Henich HaCohen of lexander, who, when one of his friends passed away, did not show any signs of sorrow ntil a few hours later when he burst out in tears. He said to the Creator, "I know that verything is for the good, but can I please not have this part of the good (this sadness). know that it is good, but can I just have the good where the good is good."

HARACHAMAN

1 this section, we refer to Abraham (loving kindness), Isaac (judgment), and Jacob 'alance). There is no way we can reach the spiritual level of these patriarchs, but if we re a level where there is some kind of affinity and some kind of sharing, where we have idgment and are not afraid to rebuke and have confrontation, where we have some kind f balance and truth—then we can at least share some of their qualities.

us forever to the ultimate ends, and be honored through us forever and for all eternity. The compassionate One! May He sustain us in honor. The compassionate One! May He break the yoke of oppression from our neck and guide us erect to our land. The compassionate One! May He send us abundant blessing to this house and upon this table at which we have eaten. The compassionate One! May He send us Elijah the Prophet—who is remembered for good—to proclaim to us good tidings, salvations, and consolations. The compassionate One! May He bless the Rav, my teacher, the master of this house, and the Rav's wife, my teacher, the lady of the house: them, their house, their family, and all that is theirs. All our friends wherever they are: them, their house, their family, and all that is theirs.

It says that when Abraham took Isaac to sacrifice him on Mount Moriah, they were originally on the other side of the river. There are two important lessons here.

First, like the river divides the two banks, to connect to holiness or anything of Light there must be a clear definition of good and evil—there needs to be clear divide. Our problem is that everything is grey because Satan clouds things. We need to aspire to go to a level where the divide between good and evil is completely clear.

The second lesson is about King David, who is the source of the Final Redemption. King David's lineage came from two illicit relationships. First, Lot slept with his two daughters and from that incestuous liaison, generations later, came Ruth, King David's great grandmother. Genesis also recounts how later in the time of Joseph, a man named Yehuda slept with Tamar, his daughter-in-law, and from that illicit union came Boaz, King David's great-grandfather. This teaches us that no matter how far we are from the other side of the river, no matter how wide the divide is, the Light can take us to the other side.

In these next blessings, we ask God for everything—health, happiness, sustenance, and the Final Redemption. You name it, we're asking for it. The kabbalists ask, "What the point in praying for anything? It's either in the cards for us, or it's not." The reason for asking has to do with ego, which is our only stumbling block to receiving lasting fulfillment. If a person can't admit to himself that he needs Light, then he can never receive Light. No matter how many positive actions we do or how smart we may be, without admitting and recognizing the need for the Light of the Creator, we can never receive permanent fulfillment.

וּלְנַצֵּחַ נִצָּחִים, וְיִתְהַדַּר בָּנוּ לָעַד ב"פ ב"ן וּלְעוֹלְמֵי עוֹלָמִים.

הָרַחֲמָן, הוּא יְפַרְנְסֵנוּ בְּכָבוֹד בוכו.

הָרַחֲמָן, הוּא יִשְׁבּוֹר עֻלֵּנוּ מֵעַל עלם צַוָּארֵנוּ וְהוּא יוֹלִיכֵנוּ קוֹמְמִיּוּת לְאַרְצֵנוּ.

הָרַחֲמָן, הוּא יִשְׁלַח לָנוּ מום, אלהים בְּרָכָה מְרֻבָּה בַּבַּיִת ב"פ רא הַזֶּה והו וְעַל שֻׁלְחָן זֶה שֶׁאָכַלְנוּ עָלָיו.

הָרַחֲמָן, הוּא יִשְׁלַח לָנוּ מום, אלהים אֶת אֵלִיָּהוּ ב"ן, לכב, יבמ הַנָּבִי זָכוּר יהי אור ע"ה לַטּוֹב והו וִיבַשֶּׂר לָנוּ מום, אלהים בְּשׂוֹרוֹת טוֹבוֹ יְשׁוּעוֹת וְנֶחָמוֹת.

הָרַחֲמָן, הוּא יְבָרֵךְ עסמ"ב אֶת הָרַב ע"ב ורבוע מ"ה רַבִּי מוֹרִי בַּעַ הַבַּיִת ב"פ ראה הַזֶּה והו, וְאֶת הָרַבָּנִית מוֹרָתִי בַּעֲלַת הַבַּיִת ב ראה הַזֶּה והו. אוֹתָם וְאֶת בֵּיתָם וְאֶת זַרְעָם וְאֶת כָּל יל אֲשֶׁ לָהֶם.

---

t does the Creator need our recognition? The kabbalists teach us that by understanding
d acknowledging that it is our denial and our doubts concerning the reality of the
reator that give rise to Satan, we weaken Satan's influence and presence in our lives.

the middle of *Birkat HaMazon,* we ask for all kinds of things, both personal and global.
e ask to be miracle makers. Each and every one of us can create miracles if we really
el the pain of the other person. If I feel your pain, I can create miracles for other
:ople. Everybody can be a miracle maker if they feel for the other person.

t the end of *Birkat haMazon,* we say we were young and now we are old. This is about
iving the same excitement and connection to the work we can do when we are older as
e have when we are younger.

ne Rav was already in his sixties when the Rav really started to do the spiritual work of
inging Kabbalah to humanity, teaching us that not only is it never too late but that we
n also affect many people even when we think our time has run out. Unfortunately,
hen people get older, nothing excites them. Just knowing that it's never too late helps us
connect to some of what the Rav has done and what Karen continues to do today.

The compassionate One! (If dining on one's own: May He bless me, [my father and mother,] my wife, my children, and all that is mine.)

All the guests here: them, their houses, their families, and all that is their us and all that is ours, just as our forefathers Abraham, Isaac, and Jace were blessed in everything, from everything, with everything. So may H bless us all together with a perfect blessing, and let us say: Amen!

On high, may merit be pleaded upon them and upon us, for a safeguard of peace. May we receive a blessing from Hashem, and favor from the God of our salvation, and find the secrets (of the Torah) and common sense in the eyes of God and man.

ON SHABBAT

The compassionate One! May He cause us to inherit a day which is completely Shabbat and rest for eternal life.

The compassionate One! May He cause us to inherit a day which completely good. The compassionate One! May He make us worthy of the days of Messiah and the life of the World to Come (the true world). From the greatness of His majestic salvations and kind favors to His anointe to David and to his descendants forever. The One that makes peace in H heights shall make peace upon us and upon all Israel. Now say: Amen Fear Hashem, all His holy ones, for there is no deprivation for the on who fear him. Young lions may become poor and hungry, but the seekers of Hashem will not lack any good. Thank Hashem, for He is good, for H kindness endures forever.

הָרַחֲמָן, הוּא יְבָרֵךְ עסמ״ב אוֹתִי וְאֶת אָבִי וְאֶת אִמִּי וְאֶת אִשְׁתִּי וְזַרְעִי וְאֶ

כָּל יל׳ אֲשֶׁר לִי. וְאֶת כָּל יל׳ הַמְּסֻבִּין כַּאן אוֹתָם וְאֶת בֵּיתָ

וְאֶת זַרְעָם וְאֶת כָּל יל׳ אֲשֶׁר לָהֶם אוֹתָנוּ וְאֶת כָּל יל׳ אֲשֶׁר לָ

מום, אלהים, כְּמוֹ שֶׁנִּתְבָּרְכוּ אֲבוֹתֵינוּ אַבְרָהָם רמ״ח, וה״פ אל יצֲ

ד״פ ב״ן וְיַעֲקֹב ז״פ יהוה, יאהדונהי אידהנויה בַּכֹּל ב״ן, לכבב, יבמ, מִכֹּל יל׳, כ

יל׳, כֵּן יְבָרֵךְ עסמ״ב אוֹתָנוּ כֻּלָּנוּ יַחַד בִּבְרָכָה שְׁלֵמָה, וְנֹאמַ

אָמֵן יאהדונהי:

בַּמָּרוֹם יְלַמְּדוּ עֲלֵיהֶם וְעָלֵינוּ ריבוע ס״ג זְכוּת, שֶׁתְּהֵא לְמִשְׁמֶרֶ

שָׁלוֹם, וְנִשָּׂא בְרָכָה מֵאֵת יְהוָֹאהדונהי, וּצְדָקָה מֵאֱלֹהֵי דמב, יל׳ה

יִשְׁעֵנוּ, וְנִמְצָא חֵן מוזי וְשֵׂכֶל טוֹב והו׳ בְּעֵינֵי מ״ה בריבוע אֱלֹהִים מום,

אהיה אדני, ילה וְאָדָם מ״ה.

ON SHABBAT

הָרַחֲמָן, הוּא יַנְחִילֵנוּ יוֹם ע״ה = נגד, זן, מזבח שֶׁכֻּלּוֹ שַׁבָּת וּמְנוּחָה

לְחַיֵּי הָעוֹלָמִים.

הָרַחֲמָן, הוּא יַנְחִילֵנוּ יוֹם ע״ה = נגד, זן, מזבח שֶׁכֻּלּוֹ טוֹב והו׳.

הָרַחֲמָן, הוּא יְזַכֵּנוּ לִימוֹת הַמָּשִׁיחַ וּלְחַיֵּי הָעוֹלָם הַבָּא.

מִגְדּוֹל יְשׁוּעוֹת מַלְכּוֹ פי׳ וְעוֹשֶׂה חֶסֶד ע״ב, ריבוע יהוה לִמְשִׁיחוֹ לְדָוִ

וּלְזַרְעוֹ עַד עוֹלָם: עוֹשֶׂה שָׁלוֹם בִּמְרוֹמָיו, הוּא יַעֲשֶׂה שָׁלוֹם

עָלֵינוּ ריבוע ס״ג וְעַל כָּל יל׳ יִשְׂרָאֵל, וְאִמְרוּ אָמֵן יאהדונהי: יְראוּ אֶ

יְהוָֹאהדונהיאהדונהי קְדֹשָׁיו, כִּי אֵין מַחְסוֹר לִירֵאָיו: כְּפִירִים רָשׁ

וְרָעֵבוּ וְדֹרְשֵׁי יְהוָֹאהדונהיאהדונהי לֹא יַחְסְרוּ כָל יל׳ טוֹב והו׳: הוֹדוּ אד

לַיהוָֹאהדונהיאהדונהי כִּי טוֹב והו׳, כִּי לְעוֹלָם והו׳ וְחַסְדּוֹ ג״פ יהוה:

Poteach Et Yadecha

You open your hands

פאי סאל וזתך

Sustenance through tithing

And satisfy the needs of every living thing

Blessed is the man that trusts in Hashem, then Hashem will be his security. I was a youth and also have aged, yet I have not seen a righteous man forsaken and his children begging for bread. Hashem will give might to Its people. Hashem will bless Its people with peace.

LeShem Yichud

For the sake of unifying The Holy One, blessed be He, and His Shechina, with fear and mercy, and with mercy and fear, to unify the name of Yud Key with Vav Key completely, in the name of all Israel, I am ready and willing to apply the connection of Third Cup out of Four Cups, and may the pleasantness of Hashem, our God, be upon us, and establish the action of our hands upon us and establish the action of our hands.

LeShem Yichud unites our thoughts and our actions with the Light and the Upper Worlds. For this reason, it precedes the prayers. Many times, we have a thought to do the right thing, but our actions contradict our original thought and intention. Throughout the *Seder*, we need to make a conscious effort to improve ourselves spiritually. *LeShem Yichud* helps keep us true to our positive thoughts and intentions, especially the day after the *Seder*.

POTEACH ET YADECHA

פּוֹתֵחַ אֶת יָדֶךָ ר״ת פאי, ס״ת וזתך (יוֹהָתוּכֶה)

You open your hands

פאי סאל וזתך

Sustenance through Tithing

וּמַשְׂבִּיעַ וזתך לְכָל יה אדני וַזִי רָצוֹן מהשע ע״ה, אל שדי ע״ה, ר״ת רוזל:

בָּרוּךְ יהוה ע״ב ורבוע מ״ה הַגֶּבֶר אֲשֶׁר יִבְטַח בַּיהוֹוָאהדונהי וְהָיָה יה
יְהוֹוָאהדונהי מִבְטַחוֹ: נַעַר ש״ך הָיִיתִי גַּם יכל זָקַנְתִּי וְלֹא רָאִיתִי
צַדִּיק נֶעֱזָב וְזַרְעוֹ מְבַקֶּשׁ לָחֶם ג״פ יהוה: יְהוֹוָאהדונהי עֹז אני יה
לְעַמּוֹ יִתֵּן יְהוֹוָאהדונהי יְבָרֵךְ עסמ״ב אֶת עַמּוֹ בַשָׁלוֹם ר״ת ע״ב:

LeShem Yichud

לְשֵׁם יהוה שדי יִוֹוֹד קוּדְשָׁא בְּרִיךְ הוּא וּשְׁכִינְתֵּיהּ (יאהדונהי) בִּדְוֹזִיל
וּרְוֹזִימוּ (יאההויהה) וּרְוֹזִימוּ וּדְוֹזִילוּ (איההויהה) לְיַוֹזְדָא שֵׁם יהוה שדי יוֹ
קֵי בְּוָאו קֵי בְּיִוֹזוּדָא שְׁלִים (יהוה) בְּשֵׁם יהוה שדי כָּל ילי יִשְׂרָאֵל
הִנְנִי מוּכָן וּמְזוּמָן לְקַיֵּם מִצְוַת כּוֹס מום, אלהים שְׁלִישִׁי שֶׁל אַרְבַּע
כּוֹסוֹת, וִיהִי אל נעם נוֹעַם ע״ה קס״א אֲדֹנָי לכה אֱלֹהֵינוּ ילה עָלֵינוּ ריבוע ס
וּמַעֲשֵׂה יָדֵינוּ יהוה אדני כּוֹנְנָה רבוע מ״ה עָלֵינוּ ריבוע ס״ג וּמַעֲשֵׂה יָדֵינוּ יה
אדני כּוֹנְנֵהוּ:

The Third Cup of Wine—Formation (Yetzirah)

We make the blessing on the third cup and drink it while leaning to the left.

Blessed are You, Hashem, our God, King of the universe, Who creates the fruit of the vine.

Shefoch Chamatcha

We fill up the cup of Elijah the Prophet and open the door to invite
Elijah to our Seder, and recite the following:

Pour your wrath upon the nations that do not recognize You and upon kingdoms that do not invoke Your Name. For they have devoured Jacob and turned his habitation into a wilderness. Pour Your anger upon them and let Your fiery wrath overtake them. Pursue them with wrath, and annihilate them from beneath the heavens of Hashem.

We close the door.

The Third Cup of Wine—Formation (Yetzirah)

Shefoch Chamatcha

"Pour your wrath upon the nations…" The nations mentioned here are the Babylonians and Romans, the nations that destroyed the Temple. The kabbalists say that if these nations had known that the Light of the world came from the Temple, not only would they not have destroyed the Temple, they would have set their armies to protect it. Instead, they destroyed their own Light because their Light, too, came from there. The lesson for us is that not only do we lack appreciation for those who do for us, but we also destroy those people who are our Light.

The kabbalists ask why Jacob didn't dream that he was going up the ladder. The answer is because there was a lesson to learn from Jacob's dream—that there is a ladder and there is a system. Once we know there is a system, there is no question that we will go up the ladder. When we talk about whisking people from the darkness and the emptiness, it's about knowing that there is a system. As long as there in an elevator, a person can get to any floor. Our job is to make everyone aware there is an elevator; there is a system.

THE THIRD CUP OF WINE – FORMATION (YETZIRAH)

> יכוויין שֶׁעֶתָה בכוס שׁלִישִׁי נֶכֶס קְטָנות רִאשׁון דאימא
>
> ## אלף למד הא יוד מם
>
> (ציור הא' היא יו"י ויוד כלול עמו)

We make the blessing on the third cup and drink it while leaning to the left.

בָּרוּךְ יהוה ע"ב ורבוע מ"ה אַתָּה יְהֹוָאֵהֵהּהויאהדונהי אֱלֹהֵינוּ ילה מֶלֶךְ הָעוֹלָם בּוֹרֵא פְּרִי ע"ה אלהים דאלפין הַגָּפֶן:

SHEFOCH CHAMATCHA

We fill up the cup of Elijah the Prophet and open the door to invite
Elijah to our Seder, and recite the following:

שְׁפֹךְ חֲמָתְךָ אֶל הַגּוֹיִם אֲשֶׁר לֹא יְדָעוּךָ וְעַל מַמְלָכוֹת אֲשֶׁר בְּשִׁמְךָ לֹא קָרָאוּ: כִּי אָכַל אֶת יַעֲקֹב ז"פ יהוה, יאהדונהי איהדונהי וְאֶת נָוֵהוּ הֵשַׁמּוּ: שְׁפָךְ עֲלֵיהֶם זַעְמֶךָ וַחֲרוֹן אַפְּךָ יַשִּׂיגֵם: תִּרְדֹּף בְּאַף וְתַשְׁמִידֵם מִתַּחַת שְׁמֵי יְהֹוָאֵהּהויאהדונהי:

We close the door.

___

We invite Elijah the Prophet to the *Seder* table on the night of the *Pesach Seder* because he is the one who will greet the Messiah (*Mashiach*) when he arrives. Elijah was chosen because he has the ability to protect us from the Negative Side during times of a great revelation of Light.

There are two levels of *Mashiach*—personal and global. Each of us can achieve our own personal *Mashiach* in our lifetime by achieving a complete transformation of character. When enough individuals achieve their own personal *Mashiach*, this critical mass will produce the global *Mashiach*, bringing about the Final Redemption with peace, fulfillment, and immortality for the entire world.

There is a story about Elijah the Prophet who met a fisherman and asked, "Have you studied? Have you connected with the mysteries of the world?" The fisherman said, "No. I have tried, but nothing worked." "Tell me, are you a good fisherman?" Eliyahu asked the man. "I am the best," he replied, to which Eliyahu said, "If only you studied like you fished; if only you connected like you fished." We need to ask ourselves a simple question: Is study and connection as important as our livelihood, or is it something that is a second thought; something that comes afterward?

Stage Fourteen:

HALEL

We pour the fourth cup and complete the Halel.

Tiferet – Lo Lanu

Not for our sake, Hashem, not for our sake, but for the sake of Your Name give glory, for the sake of Your kindness and Your truth. Why should the nations say: Where is their God? Our God is in the Heavens, He formed all that He desired. Their idols are of silver and gold, the work of the hands of man. They have mouths but cannot speak. They have eyes but cannot see. They have noses but cannot smell. Their hands cannot touch, their legs cannot walk. They utter no sounds from their throats. May their makers be like them and whoever trusts in them. Israel, place your trust in Hashem. He is your helper and protector. The House of Aaron place your trust in Hashem. He is your helper and protector. Those who fear Hashem, place your trust in Hashem. He is your helper and protector. (Psalms 115:1-11)

Stage Fourteen: Halel

Tiferet – Lo Lanu

In the beginning of the *Halel*, we ask where the Creator is. The truth here is that not only is revelation of Light the Light, but that concealment from Light is also Light. When the Creator reveals Light, that Light comes from the Creator; similarly, when there appears to be a disappearance of Light, this concealment is also from the Creator. Thus, even when it looks as if the Creator is not supporting us, He is still, in truth, supporting us. Even when it appears that He is pushing us down, He is actually supporting us. Sometimes it looks like this for us with our teacher. Our teacher is like an angel. The only teacher a person must have should be like an angel, and if our teacher is not like an angel for us, then we should not have that teacher.

STAGE FOURTEEN:

הלל

We pour the fourth cup and complete the Halel.

הלל ‑ מווי גבורות מאימא.

גדלות א' דאר"א,

יוד הה וו הה, יוד הא ואו הא.

יוד הה וו הה, יוד הא ואו הא.

קטנות ב' דאר"א,

ע"ד ע"ה, ע"ד ע"ה.

גדלות ב' דאימא,

יוד הה וו הה. יוד הא ואו הא.

TIFERET - LO LANU

לֹא כָּנֽוּ מוס, אלהים יְהֹוָאֽדנֽיֽאֽהֽדֹונֽהֽי לֹא כָּנֽוּ מוס, אלהים כִּי לְשִׁמְךָ תֵּן כָּבוֹ

ל"ב עַל חַסְדְּךָ עַל אֲמִתֶּךָ: לָמָּה יֹאמְרוּ הַגּוֹיִם אַיֵּה נָא אֱלֹהֵיהֶם יו

וֵאלֹהֵינוּ יֵלֹה בַשָּׁמָיִם י"פ טל, י"פ כוו, י"פ כוו כֹּל י יֵלֹי אֲשֶׁר חָפֵץ עָשָׂה: עֲצַבֵּיהֶ

כֶּסֶף וְזָהָב מַעֲשֵׂה יְדֵי אָדָם מ"ה: פֶּה מילה, פֶּה אלהים, ע"ה אלהים, ע"ה מוס לָהֶם וְל

יְדַבֵּרוּ ראה עֵינַיִם רביע מ"ה לָהֶם וְלֹא יִרְאוּ: אָזְנַיִם לָהֶם וְלֹא יִשְׁמָע

אַף לָהֶם וְלֹא יְרִיחוּן: יְדֵיהֶם וְלֹא יְמִישׁוּן רַגְלֵיהֶם וְלֹא יְהַלֵּ

לֹא יֶהְגּוּ בִּגְרוֹנָם: כְּמוֹהֶם יִהְיוּ אל עֹשֵׂיהֶם כֹּל יֵלֹי אֲשֶׁר בֹּטֵ

בָּהֶם: יִשְׂרָאֵל בְּטַח בַּיהֹוָאֽדנֽיֽאֽהֽדֹונֽהֽי עֶזְרָם וּמָגִנָּם הוּא: בֵּית ב

ראה אַהֲרֹן ע"ב ורביע ע"ב בִּטְחוּ בַיהֹוָאֽדנֽיֽאֽהֽדֹונֽהֽי עֶזְרָם וּמָגִנָּם הוּ

יִרְאֵי יְהֹוָאֽדנֽיֽאֽהֽדֹונֽהֽי בִּטְחוּ בַיהֹוָאֽדנֽיֽאֽהֽדֹונֽהֽי עֶזְרָם וּמָגִנָּם הוּא:

Netzach – Adonai Zachranu

Hashem, Who remembers us, blesses. He blesses the House of Israel. He blesses the House of Aaron. He blesses those who fear Hashem, the small as well as the great. May Hashem add more upon you. Upon you and upon your children. Blessed are you to Hashem, Creator of Heaven and earth. The Heavens are the Heavens of Hashem, and the earth He gave to mankind. The dead do not praise Hashem, nor do those who descend to the grave. And we will bless God from now and forever, Praise God. (Psalm 115:12–end)

Hod – Ahavti

I wanted that Hashem would listen to my voice and to my supplication and turn His Ear toward me on my days I would call. Pangs of death have surrounded me and the misery of the grave has found me. I found trouble and sorrow. Then, I called the Name of Hashem: Please, Hashem

---

Netzach – Adonai Zachranu

When we connect to the Creator, the Creator will help us and protect us. The kabbalists say this does not mean only on a metaphysical level. When a person is really connected the Creator, animals, plants, and even inanimate objects become servants to him. Imagine that two people are traveling and one is coming to hurt the other. A nail might damage his wheel and stop his car, thereby saving the other person—this nail is working for the person who is connected. In this way, all things become servants to us.

The Creator listens to the big and the small. Big actions and small actions have the same effect. Just because someone has a better job does not mean they are better. Imagine the bottom feeders in this world became extinct: The worst of the worst are integral our eco-system—and to the functioning of our universe. Yes, there are people with better positions and better jobs, but if you take anyone out of the equation, the world descend into chaos.

The Kotzke Rebbe said that he learned from his teacher that the heavens are the domain of the Creator and the land is the domain of the people and that we need to strive reach the heavens—the 99 Percent Realm. "But," the students of the Kotzke Rebbe teacher said, "how, when there is no ladder?" The answer was, "Start jumping." To which

NETZACH – ADONAI ZACHRANU

יְהֹוָ֖אֲדֹנָי זְכָרָנוּ יְבָרֵךְ עסמ״ב יְבָרֵךְ: עסמ״ב אֶת בֵּית בִּ״פ ראה יִשְׂרָאֵל
יְבָרֵךְ עסמ״ב אֶת בֵּית בִּ״פ ראה אַהֲרֹן ע״ב ורבוע ע״בּ: יְבָרֵךְ עסמ״ב יִרְאֵי
יְהֹוָ֖אֲדֹנָי ר״ת ייי הַקְּטַנִּים עִם הַגְּדֹלִים: גּ״פ אלהים יֹסֵף יְהֹוָ֖אֲדֹנָי
עֲלֵיכֶם עֲלֵיכֶם וְעַל בְּנֵיכֶם: בְּרוּכִים אַתֶּם לַיהֹוָ֖אֲדֹנָי עֹשֵׂה
שָׁמַיִם י״פ טל, י״פ כוזו וָאָרֶץ: אלהים דאלפין הַשָּׁמַיִם י״פ טל, י״פ כוזו שָׁמַיִם
י״פ טל, י״פ כוזו לַיהֹוָ֖אֲדֹנָי וְהָאָרֶץ אלהים דההין ע״ה נָתַן לִבְנֵי אָדָם: מ״ד
לֹא הַמֵּתִים יְהַלְלוּ יָהּ ההה וְלֹא כָּל יכ יֹרְדֵי דוּמָה: וַאֲנַחְנוּ נְבָרֵךְ יָ
מֵעַתָּה וְעַד עוֹלָם הַלְלוּיָהּ מום, אלהים, אהיה אדני; ילה; ללה: ההה

HOD – AHAVTI

אָהַבְתִּי כִּי יִשְׁמַע יְהֹוָ֖אֲדֹנָי אֶת קוֹלִי תַּחֲנוּנָי: כִּי הִטָּ
אָזְנוֹ לִי וּבְיָמַי אֶקְרָא: בּ״ן קנ״א אֲפָפוּנִי חֶבְלֵי מָוֶת וּמְצָרֵי מצר שְׁאוֹל
מְצָאוּנִי צָרָה אלהים דההין וְיָגוֹן אֶמְצָא: וּבְשֵׁם יהוה שדי יְהֹוָ֖אֲדֹנָי

---

he Kotzker Rebbe added "So we started jumping and the more we jumped, the more
e got hurt. We got higher and hit the ground harder." A student came to the Kotzker
ebbe's teacher and asked, "How come you went to Heaven and I didn't?" The teacher
nswered, "When you got hurt, you stopped jumping. I did not stop jumping. I got up
nd got up, until they took me."

Our job is to connect Heaven and Earth—the 99 Percent Reality to the 1 Percent Reality.
rayer is our connector; it helps us to have the elevation.

HOD – AHAVTI

For You have salvaged my soul from death and my eyes from tears..." This section of the *Halel*
peaks about tears and feeling someone else's pain.

Once a great kabbalist died, and his son waited, certain that his father would soon appear
o him in a dream and report from the Next World. But his father never came. The son
ecided that he needed to go to visit his father and requested the permission of the
Heavenly Court to do so.

rescue my soul. For God is gracious and righteous and our God is mercifu
Hashem watches over the simple people. I became destitute and He save
me. My soul return to your peacefulness, for Hashem has dealt kindly wit
you. For You have salvaged my soul from death and my eyes from tears, an
my feet from falling. I shall walk before Hashem in the land of the living
I believed even as I spoke, when I was greatly impoverished, and I said i
my haste, all men are treacherous. (Psalms 116:1-11)

When he arrived at the gates of Heaven, he asked the angels what had become of h
father. "He was here," they replied, "but he did not stay." So the son searched every regio
of Heaven, inquiring of the angels if they had seen his father. Wherever he went, th
angels gave the same answer: "Your father was here, but he continued walking." Finall
the son came upon a man sitting at the entrance to a forest and asked, "Have you seen m
father?" This man, too, answered, "Yes, he was here, but he continued walking." Then h
added, "You will find him on the other side of the forest."

The son trekked through the forest, finally reaching the place where the trees ende
There, stretching as far as the eye could see was a vast, heaving ocean with waves as ta
as mountains. His father was standing at the edge of the water, staring into the turbulen
waves. The son approached him and took his father's arm. "What are you doing here?" h
asked. "We were all worried. You did not return to us in a dream."

Without taking his eyes off the ocean, his father said, "Do you know what this ocean i
my son? This is the ocean of all the tears of all the people of the world, and I have swor
before God that I will never leave this ocean until He dries up all their tears."

Karen Berg tells us how the Gate of Tears is sometimes open and sometimes close
When we cry to complain or just cry for the sake of crying and we do not do anything t
change our situation, the Gate of Tears is closed to us. But when we cry for the sake o
changing—crying with a broken heart and begging to change—the Gate of Tears open
to us and never closes.

The Creator has mercy on us if we have mercy towards others. And even if the univers
is supposed to give us judgment, because we gave mercy to someone else, our judgmen
is sweetened.

When we rebuke someone, if it comes from the heart, it goes into the heart—out of th
heart into the heart. If it doesn't come from our heart, the other person won't listen

אֶקְרָא ב״פ קנ״א אָנָּה יְהֹוָהאדניאתהדונהי מַלְּטָה נַפְשִׁי: וְזָנוּן יהוה ע״ה ואלה ע״ה

יְהֹוָהאדניאתהדונהי וְצַדִּיק וֵאלֹהֵינוּ מְרַחֵם אברהם, רמו״ח, וז״פ אל: שֹׁמֵר

פְּתָאִים יְהֹוָהאדניאתהדונהי דַּלּוֹתִי וְלִי יְהוֹשִׁיעַ: שׁוּבִי נַפְשִׁי לִמְנוּחָיְכִי כ

יְהֹוָהאדניאתהדונהי גָּמַל עָלָיְכִי: כִּי חִלַּצְתָּ נַפְשִׁי מִמָּוֶת אֶת עֵינִי רבוע מ

מִן דִּמְעָה אֶת רַגְלִי מִדֶּחִי: אֶתְהַלֵּךְ לִפְנֵי וחכמה בינה יְהֹוָהאדניאתהדונה

בְּאַרְצוֹת הַחַיִּים בינה ע״ה: הֶאֱמַנְתִּי כִּי אֲדַבֵּר רַאה אֲנִי אני, טדהד כו

עָנִיתִי מְאֹד מ״ה: אֲנִי אני, טדהד כו״ו אָמַרְתִּי י״פ אדני ע״ה בְּחָפְזִי כָּל

הָאָדָם מ״ה כֹּזֵב:

) we have to be especially careful about what we say and how we say it, as well as ask urselves where we are coming from.

ometimes, a righteous person (*tzadik*) can say the exact same words as a wicked person *asha*), and a wicked person can say the exact same words as a *tzadik*. But when the *tzadik* ys them, this is the Holy of Holies, while when the *rasha* says them, this is the Angel of eath. It's not about the words themselves; it is about who says them. The *rasha* does ot feel that spiritual work is for him because he is so far away and doesn't feel that he is art of the system. He has taken himself out of the picture. The truth is that there is o such thing as "far away." No matter how far you are from the Light, you can still do te work. About the *rasha*, it's not that he cannot do the work or is too far; it is that he iinks he cannot.

here is no one who will not be part of the Final Redemption. Even a wicked person is romised that he will be redeemed. The process may take a long time, but everyone will e part of the Final Redemption

av Elimelech of Lizensk, a great kabbalist who lived about some 200 years ago, teaches s that while we pray, Satan often comes to us saying, "Why are you bothering to stand ere and pray? You don't really want to change. It's too difficult. So why bother with all this omplicated spiritual work? There's too much to learn, too much to do. You'll never make . And with all the negative actions you did before, your personal situation is hopeless." ut it does not matter what we did before. If we really want to—from this moment orward—we can change and transform our nature. Every person can change. Everyone as an opening. This prayer shuts down Satan's negative and destructive influence.

Yesod – Ma Ashiv

How can I repay God for all that He had bestowed upon me? I raise a cu of salvation and call out in the Name of God. I shall pay my vows to God before all His people. It is difficult in the Eyes of God, the death of H pious ones. Please, God, I am Your servant. I am Your servant, then a so of Your handmaid. You have untied my bonds. To You I shall sacrifice thanksgiving-offering and call out in the Name of Hashem. I shall pay m vows to God before all His People, in the Courtyards of Hashem, with Jerusalem, Praise God. (Psalm 116:12–end)

Malchut – Halelu

Praise Hashem, all nations. Exalt Him, all peoples. For His kindness ha overwhelmed us and the truth of Hashem is eternal, Praise God. (Psalms 117)

Yesod – Ma Ashiv

The miracles visited on us, like the miracles in Egypt, are a crutch to get us to believe i the Creator. The closer a person is to the Creator, the fewer miracles they need or receiv In Egypt, the Israelites believed in God, so why did they need Moses? The only path the Creator is through a *tzadik*—we have to have a teacher.

In this section, we have the phrase *Ana haShem*, the name of an inspiring melody sun frequently at The Kabbalah Centre. Here we are asking the Creator to give us sign teachers, directions, and pathways that will lead us to the Light. We are asking the Creat to be a true spiritual master who teaches disciples in the ways of the good—not via master-and-slave relationship, but through a master-and-student relationship in which th master mentors his students each step of the way.

Malchut – Halelu

"And the truth of God is forever." (Psalms 117:2) Truth is something that does not chang and stays forever. What the *Zohar* says is still the same today as it was yesterday and wi be for billions of years to come. There are few books that are read today that have bee around for thousands of years. If we want to live an ever-lasting life, we need to connec to truth.

YESOD - MA ASHIV

מָה מ"ה אָשִׁיב לַיהֹוָֽואֲדנֵּיאהדונֵהי כָּל יּבֹי תַּגְמוּלוֹהִי עָלָֽי: כּוֹס מום, אלה

יְשׁוּעוֹת אֶשָּׂא וּבְשֵׁם יהוה עדי יְהֹוָֽואֲדנֵּיאהדונֵהי אֶקְרָא ב"פ קנ"א: נְדָרַ

לַיהֹוָֽואֲדנֵּיאהדונֵהי אֲשַׁלֵּם נֶגְדָה נָּא לְכָל יה אדני עַמּוֹ: יָקָר בְּעֵינֵי רבוע ב

יְהֹוָֽואֲדנֵּיאהדונֵהי הַמָּֽוְתָה לַחֲסִידָֽיו: אָנָּה יְהֹוָֽואֲדנֵּיאהדונֵהי כִּי אֲנִי אני, טרה

כווז עַבְדֶּֽךָ פּי אֲנִי אני, טדה"ד כווז"ד עַבְדְּֽךָ פּי בֶּן אֲמָתֶֽךָ פִּתַּֽחְתָּ לְמוֹסֵרָ

לָךְ אֶזְבַּֽח זֶֽבַח תּוֹדָה וּבְשֵׁם יהוה עדי יְהֹוָֽואֲדנֵּיאהדונֵהי אֶקְרָא ב"פ קנ"א

נְדָרַי לַיהֹוָֽואֲדנֵּיאהדונֵהי אֲשַׁלֵּם נֶגְדָה נָּא לְכָל יה אדני עַמּוֹ: בְּחַצְרוֹ

בֵית ב"פ ראה יְהֹוָֽואֲדנֵּיאהדונֵהי בְּתוֹכֵֽכִי יְרוּשָׁלָֽםִ הַלְלוּיָהּ מום, אלהים ; יּ

לְלה:

MALCHUT - HALELU

הַלְלוּ אֶת יְהֹוָֽואֲדנֵּיאהדונֵהי כָּל יּבֹי גּוֹיִם שַׁבְּחֽוּהוּ כָּל יּבֹי הָאֻמִּים: פ

גָּבַר עָלֵֽינוּ ריבוע ס"ג וַחַסְדּוֹ ג"פ יהוה יְהוה וֶאֱמֶת אהיה פעמים אהיה, ד"פ ס"ג יְהֹוָֽואֲדנֵּיאהדונֵ

לְעוֹלָם הַלְלוּיָהּ מום, אלהים, אלהים ; ילה ; לְלה:

---

ccording to Kabbalah, prayer, the Torah, and the *Zohar* were given not only to the
raelites but to all of humanity to connect to. Each religion has its own path to the Light.
ut the one connection that applies to all nations of the world is "Love your neighbor
 yourself." Regardless of religion, all people are to be treated with human dignity. The
ly reason there is war between nations and chaos in society is because of the lack of
lerance and compassion among people.

roblems only come when there is separation, not when there is unity. There are two faces
negativity and negative people: one is dirty and disgusting, and if you oppose this kind of
erson, you are going to get dirty; the other face of negativity looks totally clean.

Malchut – Hodu

The next four lines connect to four spiritual worlds.

Give thanks to God, for He is good, for His kindness is forever.

Let Israel say so now, for His kindness is forever.

Let the House of Aaron say so now, for His kindness is forever.

Let those who fear God say so now, for His kindness is forever.

Min Hameitzar

Greatly from my distress I called out to God. Patient God answered me i
His expansiveness. God is with me, I shall not fear those who bear iniquitie.
What can man do to me? And sins, God shall come to my rescue and cleans

---

Malchut – Hodu

The *Halel* connects us to *Malchut*, our physical world. The letters of the word *Halel* can b
re-arranged to give us the 72 Name of God for dream state—*Lamed, Lamed, Hei* ללה. *Ha*
also has the same numerical value as *Alef, Dalet, Nun, Yud* אדני (65), the Name of God tha
transmits energy into our physical world.

The next four lines connect us to the four *Sefirot* of *Chochmah, Binah, Zeir Anpin,* an
Malchut. Spiritually speaking, some people in our world connect to the highest world
while others connect to the middle and lower realms. The only way humanity can achiev
true unity is for each of us to let go of our ego and accept the fact that no one is highe
or lower. It is only the ego that creates this distinction. If we consider ourselves on th
exact same level as our fellowman, energy can reach us on our own level.

The *Talmud* reinforces this concept. We learn that an ant is actually on a much highe
spiritual level than someone who isn't pursuing their spiritual work. An ant has a missio
and fulfills it, yet we as humans do not always complete our life's tasks.

Min Hameitzar

"From my great distress I called out to God." The kabbalists say that every time there is pain, it is th
Universe preparing us for something bigger. And when it does come, we see the pain was ju
to strengthen us; that the pain was just preparing us, and making our Vessel bigger.

We need to view this entire world as if there is no one else out there—just me and th
Creator. It is as if all the people are trees in the forest and it is only me and the Creato

MALCHUT – HODU

The next four lines connect to four spiritual worlds.

הוֹדוּ אהיה לַיהֹוָֹואדניאהדונהי כִּי
טוֹב והו כִּי לְעוֹלָם וַֽסְדּוֹ ג״פ יהוה:

יוד הי ויו הי
אלף הי יוד הי

יֹאמַר נָא יִשְׂרָאֵל כִּי לְעוֹלָם
וַֽסְדּוֹ ג״פ יהוה:

יוד הי ואו הי
אלף הי יוד הי

יֹאמְרוּ נָא בֵית ב״פ ראה אַֽהֲרֹן ע״ב ורבוע ע״ב
כִּי לְעוֹלָם וַֽסְדּוֹ ג״פ יהוה:

יוד הא ואו הא
אלף הא יוד הא

יֹאמְרוּ נָא יִרְאֵי יְהֹוָֹואדניאהדונהי
כִּי לְעוֹלָם וַֽסְדּוֹ ג״פ יהוה:

יוד הה וו הה
אלף הה יוד הה

MIN HAMEITZAR

מִן הַמֵּצַר מצר קָרָֽאתִי יָהּ ההה עָנָֽנִי בַמֶּרְחָב יָהּ ההה: יְהֹוָֹואדניאהדונהי
לִי לֹא אִירָא מה מ״ה יַֽעֲשֶׂה לִּי אָדָם מ״ה: יְהֹוָֹואדניאהדונהי לִי בְּעֹזְרָי
וַֽאֲנִי אני, טדה״ד כוז״ו אֶרְאֶה ראה בְשֹׂנְאָי: טוֹב והו לַֽחֲסוֹת בַּיהֹוָֹואדניאהדונהי

When we do this we connect with the Creator and not with people. My work is just for
me, and if I don't do it, then no one does. If we don't do our work, we are cooked.

Unfortunately, most of us call upon God only when we are in dire straits, forgetting that
is the Light—and not us—during our good times that creates our good fortune.

Open for me the gates of righteousness...." The Zohar also teaches us that if we create a
spiritual opening within ourselves no wider than the eye of a needle, God will show us
the Supernal Gates. Why does the Zohar use the metaphor of the eye of a needle when it
could just as easily have said "make a tiny opening?" The eye of a needle might be small,
but it is a complete and pure opening. Our opening for spirituality may be tiny, but there
can be no doubt that it is a complete and pure opening.

me. And I shall look upon my enemies. It is good to take refuge in God rather than to trust in man. It is better to take refuge in God than to trust in noblemen. All the nations surrounded me. In the Name of God, I shall cut them down. They surrounded me again and again. In the Name of God I shall cut them down. They surrounded me like bees, but are extinguished like a fire on thorns. With the Name of God, I shall cut them down. They pushed me time and again to fall and Hashem came to my aid. The strength and cutting power of God were for me a salvation. The sound of song and salvation is in the tents of the righteous. The Right of God does mighty things. The Right of God is raised. The Right of God does mighty things. I shall not die, But rather I shall live and tell of the deeds of God. God has chastised me again and again, but He has not surrendered me to death. Open for me the gates of righteousness. I will go through them and give thanks to God. This is the Gate of the Lord, the righteous may go through it.

ODECHA

We have four verses that connect us to the the four letters in Yud Hei Vav Hei, each verse is recited twice.

I am grateful to You, for You have answered me and have become my salvation. The stone that was rejected by the builders has become the main cornerstone. This came about from God, it is wondrous in our eyes. God has made this day, let us be glad and rejoice in it.

We always need to feel as if we are on the other side the door. If we are inside, we become complacent and are done for; we always have to feel that we are not in.

Nowadays, our "gates" to the Promised Land are the *tzadikim* (righteous people). The reason there is a gate and gate keepers is because the gate keepers don't just pop in, do work and leave—they work over a long period of time. They don't just wake up one day and get excited about something they are doing; they work for a long, long time. They are in it for the long haul. When we emulate the tzadikkim and we connect to the Promised Land.

מִבְטוֹחַ בָּאָדָם מ״ה: טוֹב יהו לַחֲסוֹת בַּיהֹוָאדניאהדונהי מִבְּטֹחַ בִּנְדִיבִים

כָּל יּלי גּוֹיִם סְבָבוּנִי בְּשֵׁם יהוה עדי יְהֹוָאדניאהדונהי כִּי אֲמִילַם

סַבּוּנִי גַם יֵּל סְבָבוּנִי בְּשֵׁם יהוה עדי יְהֹוָאדניאהדונהי כִּי אֲמִילַם

סַבּוּנִי כִדְבֹרִים דֹּעֲכוּ כְּאֵשׁ אלהים דיודין ע״ה קוֹצִים בְּשֵׁם יהו

עדי יְהֹוָאדניאהדונהי כִּי אֲמִילַם: דָּחֹה דְחִיתַנִי לִנְפֹּל וַיהֹוָאדניאהדונ

עֲזָרָנִי: עָזִּי אלהים, מוב ע״ה וְזִמְרָת יָהּ ההה אל כי לִישׁוּעָה: קוֹל ע

ס״ג ע״ה רִנָּה וִישׁוּעָה בְּאָהֳלֵי צַדִּיקִים יְמִין יְהֹוָאדניאהדונהי עֹשָׂה וָזי

ומב: יְמִין יְהֹוָאדניאהדונהי רוֹמֵמָה יְמִין יְהֹוָאדניאהדונהי עֹשָׂה וָזִיל ומב: לֹ

אָמוּת כִּי אֶחְיֶה וַאֲסַפֵּר מַעֲשֵׂי יָהּ ההה: יַסֹּר יִסְּרַנִּי יָּהּ ההה: ר״ת ההה

וְלַמָּוֶת לֹא נְתָנָנִי: פִּתְחוּ לִי שַׁעֲרֵי צֶדֶק אָבֹא בָם מ״ב אוֹדֶה יָ

ההה: זֶה הַשַּׁעַר לַיהֹוָאדניאהדונהי צַדִּיקִים יָבֹאוּ בוֹ:

ODECHA

We have four verses that connect us to the the four letters in Yud Hei Vav Hei, each
verse is recited twice.

י אוֹדְךָ כִּי עֲנִיתָנִי וַתְּהִי לִי לִישׁוּעָה: 2X

ה אֶבֶן יוד הה ואו הה מָאֲסוּ הַבּוֹנִים הָיְתָה לְרֹאשׁ
ריבוע אלהים ואלהים דיודין ע״ה פִּנָּה: 2X

ו מֵאֵת יְהֹוָאדניאהדונהי הָיְתָה זֹּאת הִיא נִפְלָאת
בְּעֵינֵינוּ יהוה ע״ב ורבוע מ״ה: 2X

ה זֶה הַיּוֹם ע״ה = נגד, זן, מזבח עָשָׂה יְהֹוָאדניאהדונהי
נָגִילָה וְנִשְׂמְחָה בוֹ: 2X

ODECHA

We have four verses that connect us to the four letters of the Tetragrammaton—*Yud*, *Hei*,
Vav, and *Hei*. Each verse is recited twice.

ANA

We beseech You, God, save us now.
We beseech You, God, save us now.
We beseech You, God, give us success now.
We beseech You, God, give us success now.

BARUCH HABA

These next four verses are the regular connections to the *Yud, Hei, Vav,* and *Hei.*

Each verse is recited twice.

CHOCHMAH

Blessed is the one who comes in the Name of Hashem. We bless you from The House of God.

BINA

The Lord is God, He illuminates for us. Tie the holiday-offering with rope until the corners of the Altar.

ZEIR ANPIN

You are my God and I thank You, my God, and I shall exalt You.

MALCHUT

Be grateful to God for He is good. For His kindness is forever. (Psalms 118)

ANA

These four verses offer us a different pathway to connect to the Light. The numerical equivalent of twice *Yud, Hei, Vav,* and *Hei* is 26 x 2=52, the numerical value of our physical realm of *Malchut.* Like the moon, *Malchut* has no Light of its own. These four verses help us, the *Malchut,* receive Light via the paths of the other *Sefirot:*

ANA

אָנָּא ב"ן, לכב, יבמ יְהֹוָאדֹנָיאהדונהי יהוה ועי"ע נהורין הוֹשִׁיעָה נָּא:

אָנָּא ב"ן, לכב, יבמ יְהֹוָאדֹנָיאהדונהי יהוה ועי"ע נהורין הוֹשִׁיעָה נָּא:

אָנָּא ב"ן, לכב, יבמ יְהֹוָאדֹנָיאהדונהי הַצְלִיחָה נָּא:

אָנָּא ב"ן, לכב, יבמ יְהֹוָאדֹנָיאהדונהי הַצְלִיחָה נָּא:

BARUCH HABA

These next four verses are the regular connections to the *Yud*, *Hei*, *Vav*, and *Hei*.
Each verse is recited twice.

CHOCHMAH

י בָּרוּךְ יהוה ע"ב ורביע מ"ה הַבָּא בְּשֵׁם יהוה עדי יְהֹוָאדֹנָיאהדונהי בֵּרַכְנוּכֶם מִבֵּית ב"פ ראה יְהֹוָאדֹנָיאהדונהי 2X:

BINA

ה אֵל יא"י יְהֹוָאדֹנָיאהדונהי וַיָּאֶר כף ויו זין ויו לָנוּ מום, אלהים אִסְרוּ וַ בַּעֲבֹתִים עַד קַרְנוֹת הַמִּזְבֵּחַ נגד, זן 2X:

ZEIR ANPIN

ו אֵלִי אַתָּה וְאוֹדֶךָּ אֱלֹהַי דמב, ילה אֲרוֹמְמֶךָּ 2X:

MALCHUT

ה הוֹדוּ אהיה לַיְהֹוָאדֹנָיאהדונהי כִּי טוֹב והו כִּי לְעוֹלָם וַחַסְדּוֹ ג"פ יהוה 2X:

The first verse is *Malchut* receiving from *Chochmah*.
The second verse is *Malchut* receiving from *Binah*.
The third verse is *Malchut* receiving from *Zeir Anpin*.
The fourth verse is *Malchut* receiving from *Chochmah*, *Binah*, and *Zeir Anpin*.

Hodu

לֹ

אַדְרִיאֵל

Give thanks to Hashem for He is good,
for His kindness endures forever.

בְּרְכִיאֵל

Give thanks to the God of all the heavenly powers,
for His kindness endures forever.

גּוּעְיָאֵל

Give thanks to the Master of all masters,
for His kindness endures forever.

דּוּרְעִיאֵל

To the One Who alone performs great wonders,
for His kindness endures forever.

הֹדְרִיאֵל

To the One Who made the Heavens with understanding,
for His kindness endures forever.

וּעְדִיאֵל

To the One Who spreads out the earth upon the waters,
for His kindness endures forever.

Hodu

This section contains 26 verses giving us a connection to 26 different angels plus the Tetragrammaton (*Yud, Hei, Vav,* and *Hei*), which has a numerical value of 26.

HODU

לֹ

אֲדְרִיאֵל

הוֹדוּ אהיה לַיהֹוָה אדני ואהיאהרונהי כִּי טוֹב והו אום
כִּי לְעוֹלָם וְחַסְדּוֹ ג"פ יהוה: יוֹד

בְּרְכִיאֵל

הוֹדוּ אהיה לֵאלֹהֵי דמב, ילה הָאֱלֹהִים מום, אלהים, אלהים ; ילה
כִּי לְעוֹלָם וְחַסְדּוֹ ג"פ יהוה: יוֹד

גּוֹעֵיאֵל

הוֹדוּ אהיה לַאֲדֹנֵי הָאֲדֹנִים
כִּי לְעוֹלָם וְחַסְדּוֹ ג"פ יהוה: יוֹד

דּוֹרְעֵיאֵל

לְעֹשֵׂה נִפְלָאוֹת גְּדֹלוֹת לְבַדּוֹ מ"ב
כִּי לְעוֹלָם וְחַסְדּוֹ ג"פ יהוה: יוֹד

הֲדְרִיאֵל

לְעֹשֵׂה הַשָּׁמַיִם י"פ טל, י"פ כוזו בִּתְבוּנָה
כִּי לְעוֹלָם וְחַסְדּוֹ ג"פ יהוה: יוֹד

וְועֵדִיאֵל

לְרֹקַע הָאָרֶץ אלהים דההין ע"ה עַל הַמָּיִם
כִּי לְעוֹלָם וְחַסְדּוֹ ג"פ יהוה: יוֹד

זבדיאל

To the One Who made great Lights,
for His kindness endures forever.

וזניאל

The sun for the reign of the day,
for His kindness endures forever.

טהוריאל

The moon and the stars for the reign of the night,
for His kindness endures forever.

ידידיאל

To the One Who smote Egypt through their firstborn,
for His kindness endures forever.

ה

כרוביאל

And Who took Israel out of their midst,
for His kindness endures forever.

להטיאל

With a strong Hand and with an outstretched Arm,
for His kindness endures forever.

מהגביאל

To the One Who divided the Sea of Reeds into parts,
for His kindness endures forever.

וּבדִיאֵל

לְעֹשֵׂה אוֹרִים גְּדֹלִים
כִּי לְעוֹלָם וַחַסְדּוֹ גּ״פ יהוה: יוֹד

וזניאל

אֶת הַשֶּׁמֶשׁ ב״פ שׁ״ך לְמֶמְשֶׁלֶת בַּיּוֹם ע״ה = נגד, זך, מזבוז
כִּי לְעוֹלָם וַחַסְדּוֹ גּ״פ יהוה: יוֹד

טהוריאל

אֶת הַיָּרֵחַ וְכוֹכָבִים לְמֶמְשְׁלוֹת בַּלָּיְלָה מלה
כִּי לְעוֹלָם וַחַסְדּוֹ גּ״פ יהוה: יוֹד

ידידיאל

לְמַכֵּה מִצְרַיִם מצר בִּבְכוֹרֵיהֶם
כִּי לְעוֹלָם וַחַסְדּוֹ גּ״פ יהוה: יוֹד

ה

כרוביאל

וַיּוֹצֵא יִשְׂרָאֵל מִתּוֹכָם
כִּי לְעוֹלָם וַחַסְדּוֹ גּ״פ יהוה: הָי

להטיאל

בְּיָד חֲזָקָה וּבִזְרוֹעַ נְטוּיָה
כִּי לְעוֹלָם וַחַסְדּוֹ גּ״פ יהוה: הָי

מהגביאל

לְגֹזֵר יַם יל״י סוּף לִגְזָרִים
כִּי לְעוֹלָם וַחַסְדּוֹ גּ״פ יהוה: הָי

נּוּרִיאֵל

And Who caused Israel to pass through It,
for His kindness endures forever.

נוֹצְצִיאֵל

And threw Pharoah and his army into the Sea of Reeds,
for His kindness endures forever.

ו

נוּדִיאֵל

To the One Who led His Nation, Israel, through the wilderness,
for His kindness endures forever.

סרְעִיאֵל

To the One Who smote kings,
for His kindness endures forever.

עֲטִיאֵל

And slew mighty kings,
for His kindness endures forever.

פַּקְדִיאֵל

Sichon, the king of the Emorites, because of
His kindness endures forever.

צְרוּפִיאֵל

And Og, the king of Bashan,
for His kindness endures forever.

נוריאל

וְהֶעֱבִיר יִשְׂרָאֵל בְּתוֹכוֹ

כִּי לְעוֹלָם וַחַסְדוֹ ג״פ יהוה: הֵי

נוצציאל

וְנִעֵר פַּרְעֹה שׁ״ך וְחֵילוֹ ומ״ב בְיַם יל׳ סוּף

כִּי לְעוֹלָם וַחַסְדוֹ ג״פ יהוה: הֵי

ו

נודיאל

לְמוֹלִיךְ עַמּוֹ בַּמִּדְבָּר אברהם, רמ״ווו, וז״פ אל

כִּי לְעוֹלָם וַחַסְדוֹ ג״פ יהוה: וִיֵן

סרעיאל

לְמַכֵּה מְלָכִים גְּדֹלִים

כִּי לְעוֹלָם וַחַסְדוֹ ג״פ יהוה: וִיֵן

עעׂאל

וַיַּהֲרֹג מְלָכִים אַדִּירִים הרי

כִּי לְעוֹלָם וַחַסְדוֹ ג״פ יהוה: וִיֵן

פקדיאל

לְסִיחוֹן מֶלֶךְ הָאֱמֹרִי

כִּי לְעוֹלָם וַחַסְדוֹ ג״פ יהוה: וִיֵן

צרופיאל

וּלְעוֹג מֶלֶךְ הַבָּשָׁן

כִּי לְעוֹלָם וַחַסְדוֹ ג״פ יהוה: וִיֵן

קְדוֹשִׂיאֵל

And presented their land as a heritage,
for His kindness endures forever.

רוּמְמִיאֵל

A heritage for Israel, His servant,
for His kindness endures forever.

שׂוֹמְריאֵל

In our lowliness He remembered us,
for His kindness endures forever.

שׂוֹמְריאֵל

And released us from our tormentors,
for His kindness endures forever.

תוֹמְכִיאֵל

He gives nourishment to all flesh,
for His kindness endures forever.

תהֹפִיאֵל
Give thanks to the God of the Heavens,
for His kindness endures forever.
(Psalm 136)

קְדוּשִׁיאֵל

וְנָתַן אַרְצָם לְנַחֲלָה

כִּי לְעוֹלָם וְחַסְדּוֹ ג״פ יהוה: וַיִו

ה

רוֹמְמִיאֵל

נַחֲלָה לְיִשְׂרָאֵל עַבְדּוֹ

כִּי לְעוֹלָם וְחַסְדּוֹ ג״פ יהוה: הָי

שׁוֹמְרִיאֵל

שֶׁבְּשִׁפְלֵנוּ זָכַר לָנוּ מום, אלהים, אהיה אדני

כִּי לְעוֹלָם וְחַסְדּוֹ ג״פ יהוה: הָי

שׁוֹמְרִיאֵל

וַיִּפְרְקֵנוּ מִצָּרֵינוּ

כִּי לְעוֹלָם וְחַסְדּוֹ ג״פ יהוה: הָי

תוֹמְכִיאֵל

נֹתֵן אבג״ית״ץ, ושׂ״ר, אהבת וחן לֶחֶם ג״פ יהוה לְכָל יה אדני בָּשָׂר

כִּי לְעוֹלָם וְחַסְדּוֹ ג״פ יהוה: הָי

תַּהְפִּיאֵל

הוֹדוּ אהיה לְאֵל יי״י הַשָּׁמָיִם י״פ טל, י״פ כוזו

כִּי לְעוֹלָם וְחַסְדּוֹ ג״פ יהוה: הָי

Nishmat Kol Chai

The soul of every living thing shall bless Your Name, Hashem, our God and the spirit of all flesh shall always glorify and exalt Your remembrance our King. From (this) world to the world (to come), You are God. And other than You, we have no redeeming or saving king. Liberator, rescuer sustainer, and merciful. At any time of distress and anguish.

We have no helping or supporting king other than You. God of the first and of the last, God of all creatures, Master of all generations, Which is extolled through a multitude of praises, Which guides Its world with kindness and Its creatures with mercy. Hashem is a God of truth. It is awake, neither slumbers nor sleeps. It rouses the sleepers and awakens the slumberers, resuscitates the dead, heals the sick, gives sight to the blind straightens the bent, makes the mute speak, deciphers the unknown—and

Nishmat Kol Chai

"In famine You nourished us…" In this next section of the *Halel*, we thank the Creator for the fact that there is hunger. A lack of something seems like an unusual thing to thank the Creator for, but the kabbalists teach that we are really thanking the Creator for giving us desire. If we would never be hungry, would we have desire for food? Of course not Part of what the Creator is doing is ensuring lack so that we never shut down our desire It's part of His gift to us, and it doesn't come from any actions we do, it is an attribute of the Creator.

Every person is worthy of a miracle—miracles are not just for special people. Every person is worthy of the connection with the Creator.

We know where we come from, and we know how it will all end. It was part of the Divine Plan that Adam and Eve would taste of the fruit from the Tree of Knowledge, and it's equally part of the Divine Plan that the Final Redemption will come. So in essence, the end is here. Our problem is that we get lost in the process and lose sight of the fact that we'll get to the end, no matter what. How we get there is what's in our power. But if we

Nishmat Kol Chai

נִשְׁמַת כָּל יְלי וָזֹי ר"ת ג הוויות תְּבָרֵךְ אֶת שִׁמְךָ יְהוָֹאדנהיאהדונהי אֱלֹהֵינ
יְלה וְרוּוַז מלוי אלהים דיודין כָּל יְלי בָּשָׂר תְּפָאֵר וּתְרוֹמֵם זִכְרְךָ מַלְכֵּנ
תָּמִיד ע"ה נתה, קס"א קנ"א קמ"ג. מִן הָעוֹלָם וְעַד הָעוֹלָם אַתָּה אֵל יי"א
וּמִבַּלְעָדֶיךָ אֵין לָנוּ אלהים מום, מֶלֶךְ גּוֹאֵל וּמוֹשִׁיעַ. פּוֹדֶה וּמַצִּיל
וְעוֹנֶה וּמְרַחֵם אברהם, רמ"וז, וז"פ אל. בְּכָל ב"ן, לכב, יבם עֵת יְ"פ אהיה י הויות צָרָ
אלהים דההין וְצוּקָה. אֵין לָנוּ אלהים מום, מֶלֶךְ עוֹזֵר וְסוֹמֵךְ ריבוע אדני, כ
אֶלָּא אָתָּה: אֱלֹהֵי דמב, ילה הָרִאשׁוֹנִים וְהָאַחֲרוֹנִים. אֱלוֹהַ מ
כָּל יְלי בְּרִיּוֹת. אֲדוֹן אני כָּל יְלי תּוֹלָדוֹת. הַמְהֻלָּל בְּכָל ב"ן, לכב, יב
הַתִּשְׁבָּחוֹת. הַמְנַהֵג עוֹלָמוֹ בְּחֶסֶד ע"ב, ריבוע יהוה וּבְרִיּוֹתָיו בְּרַחֲמִים
אלהים דיודין, מצפצ, י"פ ייי. וַיהוֹאדנהיאהדונהי אֱלֹהִים מום, אלהים ; ילה אֱמ
אהיה פעמים אהיה, ז"פ ס"ג לֹא יָנוּם וְלֹא יִישָׁן. הַמְּעוֹרֵר יְשֵׁנִים וְהַמֵּקִי
נִרְדָּמִים. מְוַזֹּיֶה ס"ג מֵתִים. וְרוֹפֵא וְזֹולִים מ"ה יהוה. פּוֹקֵחַ עִוְרִים

---

eep our eyes on the prize (the Redemption), and remember that it's ours, no matter what,
e literally speed up the process—that middle part where we lose our consciousness,
xcitement, and motivation.

his section is recited on all holidays and on Shabbat. It is our connection, our Vessel, to
apture the additional spiritual energy that is made available on holidays and Shabbat. We
enerally recite these verses in the morning—except on Passover, when we recite them
t night.

av Avraham Azulai teaches us that when nightfall arrives, a part of our soul leaves us for
e Upper Worlds even when we are awake, and at midnight, the soul returns, which is why
e feel tired as the evening grows on. Before we go to bed, there is a special connection
e make, known as the *Shema*, which helps to remove the negativity accumulated during
e day so that the soul can elevate higher and recharge. The *Shema* also protects the body
hile the soul is away.

While on all the other nights of the year our soul leaves us, on *Pesach*, our soul does not
eed recharging because the holiday itself provides us with that charge. So we do not have
 recite the *Shema* on *Pesach* because our soul remains with us, and we do not require any
xtra protection.

to You alone we give thanks. Were our mouth full of songs as the sea and our tongue as full of joyous song as its multitude of waves, and our lips as full of praise as the breadth of the sky, and our eyes as brilliant as the sun and the moon, and our hands as outspread as eagles of the sky and our feet as swift as hinds, we still could not thank You sufficiently Hashem, our God, and bless Your Name, Our King, for even one of th thousand, thousands of thousands, and myriad of times (that You hav granted us) favors, miracles, and wonders that You performed for us and fo our forefathers.

At first You redeemed us from Egypt, Hashem, our God, and liberated u from the house of bondage. In famine You nourished us, and in plenty You sustained us. From the sword You saved us; from plague You let us escape and from severe and numerous diseases You spared us. Until now Your mercy has helped us, and Your kindness has not forsaken us. Therefore, th organs that You differentiated within us, spirit and soul that You breathed into our nostrils, and the tongue that You placed in our mouth, all of them shall thank and bless, praise and glorify Your Name, our King continuously. For every mouth shall thank You, every tongue shall praise You, every eye shall look forward to You, every knee shall bend to You every erect spine shall prostrate itself before You; the hearts shall fear You the guts and kidneys shall sing (praises) to Your Name, as it is written "All my bones shall say: 'Hashem, who is like You?' You save the poor man from one stronger than him; the poor and destitute from one who would rob him." The outcry of the poor You hear. The screams of the destitute You listen to and save them. As it is written: Sing, righteous of Hashem the straight are praiseworthy.

וְזוֹקֵף כְּפוּפִים. הַמֵּשִׂיחַ אִלְּמִים. וְהַמַּפְעֲנֵחַ נֶעְלָמִים. וּלְךָ לְבַד
אֲנַחְנוּ מוֹדִים: וְאִלּוּ פִינוּ מָלֵא שִׁירָה כַּיָּם יליּ. וּלְשׁוֹנֵנוּ רִנָּה כַּהֲמוֹן
גַּלָּיו. וְשִׂפְתוֹתֵינוּ שֶׁבַח כְּמֶרְחֲבֵי רָקִיעַ. וְעֵינֵינוּ מְאִירוֹת כַּשֶּׁמֶשׁ
ב״פ שי״ך וְכַיָּרֵחַ. וְיָדֵינוּ פְרוּשׂוֹת כְּנִשְׁרֵי שָׁמַיִם יל״פ טל, יל״פ כווו. וְרַגְלֵי
קַלּוֹת כָּאַיָּלוֹת. אֵין אֲנַחְנוּ מַסְפִּיקִין לְהוֹדוֹת לְךָ יְהוֹ..אדני..אהדונהי
אֱלֹהֵינוּ ילה.. וּלְבָרֵךְ אֶת שְׁמֶךָ מַלְכֵּנוּ. עַל אַחַת מֵאֶלֶף אַלְפֵי
אֲלָפִים קס״א. וְרוֹב רִבֵּי רְבָבוֹת פְּעָמִים. הַטּוֹבוֹת נִסִּים וְנִפְלָאוֹת
שֶׁעָשִׂיתָ עִמָּנוּ רבוע ס״ג. וְעִם אֲבוֹתֵינוּ. מִלְּפָנִים מִמִּצְרַיִם מצר גְּאַלְתָּ
יְהוֹ..אדני..אהדונהי אֱלֹהֵינוּ ילה.. מִבֵּית ב״פ ראה עֲבָדִים פְּדִיתָנוּ. בְּרָעָב
ע״ב ורבוע אלהים זַנְתָּנוּ. וּבְשָׂבָע ע״ב ואלהים דיודין כִּלְכַּלְתָּנוּ. מֵחֶרֶב רבוע
ורבוע אהיה הִצַּלְתָּנוּ. מִדֶּבֶר ראה מִלַּטְתָּנוּ. וּמֵחֳלָאִים רָעִים וְרַבִּים
דִּלִּיתָנוּ: עַד הֵנָּה מ״ה יה עֲזָרוּנוּ רַחֲמֶיךָ וְלֹא עֲזָבוּנוּ וַחֲסָדֶיךָ. עַל כֵּן
אֵבָרִים שֶׁפִּלַּגְתָּ בָּנוּ. וְרוּחַ מילוי אלהים דיודין וּנְשָׁמָה שֶׁנָּפַחְתָּ בְּאַפֵּינוּ
וְלָשׁוֹן אלהים פשוט ויודין אֲשֶׁר שַׂמְתָּ בְּפִינוּ. הֵן הֵם, יוֹדוּ וִיבָרְכוּ
וִישַׁבְּחוּ. וִיפָאֲרוּ. אֶת שִׁמְךָ מַלְכֵּנוּ תָּמִיד ע״ה נתה, קס״א קנ״א קמ״ג. כָּ
כָּל יל״י פֶּה מילה, ע״ה אלהים, ע״ה מום יל״י לְךָ יוֹדֶה. וְכָל יל״י לָשׁוֹן יל״י אלהים פש
ויודין ע״ה לְךָ תִשָּׁבַע. וְכָל יל״י עַיִן רבוע מ״ה לְךָ תְצַפֶּה. וְכָל
בֶּרֶךְ לְךָ תִכְרַע. וְכָל יל״י קוֹמָה לְפָנֶיךָ סמ״ב תִשְׁתַּחֲוֶה. וְהַלְּבָבוֹ
יִירָאוּךָ וְהַקֶּרֶב וְהַכְּלָיוֹת יְזַמְּרוּ לִשְׁמֶךָ. כַּדָּבָר ראה שֶׁנֶּאֱמַר כָּ
יל״י עַצְמוֹתַי תֹּאמַרְנָה יְהוֹ..אדני..אהדונהי מִי יל״י כָמוֹךָ מום, אלהים, אלהים בַּצִּיל עָ
רבוע מ״ה מֵחָזָק פהל מִמֶּנּוּ וְעָנִי רבוע מ״ה וְאֶבְיוֹן מִגֹּזְלוֹ: שַׁוְעַת עֲנִיִּי
אַתָּה תִשְׁמַע. צַעֲקַת הַדַּל תַּקְשִׁיב וְתוֹשִׁיעַ: וּכְתוּב רַנְּנוּ צַדִּיקִי
בַּיהוֹ..אדני..אהדונהי לַיְשָׁרִים נָאוָה תְהִלָּה ע״ה אמת, אהיה פעמים אהיה, ז״פ ס״ג:

ISAAC AND REBECCA

R   *By the mouths of the upright, You shall be exalted.*   Y

I   I

V   *And by the lips of the righteous, You shall be blessed.*   T

                                                              Z

K   *And by the tongues of the pious, You shall be sanctified.*   C

A   H

H   *And among the holy ones, You shall be lauded.*   A

                                                              K

BEMIKEHALOT

In the assemblies of the myriads of Your people, the house of Israel. F
the duty of all creatures perform before You, Hashem, our God and th
God of our forefathers, is to thank, laud, praise, glorify, exalt, ador
and conduct all expressions of the songs and praises of David, the son o
Yishai, Your servant, Your anointed.

YISHTABACH

ISAAC AND REBECCA

We speak about the concept of holiness here, and how the way to be holy is to l
concealed. It says of Rav Yonatan ben Uziel that when he would study, birds that fle
above his head would burst into flames in mid- air. If this is the power of the studer
imagine how much more power Rav Yonatan's teacher had. And yet no birds ever die
when the teacher studied because he kept the heat and fire concealed. Rav Yonatar
teacher restricted that tremendous power.

This is true not just for learning but also for prayer. There is a story about one of th
tzadikim (righteous people) who went to see his friend. The friend's son asked th
kabbalist, "Why don't you move when you pray?" The kabbalist replied, "When you kno
how to swim and dive, you don't make any splashes or noise; it's one fluid, conceale
movement.

Isaac and Rivkah

ר	תִּתְרוֹמֵם:	לְשָׁרִים	בְּפִי	לְ
ב	תִּתְבָּרַךְ:	צַדִּיקִים	וּבְשִׂפְתֵי	צ
ק	תִּתְקַדָּשׁ:	וְחֲסִידִים שכינה ע"ה	וּבִלְשׁוֹן	וח
ה	תִּתְהַלָּל:	קְדוֹשִׁים	וּבְקֶרֶב	ק

Bemikehalot

בְּמִקְהֲלוֹת רִבְבוֹת עַמְּךָ ה' הוויות, נגמ בֵּית ב"פ ראה יִשְׂרָאֵל. שֶׁפְ
וְזֹאבֵת כָּל יל' הַיְצוּרִים לְפָנֶיךָ סמ"ב יְהֹוֹֹאדנ'אהדונהי אֱלֹהֵינוּ ילה. וֵאלֹ
דמב, ילה אֲבוֹתֵינוּ לְהוֹדוֹת. לְהַלֵּל ללה, אדני. לְשַׁבֵּחַ. לְפָאֵר. לְרוֹמֵ
לְהַדֵּר ד"פ ב"ן ע"ה. וּלְנַצֵּחַ. עַל כָּל יל' דִּבְרֵי ראה שִׁירוֹת וְתִשְׁבְּחוֹ
דָּוִד בֶּן יִשַׁי עַבְדֶּךָ פרי מְשִׁיחֶךָ:

---

aac (Yitzchak), son of the Patriarch Abraham, successfully prayed for his wife Rebecca
ivka) to have a baby. The lesson of this story is that the only way our own prayers will
answered is for us to pray for others—who are in need of financial, health, personal,
emotional sustenance—with a genuine heart.

Bemikehalot

his prayer is our connection to the spiritual essence of *Malchut*. Contrary to popular
elief, the physical world is not a hindrance or a blockage preventing us from connecting
the Creator. Instead, physical matter is our vehicle with which to make our connection.
e accomplish this through the power of mind over matter. And each time we achieve
ind over matter, we make the highest possible connection to the Creator.

May Your Name be praised forever, our King, the God, the great and ho
King, Who is in the Heavens and in the earth. For to You are befittin,
Hashem our God and the God of our fathers, forever and ever: 1) son
2) and praise 3) exultation 4) and melody 5) power 6) and dominic
7) eternity 8) greatness 9) valor 10) praise 11) and glory 12) holine
13) and sovereignty. Blessings and thanksgiving to Your great and holy Nam
from this world to the world to come. You are God. Blessed are You, Hashen.
King, Who is great and lauded with praise. God of thanksgiving.

Here we receive the energy of Abraham the Patriarch which is
spelled out in the following section

A   *Master of the wonders.*

V   *Creator of the souls.*

RA   *Master of all deeds.*

HA   *One Who chooses melodious songs of praise.*

M   *The King, the God Who gives life to all the worlds, amen.*

YISHTABACH

Here, the first word, *Uvchen*, has the numerical value of 72, linking us to the 72 Names o
God. The next word, *Yishtabach*, has the numerical value of 720—ten times the power o
the 72 Names of God.

YISHTABACH

S H L o M o H (SOLOMON)

וּבְכֵן ע״ב, ריבוע יהוה יִשְׁתַּבַּח ייפ ע״ב שִׁמְךָ לָעַד מַלְכֵּנוּ הָאֵ

לאה (אלד ע״ה) הַמֶּלֶךְ ר״ת שלמה המלך הַגָּדוֹל לההו, מבה, יזל, אום וְהַקָּדוֹשׁ

בַּשָּׁמַיִם ייפ טל, ייפ כוזו וּבָאָרֶץ אלהים דאלפין כִּי לְךָ נָאֶה יְהֹ(אדניאהדונהי)

אֱלֹהֵינוּ ילה וֵאלֹהֵי לכב, דמב, ילה אֲבוֹתֵינוּ לְעוֹלָם וָעֶד: (1) שִׁי

(2) וּשְׁבָחָה. (3) הַלֵּל אדני, ללה וְזִמְרָה. (4) עֹז אני יהוה (5) וּמֶמְשָׁלָה

(7) נֶצַח. (8) גְּדֻלָּה. (9) גְבוּרָה רי״ו. (10) תְּהִלָּה ע״ה אמת, אהיה פעמים אהיה, ז״פ ס

(11) וְתִפְאֶרֶת. (12) קְדֻשָּׁה. (13) וּמַלְכוּת. בְּרָכוֹת וְהוֹדָאוֹת לְשִׁמְךָ

הַגָּדוֹל לההו, מבה, יזל, אום וְהַקָּדוֹשׁ. וּמֵעוֹלָם וְעַד עוֹלָם אַתָּה אֵל ייא

בָּרוּךְ יהוה ע״ב ורבוע מ״ה אַתָּה יְהֹוה(אדניאהדונהי) מֶלֶךְ גָּדוֹל לההו, מבה, יזל, או

וּמְהֻלָּל בַּתִּשְׁבָּחוֹת. אֵל ייא״ הַהוֹדָאוֹת.

Here we receive the energy of Abraham the Patriarch which is
spelled out in the following section

A אֲדוֹן אני הַנִּפְלָאוֹת.

V בּוֹרֵא כָּל ילי הַנְּשָׁמוֹת.

R רִבּוֹן כָּל ילי

HA הַמַּעֲשִׂים. הַבּוֹחֵר בְּשִׁירֵי זִמְרָה.

M מֶלֶךְ אֵל ייא״ וְחֵי הָעוֹלָמִים: אָמֵן יאהדונהי:

LeShem Yichud – Preparing for the Fourth Cup of Wine

For the sake of unifying The Holy One, blessed be He, and His Shechina, with fear and mercy, and with mercy and fear, to unify the name of Yu Key with Vav Key completely, in the name of all Israel, I am ready an willing to apply the connection of Fourth Cup out of Four Cups, and me the pleasantness of Hashem, our God, be upon us, and establish the actic of our hands upon us and establish the action of our hands.

The Fourth Cup of Wine—Action (Asiyah)

Blessed are You, Hashem, our God, King of the universe, Who creates tl fruit of the vine.

We drink while leaning to the left and then recite the last blessing.

The Final Blessing

Blessed are You, Hashem, our God, King of the universe, for the vine and tl fruit of the vine, and for the produce of the field. And for a desirable, goo and spacious land that You were pleased to give our forefathers as a heritage, i eat of its fruit and to be satisfied with its goodness. Have mercy, Hashem, ol God, on us and on Israel, Your people; on Jerusalem, Your city; on the moul of Zion, the resting place of Your glory; Your altar and Your temple. Rebuil Jerusalem, the holy city, speedily, in our days. Bring us up into it, gladden us l its rebuilding, and we shall bless You upon it in holiness and purity.

LeShem Yichud and Preparation for the Fourth Cup of Wine

As mentioned previously, *LeShem Yichud* unifies our thoughts and our actions with th Light and the Upper Worlds. Here we have our final opportunity this *Seder* night t make this connection. Throughout the process, we need to make a conscious effort t improve ourselves spiritually. *LeShem Yichud* helps keep us true to our positive thought and intentions, especially the day after the *Seder*.

LeShem Yichud – Preparing for the fourth Cup of Wine

לְשֵׁם יהוה שדי יוֹחוּד קוּדְשָׁא בְּרִיך הוּא וּשְׁכִינְתֵּיהּ (יאההויהי) בִּדְחִילוּ
וּרְחִימוּ (יאההויהה) וּרְחִימוּ וּדְחִילוּ (איההויהה) לְיַחֲדָא שֵׁם יהוה שדי יוֹד כְ
בּוֹאוּ קֵי בְּיַחֲדָא שְׁלִים (יהוה) בְּשֵׁם יהוה שדי כָּל ילי יִשְׂרָאֵל, הִנְ
מוּכָן וּמְזוּמָּן לְקַיֵּים מִצְוַת כּוֹס מוּם, אלהים רְבִיעִי שֶׁל אַרְבַּע כּוֹסוֹ
וִיהִי אל נֹעַם ע"ה קס"א אֲדֹנָי לֵלה אֱלֹהֵינוּ ילה עָלֵינוּ ריבוע ס"ג וּמַעֲשֵׂה יְדֵ
יהוה אדני כּוֹנְנָה רבוע מ"ה עָלֵינוּ ריבוע ס"ג וּמַעֲשֵׂה יָדֵינוּ כּוֹנְנֵהוּ יהוה אדני:

The fourth cup of wine – Action (Asiyah)

בָּרוּך יהוה ע"ב ורבוע מ"ה אַתָּה יְהֹוָואהדונהי אֱלֹהֵינוּ ילה מֶלֶך הָעוֹלָ
בּוֹרֵא פְּרִי ע"ה אלהים דאלפין הַגָּפֶן:

> יכוון שעתה בכוס רביעי נכנס קטנות ראשון דאימא
> **אלף למד הא יוד מם**
> (ציור הא' יו"ד ויוד כלול בו)

We drink while leaning to the left and then recite the last blessing.

The final blessing

בָּרוּך יהוה ע"ב ורבוע מ"ה אַתָּה יְהֹוָואהדונהי אֱלֹהֵינוּ ילה מֶלֶך הָעוֹלָ
עַל הַגֶּפֶן וְעַל פְּרִי ע"ה אלהים דאלפין הַגָּפֶן וְעַל תְּנוּבַת הַשָּׂדֶה ש
וְעַל אֶרֶץ אלהים דאלפין חֶמְדָּה נגד, זן, מזבח וְחֶמְדָּה טוֹבָה אכא וּרְחָבָה שֶׁרָצִי
וְהִנְחַלְתָּ לַאֲבוֹתֵינוּ לֶאֱכֹל מִפִּרְיָהּ וְלִשְׂבּוֹעַ מִטּוּבָהּ אכא‑ רַחֶ
אברהם, רמ"ח, ו"פ אל יְהֹוָואהדונהי אֱלֹהֵינוּ ילה עָלֵינוּ ריבוע ס"ג וְעַל יִשְׂרָאֵ
עַמֶּךָ ה הויות, נמם וְעַל יְרוּשָׁלַיִם עִירָךְ וְעַל הַר רבוע אלהים ‑ ה צִי
יוסף, ר"פ יהוה, ה"פ אל מִשְׁכַּן ב"פ (רבוע אלהים ‑ ה) כְּבוֹדָךְ ב הויות, וְעַל מִזְבּוֹחָ

The Final Blessing

ll of the food and drink that arrives at our table especially on a holiday has a definite
urpose. There is a spark of a soul within it that requires elevation. By blessing the food and
ating it, we elevate the spark. This blessing elevates the sparks of soul within the wine.

> On Shabbat
>
> *Favor us and strengthen us on this day of Shabbat.*

And grant us happiness on the day of this feast of Matzot, on this holid
of holy reading. For You are good; You do good to all; and we thank Yo
Hashem, our God, for the land and for the fruit of the vine. Blessed a
You, Hashem, for the land and for (its) fruit of the vine.

STAGE FIFTEEN:

NIRTZAH

The Seder is now concluded in accordance with its laws, with all its ordinan
and statutes. Just as we were privileged to arrange it, so may we merit
perform it. O Pure One, Which dwells on high, raise up the countle
congregation; soon guide the offshoots of Your plants, redeemed, to Zia
with glad song.

LESHANAH HABA'A

Next year in rebuilt Jerusalem

(We repeat this three times.)

STAGE FIFTEEN: NIRTZAH

Before we recite *Nirtzah*, we remove any uncertainty or doubts from our consciousnes
thus ensuring that all the efforts and requests we have made thus far are fulfilled in
lasting manner. We are using the power of certainty to guarantee that we have the streng
to get out of our own personal "Egypt" (chaos). As we inject certainty into the proce
and into the outcome, we meditate that all those around the world who are taking part i
a *Pesach Seder* will successfully complete their job as well.

LESHANA HABA'A

One of the ways to connect to the Creator is with song. The Ari says the way th
angels elevate is through song, and it is so important to sing in prayer because there
an elevation that happens to the soul through song, and this is why both the Ari an
Rav Ashlag composed songs.

וְעַל הֵיכָלֶךָ. וּבְנֵה יְרוּשָׁלַיִם עִיר בַּוְזְוָךְ, סַנְדְלְפוֹן, עָרֵי הַקֹּדֶשׁ בִּמְהֵרָה בְּיָמֵינוּ. וְהַעֲלֵנוּ לְתוֹכָהּ. וְשַׂמְּחֵנוּ בְּבִנְיָנָהּ. וּנְבָרֶכְךָ עָלֶיהָ פו בִּקְדֻשָּׁה וּבְטָהֳרָה.

On Shabbat
וּרְצֵה אלהים דההין וְהַחֲלִיצֵנוּ בְּיוֹם ע״ה = נגד, זן, מזבח הַשַּׁבָּת הַזֶּה והו.

וְשַׂמְּחֵנוּ בְּיוֹם ע״ה = נגד, זן, מזבח וְחַג הַמַּצּוֹת הַזֶּה והו. בְּיוֹם ע״ה = נגד, זן, מזב טוֹב והו מִקְרָא קֹדֶשׁ הַזֶּה והו. כִּי אַתָּה טוֹב והו וּמֵטִיב לַכֹּל יה אד וְנוֹדֶה לְּךָ יְהֹוָהאהדונהי אֱלֹהֵינוּ ילה עַל הָאָרֶץ אלהים דההין ע״ה וְעַל פְּרִי ע״ה אלהים דאלפין הַגָּפֶן. בָּרוּךְ, יהוה ע״ב ורבוע מ״ה אַתָּה יְהֹוָהאהדונה עַל הָאָרֶץ אלהים דההין ע״ה וְעַל פְּרִי ע״ה אלהים דאלפין גַּפְנָה (הַגָּפֶן).

STAGE FIFTEEN:

נִרְצָה

וְחֲסַל סִדּוּר פֶּסַח כְּהִלְכָתוֹ כְּכָל מִשְׁפָּטוֹ וְחֻקָּתוֹ. כַּאֲשֶׁר זָכִינוּ לְסַדֵּר אוֹתוֹ. כֵּן נִזְכֶּה לַעֲשׂוֹתוֹ. זָךְ יי שׁוֹכֵן מְעוֹנָה. קוֹמֵם קְהַל ע״ב ס״ג עֲדַת מִי ילי מָנָה ע״ה פוי. בְּקָרוֹב נַהֵל נִטְעֵי כַנָּה. פְּדוּיִם לְצִיּוֹן יוסף, ו״פ יהוה, ה״פ אל בְּרִנָּה:

LeShanah Haba'a

לְשָׁנָה אלהים פשוט וירדין הַבָּאָה בִּירוּשָׁלַיִם הַבְּנוּיָה: ג״פ
(We repeat this three times.)

We sing "*Next year in Jerusalem*" because we can bring about the Age of Messiah and the Temple in Jerusalem if we just keep the consciousness of *Pesach*. Although this is a simple enough idea, it is one that requires extraordinary spiritual strength. The problem is further compounded by our short memory. We tend to forget the intensity of energy aroused in the *Seder* as soon as we go back to the mundane world. It is easy to fall prey to the illusions, chaos, and pressures that confront us in our daily lives. The moment we react to these illusions, we allow the doubts to set in—and then the game is over.

Uvchen

This connects us to the actual point at midnight when chaos was removed from the lives of the Israelites some 3,400 years ago

It came to pass at midnight.

You have, then, performed many wonders by night. At the head of th watchers of this night. To the righteous convert (Abraham) You gai triumph by dividing for him the night. It came to pass at midnight. Yc judged the king of Grar (Avimelech) in a dream by night. You frighten the Aramean (Laban) in the dark of night. Israel (Jacob) fought with a angel and overcame him by night. It came to pass at midnight.

You judged the king of Grar (Avimelech) in a dream by night. Yc frightened the Aramean (Laban) in the dark of night. Israel (Jacob) fougi with an angel and overcame him by night. It came to pass at midnight. Egypt's firstborn You crushed at midnight. Their host they found not upc arising at night. The army of the prince of Charosheth (Sisra) You swej away with stars of the night. It came to pass at midnight.

The blasphemer (Sancheriv) planned to raise his hand against Jerusalen but You withered his corpses by night. Bel was overturned with its pedesta in the darkness of night. To the man of Your delight (Daniel) was reveale the mystery of the visions of night. It came to pass at midnight.

He (Belshatzar), who caroused from the holy vessels, was killed that ver night. From the lion's den was rescued he (Daniel) who interpreted th "terrors" of the night. The Agagite (Haman) nursed hatred and wro. decrees at night. It came to pass at midnight.

Uvchen

Both Uvchen songs are structured according to the 22 letters of the Aramaic alphabet.

UVCHEN

This connects us to the actual point at midnight when chaos was removed from the lives of the Israelites some 3,400 years ago

וּבְכֵן ע"ב, ריבוע יהוה וַיְהִי אל בַּחֲצִי הַלַּיְלָה מלה:

אָז רוֹב נִסִּים הִפְלֵאתָ בַּלַּיְלָה מלה. בְּרֹאשׁ ריבוע אלהים ואלהים דיודין ע' אַשְׁמוֹרֶת זֶה הַלַּיְלָה מלה. גֵּר בן קנ"א צֶדֶק נִצַּחְתּוֹ כְּנֶחֱלַק לוֹ לַיְלָ מלה. וַיְהִי אל בַּחֲצִי הַלַּיְלָה מלה:

דַּנְתָּ מֶלֶךְ גְּרָר בַּחֲלוֹם הַלַּיְלָה מלה. הִפְחַדְתָּ אֲרַמִּי בְּאֶמֶשׁ לַיְלָה מלה. וַיָּשַׂר יִשְׂרָאֵל לְאֵל ייא" וַיּוּכַל לוֹ לַיְלָה מלה. וַיְהִי אל בַּחֲצִי הַלַּיְלָה מלה:

זֶרַע בְּכוֹרֵי פַתְרוֹס מָחַצְתָּ בַּחֲצִי הַלַּיְלָה מלה. חֵילָם לֹא מָצְאוּ בְּקוּמָם בַּלַּיְלָה מלה. טִיסַת נְגִיד וְחֲרֹשֶׁת סִלִּיתָ בְּכוֹכְבֵי לַיְלָ מלה. וַיְהִי אל בַּחֲצִי הַלַּיְלָה מלה:

יָעַץ מְחָרֵף לְנוֹפֵף אִוּוּי הוֹבַשְׁתָּ פְגָרָיו בַּלַּיְלָה מלה. כָּרַ בֵּל וּמַצָּבוֹ בְּאִישׁוֹן לַיְלָה מלה. לְאִישׁ ע"ה קנ"א קס"א וְזְמוּדוֹ נִגְלָה רָז אור, אין סוף וְחֲזוֹת לַיְלָה מלה. וַיְהִי אל בַּחֲצִי הַלַּיְלָה מלה:

מִשְׁתַּכֵּר בִּכְלֵי קֹדֶשׁ נֶהֱרַג בּוֹ בַּלַּיְלָה מלה. נוֹשַׁע מִבּוֹר אֲרָיוֹ פּוֹתֵר בִּעֲתוּתֵי לַיְלָה מלה. שִׂנְאָה נָטַר אֲגָגִי וְכָתַב סְפָרִים בַּלַּיְלָ מלה. וַיְהִי אל בַּחֲצִי הַלַּיְלָה מלה:

עוֹרַרְתָּ נִצְחֲךָ עָלָיו בְּנֶדֶד שְׁנַת לַיְלָה מלה. פּוּרָה תִדְרוֹךְ לְשׁוֹמֵ מַה מ"ה מִּלַּיְלָה מלה. צָרַח כַּשּׁוֹמֵר וְשָׂח אָתָא בֹקֶר וְגַם יג"ל לַיְלָ מלה. וַיְהִי אל בַּחֲצִי הַלַּיְלָה מלה:

קָרֵב יוֹם ע"ה = נגד, זן, מזבזו אֲשֶׁר הוּא לֹא יוֹם ע"ה = נגד, זן, מזב וְלֹא לַיְלָה מלה. רָם הוֹדַע כִּי לְךָ הַיּוֹם ע"ה = נגד, זן, מזבזו אַף לְ הַלַּיְלָה מלה. שׁוֹמְרִים הַפְקֵד לְעִירְךָ כָּל יל" הַיּוֹם ע"ה = נגד, זן, מזב

You began Your triumph over him, when You disturbed (Ahashverosh')
sleep at night. Trample the wine-press to help those who ask the watchman
"What of the long night?" He will shout like a watchman and say
"Morning shall come after night." It came to pass at midnight.

Hasten the day (of Messiah), that is neither day nor night. Most High
make known that Yours are day and night. Most High, make known that
Yours are day and night. Brighten like the light of day the darkness of
night. It came to pass at midnight.

And you shall say: "This is the feast of Pesach." Above all festival
You elevated Pesach. To the Oriental (Abraham) You revealed the future
midnight of Pesach. And you shall say: "This is the feast of Pesach." At
his door You knocked in the heat of the day on Pesach. He satiated the
angels with Matzah-cakes on Pesach. And he ran to the herd, symbolic of
the sacrificial beast   of Pesach. And you shall say: "This is the feast of
Pesach."

The Sodomites provoked (God) and were devoured by fire on Pesach. Lot
was withdrawn from them and he baked Matzah at the time of the end
of Pesach. You swept clean the soil of Moph and Noph (in Egypt) when
You passed through on Pesach. And you shall say: "This is the feast of
Pesach."

O God, You crushed every firstborn of On (in Egypt) on the watchful night
of Pesach. But Master, Your own firstborn You skipped by merit of the
blood of Pesach, not to allow the Destroyer to enter my doors on Pesach.
And you shall say: "This is the feast of Pesach."

The beleaguered (Jericho) was besieged on Pesach. Midian was destroyed at
the sound of Omer barely on Pesach. The mighty nobles of Pul and Lud
(Assyria) were consumed in a great conflagration on Pesach. And you shall
say: "This is the feast of Pesach."

וְכָל יֹי הַלַּיְלָה מלה. תָּאִיר כָּאוֹר רו, אין סוף יוֹם ע״ה = נגד, זן, מזבח וְשֶׁכֶד
לַיְלָה מלה. וַיְהִי אל בַּחֲצִי הַלַּיְלָה מלה:

וּבְכֵן ע״ב, ריבוע יהוה וַאֲמַרְתֶּם זֶבַח פֶּסַח:

אֹמֶץ גְּבוּרוֹתֶיךָ הִפְלֵאתָ בַּפֶּסַח. בְּרֹאשׁ ריבוע אלהים ואלהים דיודין ע
כָּל יֹי מוֹעֲדוֹת נִשֵּׂאתָ פֶּסַח. גִּלִּיתָ לְאֶזְרָחִי וְחֲצוֹת לֵיל פֶּסַח
וַאֲמַרְתֶּם זֶבַח פֶּסַח:

דְּלָתָיו דָּפַקְתָּ כְּחוֹם הַיּוֹם ע״ה = נגד, זן, מזבח בַּפֶּסַח. הִסְעִיד נוֹצְצִים
עֻגוֹת מַצּוֹת בַּפֶּסַח. וְאֶל הַבָּקָר רָץ זֵכֶר לְשׁוֹר אבגית״ץ, ושׁר, אהבת חנ
עֶרֶךְ פֶּסַח. וַאֲמַרְתֶּם זֶבַח פֶּסַח:

זוֹעֲמוּ סְדוֹמִים וְלֹהֲטוּ בָּאֵשׁ אלהים דיודין ע״ה בַּפֶּסַח. וְחֻלַּץ לוֹט מ
מֵהֶם וּמַצּוֹת אָפָה בְּקֵץ אלהים פֶּסַח. טֵאטֵאתָ אַדְמַת מוּ
וְנֹף בְּעָבְרְךָ בַּפֶּסַח. וַאֲמַרְתֶּם זֶבַח פֶּסַח:

יָהּ רֹאשׁ ההה ריבוע אלהים ואלהים דיודין ע״ה כָּל יֹי אוֹן מָחַצְתָּ בְּלֵיל שִׁמּוּ
פֶּסַח. כַּבִּיר עַל בֵּן בְּכוֹר פָּסַחְתָּ בְּדַם רביע אהיה פֶּסַח. לְבִלְתִּ
תֵּת מַשְׁחִית לָבֹא בִּפְתָחַי בַּפֶּסַח. וַאֲמַרְתֶּם זֶבַח פֶּסַח:

מְסֻגֶּרֶת סֻגָּרָה בְּעִתּוֹתֵי פֶּסַח. נִשְׁמְדָה מִדְיָן בִּצְלִיל שְׂעוֹר
עֹמֶר פֶּסַח. שֹׂרְפוּ מִשְׁמַנֵּי פּוּל וְלוּד בִּיקַד יְקוֹד פֶּסַח
וַאֲמַרְתֶּם זֶבַח פֶּסַח:

עוֹד הַיּוֹם ע״ה = נגד, זן, מזבח בְּנֹב לַעֲמוֹד עַד גָּעָה עוֹנַת פֶּסַח. פַּ
יַד כַּתְבָה לְקַעֲקֵעַ צוּל בַּפֶּסַח. צָפֹה הַצָּפִית עָרוֹךְ הַשֻּׁלְחָן
בַּפֶּסַח. וַאֲמַרְתֶּם זֶבַח פֶּסַח:

קָהָל ע״ב, ס״ג כִּנְּסָה הֲדַסָּה צוֹם לְשַׁלֵּשׁ בַּפֶּסַח. רֹאשׁ
ריבוע אלהים ואלהים דיודין ע״ה מִבֵּית ב״פ ראה רָשָׁע מָחַצְתָּ בְּעֵץ ע״ה קס״א
וְחֲמִשִּׁים בַּפֶּסַח. שְׁתֵּי אֵלֶּה רֶגַע ג״פ אלהים ט״ו אותיות תָּבִיא לְעוּצִי
בַּפֶּסַח. תָּעוֹז יָדְךָ בויכו וְתָרוּם יְמִינֶךָ כְּלֵיל הִתְקַדֶּשׁ חַג פֶּסַח
וַאֲמַרְתֶּם זֶבַח פֶּסַח:

He (Sancheriv) would have stood that day at Nov, but for the advent of Pesach. A hand inscribed the destruction of Zul (Babylon) on Pesach. As the watch was set, and the royal table decked on Pesach. And you shall say "This is the feast of Pesach."

Hadassah (Esther) gathered a congregation for a three-day fast on Pesach. You caused the head of the evil clan (Haman) to be hanged on a fifty cubit gallows on Pesach. Doubly, will you bring in an instant upon Utzit (Edom) on Pesach. Let Your hand be strong, and Your right arm exalted as on the night when You hallowed the festival of Pesach. And you shall say: "This is the feast of Pesach."

KI LO NA'EH

To It praise is due! To It praise is fitting! Powerful in majesty, perfectly distinguished, Its regiments of angels say to It: Yours and only Yours; Yours, yet Yours; Yours, surely Yours; Yours Hashem, is the sovereignty. To It praise is due! To It praise is fitting!

Supreme in kingship, perfectly glorious, Its faithful say to It: Yours and only Yours; Yours, yet Yours; Yours, surely Yours; Yours Hashem, is the sovereignty. To It praise is due! To It praise is fitting!

Pure in kingship, perfectly immune, Its angels say to It: Yours and only Yours; Yours, yet Yours; Yours, surely Yours; Yours Hashem, is the sovereignty. To It praise is due! To It praise is fitting!

KI LO NA'EH

This song speaks about God's Kingdom, and what the concept of a king and his subject is all about. A king cannot be a king without subjects and a kingdom: It is the subjects who

KI LO NA'EH

כִּי לוֹ נָאֶה. כִּי לוֹ יָאֶה:

אַדִּיר הוּא בִּמְלוּכָה. בָּחוּר כַּהֲלָכָה. גְּדוּדָיו יֹאמְרוּ לוֹ: לְךָ וּלְךָ. לְךָ כִּי לְךָ. לְךָ אַף לְךָ. לְךָ יְהוָֹאַדנֹיאהדונהי הַמַּמְלָכָה. כִּי לוֹ נָאֶה. כִּי לוֹ יָאֶה:

דָּגוּל בִּמְלוּכָה. הָדוּר כַּהֲלָכָה. וָתִיקָיו יֹאמְרוּ לוֹ: לְךָ וּלְךָ. לְךָ כִּי לְךָ. לְךָ אַף לְךָ. לְךָ יְהוָֹאַדנֹיאהדונהי הַמַּמְלָכָה. כִּי לוֹ נָאֶה. כִּי לוֹ יָאֶה:

זַכַּאי בִּמְלוּכָה. וְחָסִין כַּהֲלָכָה. טַפְסְרָיו יֹאמְרוּ לוֹ: לְךָ וּלְךָ. לְךָ כִּי לְךָ. לְךָ אַף לְךָ. לְךָ יְהוָֹאַדנֹיאהדונהי הַמַּמְלָכָה. כִּי לוֹ נָאֶה. כִּי לוֹ יָאֶה:

יָחִיד בִּמְלוּכָה. כַּבִּיר כַּהֲלָכָה. לִמּוּדָיו יֹאמְרוּ לוֹ: לְךָ וּלְךָ. לְךָ כִּי לְךָ. לְךָ אַף לְךָ. לְךָ יְהוָֹאַדנֹיאהדונהי הַמַּמְלָכָה. כִּי לוֹ נָאֶה. כִּי לוֹ יָאֶה:

מֶלֶךְ בִּמְלוּכָה. נוֹרָא ע"ה ג"פ אלהים כַּהֲלָכָה. סְבִיבָיו יֹאמְרוּ לוֹ: לְךָ וּלְךָ. לְךָ כִּי לְךָ. לְךָ אַף לְךָ. לְךָ יְהוָֹאַדנֹיאהדונהי הַמַּמְלָכָה. כִּי לוֹ נָאֶה. כִּי לוֹ יָאֶה:

עָנָיו בִּמְלוּכָה. פּוֹדֶה כַּהֲלָכָה. צַדִּיקָיו יֹאמְרוּ לוֹ: לְךָ וּלְךָ. לְךָ כִּי לְךָ. לְךָ אַף לְךָ. לְךָ יְהוָֹאַדנֹיאהדונהי הַמַּמְלָכָה. כִּי לוֹ נָאֶה. כִּי לוֹ יָאֶה:

elp define the king and give him something to rule over—there is a mutual dependency. With the Creator, however, there is no dependency on anything. To be a subject of this King (the Creator) is a rare privilege, for it is a relationship built on the greatest love of l—unconditional love.

Alone in kingship, perfectly omnipotent, Its scholars say to It: Yours an only Yours; Yours, yet Yours; Yours, surely Yours; Yours Hashem, is th sovereignty. To It praise is due! To It praise is fitting!

Commanding in kingship, perfectly wondrous, Its surroundings say 1 It: Yours and only Yours; Yours, yet Yours; Yours, surely Yours; Your Hashem, is the sovereignty. To It praise is due! To It praise is fitting!

Humble in kingship, perfectly redeeming, Its righteous say to It: Yours an only Yours; Yours, yet Yours; Yours, surely Yours; Yours Hashem, is th sovereignty. To It praise is due! To It praise is fitting!

Holy in kingship, perfectly merciful, Its troops of angels say to It: Your and only Yours; Yours, yet Yours; Yours, surely Yours; Yours Hashem, . the sovereignty. To It praise is due! To It praise is fitting!

Assertive in kingship, perfectly sustaining, Its perfect ones say to It: Your and only Yours; Yours, yet Yours; Yours, surely Yours; Yours Hashem, . the sovereignty. To It praise is due! To It praise is fitting!

ADIR HU

It is most mighty. May It soon rebuild Its House, speedily, yes, speedily, i our days, soon. God rebuild, God rebuild, rebuild Your House soon.

It is distinguished. It is great. It is exalted. May It soon rebuild Its Hous speedily, yes, speedily, in our days, soon. God rebuild, God rebuild, rebuil Your House soon.

ADIR HU

This song connects us to the absence of the physical Temple. The Creator wants to giv us everything but cannot because we don't have the Vessel of the Temple to manifest th Light. Gazing at a photograph of the Earth from space reveals a profound kabbalisti principle concerning the secret to generating spiritual Light. The Earth is illuminated lik a sparkling blue jewel, while space around the Earth remains black because there is n

קָדוֹשׁ בִּמְלוּכָה. רַחוּם כַּהֲלָכָה. שִׁנְאַנָּיו יֹאמְרוּ לוֹ: לְךָ וּלְךָ
לְךָ כִּי לְךָ. לְךָ אַף לְךָ. לְךָ יְהֹוָﬞﬞﬞﬞאֲדֹנָי הַמַּמְלָכָה. כִּי לוֹ נָאֶה
כִּי לוֹ יָאֶה:

תַּקִּיף בִּמְלוּכָה. תּוֹמֵךְ כַּהֲלָכָה. תְּמִימָיו יֹאמְרוּ לוֹ: לְךָ וּלְךָ
לְךָ כִּי לְךָ. לְךָ אַף לְךָ. לְךָ יְהֹוָﬞﬞﬞﬞאֲדֹנָי הַמַּמְלָכָה. כִּי לוֹ נָאֶה
כִּי לוֹ יָאֶה:

ADIR HU

אַדִּיר הֲרֵי הוּא יִבְנֶה בֵיתוֹ ב"פ ראה בְּקָרוֹב. בִּמְהֵרָה בִּמְהֵרָ
בְּיָמֵינוּ בְּקָרוֹב. אֵל יא"י בְּנֵה. אֵל יא"י בְּנֵה. בְּנֵה בֵיתְךָ ב"פ רא
בְּקָרוֹב:

בָּחוּר הוּא. גָּדוֹל לחוו, מבה, יזל, אום הוּא. דָּגוּל הוּא. יִבְנֶה בֵיתוֹ ב
ראה בְּקָרוֹב. בִּמְהֵרָה בִּמְהֵרָה בְּיָמֵינוּ בְּקָרוֹב. אֵל יא"י בְּנֵה. א
יא"י בְּנֵה. בְּנֵה בֵיתְךָ ב"פ ראה בְּקָרוֹב:

הָדוּר הוּא. וָתִיק הוּא. זַכַּאי הוּא. וְחָסִיד הוּא. יִבְנֶה בֵיתוֹ ב
ראה בְּקָרוֹב. בִּמְהֵרָה בִּמְהֵרָה בְּיָמֵינוּ בְּקָרוֹב. אֵל יא"י בְּנֵה. א
יא"י בְּנֵה. בְּנֵה בֵיתְךָ ב"פ ראה בְּקָרוֹב:

טָהוֹר י"פ אכא הוּא. יָחִיד הוּא. כַּבִּיר הוּא. לָמוּד הוּא. מֶלֶ
הוּא. יִבְנֶה בֵיתוֹ ב"פ ראה בְּקָרוֹב. בִּמְהֵרָה בִּמְהֵרָה בְּיָמֵינוּ בְּקָרוֹב
אֵל יא"י בְּנֵה. אֵל יא"י בְּנֵה. בְּנֵה בֵיתְךָ ב"פ ראה בְּקָרוֹב:

---

essel, no physical object in space to reflect the light. Sunlight fills the vacuum of space,
ut this light remains concealed without a Vessel to reflect it and make it shine. The
oment a Vessel reflects the Light, illumination occurs. In the same manner, the Creator
quires a Vessel to "reflect" the Light in order to generate the Light of fulfillment. The
emple was the most powerful Vessel on the planet for generating spiritual Light.

Vhen we feel the Creator's pain and frustration at not being able to give this fulfillment
 us, it will motivate us to continually change our nature. Changing our nature is how we
uild our own internal Vessel to receive and reveal God's infinite Light.

It is all glorious. It is faithful. It is faultless. It is righteous. May It soon rebuild Its House, speedily, yes, speedily, in our days, soon. God rebuild, God rebuild, rebuild Your House soon.

It is pure. It is unique. It is powerful. It is all-wise. It is King. May It soon rebuild Its House, speedily, yes, speedily, in our days, soon.

God rebuild, God rebuild, rebuild Your House soon.

It is awesome. It is sublime. It is all-powerful. It is the Redeemer. It is righteous. May It soon rebuild Its House, speedily, yes, speedily, in our days, soon. God rebuild, God rebuild, rebuild Your House soon.

It is holy. It is compassionate. It is Almighty. It is omnipotent. May It soon rebuild Its House, speedily, yes, speedily, in our days, soon. God rebuild, God rebuild, rebuild Your House soon.

ECHAD MI YODEA

Who knows one?
I know one: One is our God, in heaven and on earth.

Who knows two?
I know two: Two are the Tablets of the Covenant; one is our God, in heaven and on earth.

ECHAD MI YODEA

This song starts out with: "*Who knows one? I know one!*"

When Rav Chanoch Heinich of Alexander was a young boy, he told his father that he went to learn from his kabbalistic master. When his father asked what he learned, he replied "There is a Creator." His father laughed at him and asked the maid, "Is there a God?" When she said, "Yes," the father looked at his son and said, "You had to go all the way to a master to find out there is a God? Even our maid knows there is a God. These kabbalists don't know anything." Rav Chanoch replied, "She just says there is a God. I know there's a God." This is the point of Echad Mi Yodea—to really get to know the Creator.

נוֹרָא ע"ה ג"פ אלהים הוּא. שַׂגִּיב הוּא. עִזּוּז הוּא. פּוֹדֶה הוּא. צַדִּיק

הוּא. יִבְנֶה בֵיתוֹ ב"פ ראה בְּקָרוֹב. בִּמְהֵרָה בִּמְהֵרָה בְּיָמֵינוּ בְּקָרוֹב

אֵל יי"י בְּנֵה. אֵל יי"י בְּנֵה. בְּנֵה בֵיתְךָ ב"פ ראה בְּקָרוֹב:

קָדוֹשׁ הוּא. רַחוּם הוּא. שַׁדַּי הוּא. תַּקִּיף הוּא. יִבְנֶה בֵּיד

ב"פ ראה בְּקָרוֹב. בִּמְהֵרָה בִּמְהֵרָה בְּיָמֵינוּ בְּקָרוֹב. אֵל יי"י בְּנֵה

אֵל יי"י בְּנֵה. בְּנֵה בֵיתְךָ ב"פ ראה בְּקָרוֹב:

ECHAD MI YODEA

אֶחָד אהבה, דאגה מִי יל יוֹדֵעַ.

אֶחָד אהבה, דאגה אֲנִי אני, טדהד כוזו יוֹדֵעַ. אֶחָד אהבה, דאגה אֱלֹהֵינוּ י

שֶׁבַּשָּׁמַיִם י"פ טל, י"פ כוזו וּבָאָרֶץ אלהים דאלפין:

שְׁנַיִם מִי יל יוֹדֵעַ.

שְׁנַיִם אֲנִי אני, טדהד כוזו יוֹדֵעַ שְׁנֵי לוּחוֹת הַבְּרִית. אֶחָד אהבה, דא

אֱלֹהֵינוּ ילה שֶׁבַּשָּׁמַיִם י"פ טל, י"פ כוזו וּבָאָרֶץ אלהים דאלפין:

Who knows three? I know three! Three is for our forefathers…"

With this verse, we connect to our three forefathers: Abraham, Isaac, and Jacob, who are chariots of this world. The idea here is that when the same thing keeps happening, we need to act in a new and different way. We need to change our routine or nothing will change in our life. Sometimes, we may need to act differently even given the same situation: sometimes like Abraham and having mercy, sometimes like Isaac and executing judgment.

Who knows ten? I know ten! Ten is for the Ten Utterances…"

The Ten Utterances give us both spiritual Light and the understanding that we must know our limitations and not test them. We should not tempt tests and bring them on ourselves. In other words, if you're trying to lose weight, don't get a job at a bakery.

Who knows thirteen? I know thirteen! Thirteen is for the Attributes of God…"

This song only goes up to 13, no further. The kabbalists teach us that we stop at 13 because the number 13 is also the numerical value of the word echad, which means "one." Basically, we're going back to the beginning. In reality, we're not really counting anything—we're saying that everything is all one.

Who knows three?
I know three: Three are the Patriarchs; two are the Tablets of the Covenant; one is our God, in heaven and on earth.

Who knows four?
I know four: Four are the Matriarchs; three are the Patriarchs; two are t *Tablets of the Covenant; one is our God, in heaven and on earth.*

Who knows five?
I know five: Five are the Books of Torah; four are the Matriarchs; thr *are the Patriarchs; two are the Tablets of the Covenant; one is our God, heaven and on earth.*

Who knows six?
I know six: Six are the Orders of the Mishnah; five are the Books of Torah; four are the Matriarchs; three are the Patriarchs; two are the Tablets of the Covenant; one is our God, in heaven and on earth

Who knows seven?
I know seven: Seven are the days of the week; six are the Orders of t *Mishnah; five are the Books of Torah; four are the Matriarchs; three a* *the Patriarchs; two are the Tablets of the Covenant; one is our God, heaven and on earth.*

Who knows eight?
I know eight: Eight are the days of circumcision; seven are the days of t *week; six are the Orders of the Mishnah; five are the Books of Tora* *four are the Matriarchs; three are the Patriarchs; two are the Tablets of t* *Covenant; one is our God, in heaven and on earth.*

Who knows nine?
I know nine: Nine are the months of pregnancy; eight are the days c *circumcision; seven are the days of the week; six are the Orders of t*

שְׁלֹשָׁה מִי יָי יוֹדֵעַ.

שְׁלֹשָׁה אֲנִי אני, טדהד כוו' יוֹדֵעַ. שְׁלֹשָׁה אָבוֹת. שְׁנֵי לוּחוֹת הַבְּרִית. אֶחָד אהבה, דאגה אֱלֹהֵינוּ ילה שֶׁבַּשָּׁמַיִם יפ טל, י כוו וּבָאָרֶץ אלהים דאלפין:

אַרְבַּע מִי יי יוֹדֵעַ.

אַרְבַּע אֲנִי אני, טדהד כוו' יוֹדֵעַ. אַרְבַּע אִמָּהוֹת. שְׁלֹשָׁה אָבוֹת. שְׁנֵי לוּחוֹת הַבְּרִית. אֶחָד אהבה, דאגה אֱלֹהֵינוּ ילה שֶׁבַּשָּׁמַיִם יפ טל, יפ כו וּבָאָרֶץ אלהים דאלפין:

חֲמִשָּׁה מִי יי יוֹדֵעַ.

חֲמִשָּׁה אֲנִי אני, טדהד כוו' יוֹדֵעַ. חֲמִשָּׁה וֹזוּמִשֵׁי תוֹרָה. אַרְבַּע אִמָּהוֹת. שְׁלֹשָׁה אָבוֹת. שְׁנֵי לוּחוֹת הַבְּרִית. אֶחָד אהבה, דא אֱלֹהֵינוּ ילה שֶׁבַּשָּׁמַיִם יפ טל, יפ כוו וּבָאָרֶץ אלהים דאלפין:

שִׁשָּׁה מִי יי יוֹדֵעַ.

שִׁשָּׁה אֲנִי אני, טדהד כוו' יוֹדֵעַ. שִׁשָּׁה סִדְרֵי מִשְׁנָה שדי יה אדני. וֹחֲמִשׁ וֹזוּמִשֵׁי תוֹרָה. אַרְבַּע אִמָּהוֹת. שְׁלֹשָׁה אָבוֹת. שְׁנֵי לוּחוֹ הַבְּרִית. אֶחָד אהבה, דאגה אֱלֹהֵינוּ ילה שֶׁבַּשָּׁמַיִם יפ טל, יפ כוו וּבָאָר אלהים דאלפין:

שִׁבְעָה מִי יי יוֹדֵעַ.

שִׁבְעָה אֲנִי אני, טדהד כוו' יוֹדֵעַ. שִׁבְעָה יְמֵי שַׁבַּתָּא. שִׁשָּׁה סִדְרֵ מִשְׁנָה שדי יה אדני. וֹחֲמִשָּׁה וֹזוּמִשֵׁי תוֹרָה. אַרְבַּע אִמָּהוֹת. שְׁלֹשָׁ אָבוֹת. שְׁנֵי לוּחוֹת הַבְּרִית. אֶחָד אהבה, דאגה אֱלֹהֵינוּ ילה שֶׁבַּשָּׁמַיִם יפ טל, יפ כוו וּבָאָרֶץ אלהים דאלפין:

שְׁמוֹנָה מִי יי יוֹדֵעַ.

שְׁמוֹנָה אֲנִי אני, טדהד כוו' יוֹדֵעַ. שְׁמוֹנָה יְמֵי מִילָה אלהים עה. שִׁבְעָ יְמֵי שַׁבַּתָּא. שִׁשָּׁה סִדְרֵי מִשְׁנָה שדי יה אדני. וֹחֲמִשָּׁה וֹזוּמִשֵׁי תוֹרָה אַרְבַּע אִמָּהוֹת. שְׁלֹשָׁה אָבוֹת. שְׁנֵי לוּחוֹת הַבְּרִית. אֶחָד אהבה, דאגה אֱלֹהֵינוּ ילה שֶׁבַּשָּׁמַיִם יפ טל, יפ כוו וּבָאָרֶץ אלהים דאלפין:

Mishnah; five are the Books of Torah; four are the Matriarchs; three are the Patriarchs; two are the Tablets of the Covenant; one is our God, in heaven and on earth.

Who knows ten?
I know ten: Ten are the ten Commandments; nine are the months of pregnancy; eight are the days of circumcision; seven are the days of the week; six are the Orders of the Mishnah; five are the Books of Torah; four are the Matriarchs; three are the Patriarchs; two are the Tablets of the Covenant; one is our God, in heaven and on earth.

Who knows eleven?
I know eleven: Eleven are the stars; ten are the ten Commandments; nine are the months of pregnancy; eight are the days of circumcision;
seven are the days of the week; six are the Orders of the Mishnah; five are the Books of Torah; four are the Matriarchs; three are the Patriarchs; two are the Tablets of the Covenant; one is our God, in heaven and on earth.

Who knows twelve?
I know twelve: Twelve are the tribes; eleven are the stars; ten are the ten Commandments; nine are the months of pregnancy; eight are the days of circumcision; seven are the days of the week; six are the Orders of the Mishnah; five are the Books of Torah; four are the Matriarchs; three are the Patriarchs; two are the Tablets of the Covenant; one is our God, in heaven and on earth.

Who knows thirteen?
I know thirteen: Thirteen are the attributes of God; twelve are the tribes; eleven are the stars; ten are the ten Commandments; nine are the months of pregnancy; eight are the days of circumcision; seven are the days of the week; six are the Orders of the Mishnah; five are the Books of Torah; four are the Matriarchs; three are the Patriarchs; two are the Tablets of the Covenant; one is our God, in heaven and on earth.

תִּשְׁעָה מִי יִּלֹ יוֹדֵעַ.

תִּשְׁעָה אֲנִי אני, טדהׂד כוׂיׂ יוֹדֵעַ. תִּשְׁעָה יַרְחֵי לֵידָה. שְׁמוֹנָה יְמֵי
מִילָה אלהים עׂהׂ. שִׁבְעָה יְמֵי שַׁבַּתָּא. שִׁשָּׁה סִדְרֵי מִשְׁנָה שׂדי ׂ
אׇדׂני וַחֲמִשָּׁה וְחוּמְשֵׁי תוֹרָה. אַרְבַּע אִמָּהוֹת. שְׁלֹשָׁה אָבוֹת. שְׁ
לוּחוֹת הַבְּרִית. אֶחָד אהבה, דאגה אֱלֹהֵינוּ ילה שֶׁבַּשָּׁמַיִם ייׂפ טל, יׂפ כו
וּבָאָרֶץ אלהים דאלפין:

עֲשָׂרָה מִי יִּלֹ יוֹדֵעַ.

עֲשָׂרָה אֲנִי אני, טדהׂד כוׂיׂ יוֹדֵעַ. עֲשָׂרָה דִבְּרַיָּא. תִּשְׁעָה יַרְח
לֵידָה. שְׁמוֹנָה יְמֵי מִילָה אלהים עׂהׂ. שִׁבְעָה יְמֵי שַׁבַּתָּא. שִׁשָּׁ
סִדְרֵי מִשְׁנָה שׂדי יה אׇדׂני וַחֲמִשָּׁה וְחוּמְשֵׁי תוֹרָה. אַרְבַּע אִמָּהוֹת
שְׁלֹשָׁה אָבוֹת. שְׁנֵי לוּחוֹת הַבְּרִית. אֶחָד אהבה, דאגה אֱלֹהֵינוּ יל
שֶׁבַּשָּׁמַיִם ייׂפ טל, יׂפ כוׂזׂ וּבָאָרֶץ אלהים דאלפין:

אֶחָד אהבה, דאגה עָשָׂר מִי יִּלֹ יוֹדֵעַ.

אֶחָד אהבה, דאגה עָשָׂר אֲנִי אני, טדהׂד כוׂיׂ יוֹדֵעַ. אֶחָד אהבה, דאגה עָשָׂ
כּוֹכְבַיָּא. עֲשָׂרָה דִבְּרַיָּא. תִּשְׁעָה יַרְחֵי לֵידָה. שְׁמוֹנָה יְמ
מִילָה אלהים עׂהׂ. שִׁבְעָה יְמֵי שַׁבַּתָּא. שִׁשָּׁה סִדְרֵי מִשְׁנָה שׂדי ׂ
אׇדׂני וַחֲמִשָּׁה וְחוּמְשֵׁי תוֹרָה. אַרְבַּע אִמָּהוֹת. שְׁלֹשָׁה אָבוֹת. שְׁ
לוּחוֹת הַבְּרִית. אֶחָד אהבה, דאגה אֱלֹהֵינוּ ילה שֶׁבַּשָּׁמַיִם ייׂפ טל, יׂפ כו
וּבָאָרֶץ אלהים דאלפין:

שְׁנֵים עָשָׂר מִי יִּלֹ יוֹדֵעַ.

שְׁנֵים עָשָׂר אֲנִי אני, טדהׂד כוׂיׂ יוֹדֵעַ. שְׁנֵים עָשָׂר שִׁבְטַיָּא. אֶחָד
אהבה, דאגה עָשָׂר כּוֹכְבַיָּא. עֲשָׂרָה דִבְּרַיָּא. תִּשְׁעָה יַרְחֵי לֵידָה
שְׁמוֹנָה יְמֵי מִילָה אלהים עׂהׂ. שִׁבְעָה יְמֵי שַׁבַּתָּא. שִׁשָּׁה סִדְרֵ
מִשְׁנָה שׂדי יה אׇדׂני וַחֲמִשָּׁה וְחוּמְשֵׁי תוֹרָה. אַרְבַּע אִמָּהוֹת. שְׁלֹ
אָבוֹת. שְׁנֵי לוּחוֹת הַבְּרִית. אֶחָד אהבה, דאגה אֱלֹהֵינוּ ילה שֶׁבַּשָּׁמַיִ
ייׂפ טל, יׂפ כוׂזׂ וּבָאָרֶץ אלהים דאלפין:

CHAD GADYA

A kid, a kid that father bought for two zuzim, a kid, a kid. A cat then came and devoured the kid that father bought for two zuzim, a kid, a kid.

A dog then came and bit the cat that devoured the kid that father bought for two zuzim, a kid, a kid.

A stick then came and beat the dog that bit the cat that devoured the kid that father bought for two zuzim, a kid, a kid.

A fire then came and burnt the stick that beat the dog that bit the cat that devoured the kid that father bought for two zuzim, a kid, a kid.

Water then came and quenched the fire that burnt the stick that beat the dog that bit the cat that devoured the kid that father bought for two zuzim, a kid, a kid.

An ox then came and drank the water that quenched the fire that burnt the stick that beat the dog that bit the cat that devoured the kid that father bought for two zuzim, a kid, a kid.

CHAD GADYA

This song is written in Aramaic, and as mentioned previously, the Aramaic language is code that the angels cannot understand. Because the Negative Side also has angels that can influence and sabotage our connections, we employ Aramaic when we want to bypass all angels. In this song, God slaughters the Angel of Death, connecting us to Him and giving birth to immortality. Therefore, we do not want any negative angels interfering with this connection.

שְׁלֹשָׁה עָשָׂר מִי יֹ יֹודֵעַ.

שְׁלֹשָׁה עָשָׂר אֲנִי אֲנִי, טרדה"ר כוזו יֹודֵעַ. שְׁלֹשָׁה עָשָׂר מִדַּיָּא. שְׁנֵי עָשָׂר שִׁבְטַיָּא. אֲחַד אהבה, דאגה עָשָׂר כּוֹכְבַיָּא. עֲשָׂרָה דִבְּרַיָּא. תִּשְׁעָה יַרְחֵי לֵידָה. שְׁמוֹנָה יְמֵי מִילָה אלהים ע"ה. שִׁבְעָה יְ שַׁבַּתָּא. שִׁשָּׁה סִדְרֵי מִשְׁנָה שדי יה אדני. וַחֲמִשָּׁה וְחוּמְשֵׁי תוֹרָה אַרְבַּע אִמָּהוֹת. שְׁלֹשָׁה אָבוֹת. שְׁנֵי לוּחוֹת הַבְּרִית. אֶחָד אהבה, דא אֱלֹהֵינוּ ילה שֶׁבַּשָּׁמַיִם י"פ טל, י"פ כוזו וּבָאָרֶץ אלהים דאלפין:

CHAD GADYA

חַד גַּדְיָא, חַד גַּדְיָא. דְּזַבִּין אַבָּא בִּתְרֵי זוּזֵי. חַד גַּדְיָא, חַד גַּדְיָא. וְאָתָא שׁוּנְרָא, וְאָכְלָה לְגַדְיָא, דְּזַבִּין אַבָּא בִּתְרֵי זוּ חַד גַּדְיָא, חַד גַּדְיָא.

וְאָתָא כַלְבָּא, וְנָשַׁךְ לְשׁוּנְרָא, דְּאָכְלָה לְגַדְיָא, דְּזַבִּין אַבּ בִּתְרֵי זוּזֵי. חַד גַּדְיָא, חַד גַּדְיָא.

וְאָתָא חוּטְרָא, וְהִכָּה לְכַלְבָּא, דְּנָשַׁךְ לְשׁוּנְרָא, דְּאָכְלָה לְגַדְיָא דְּזַבִּין אַבָּא בִּתְרֵי זוּזֵי. חַד גַּדְיָא, חַד גַּדְיָא.

וְאָתָא נוּרָא ע"ה ג"פ אלהים, וְשָׂרַף לְחוּטְרָא, דְּהִכָּה לְכַלְבָּא, דְּנָשַׁ לְשׁוּנְרָא, דְּאָכְלָה לְגַדְיָא, דְּזַבִּין אַבָּא בִּתְרֵי זוּזֵי. חַד גַּדְיָא חַד גַּדְיָא.

וְאָתָא מַיָּא, וְכָבָה לְנוּרָא ע"ה ג"פ אלהים, דְּשָׂרַף לְחוּטְרָא, דְּהִכָּ לְכַלְבָּא, דְּנָשַׁךְ לְשׁוּנְרָא, דְּאָכְלָה לְגַדְיָא, דְּזַבִּין אַבָּא בִּתְר זוּזֵי. חַד גַּדְיָא, חַד גַּדְיָא.

וְאָתָא תוֹרָא, וְשָׁתָה לְמַיָּא, דְּכָבָה לְנוּרָא ע"ה ג"פ אלהים, דְּשָׂר לְחוּטְרָא, דְּהִכָּה לְכַלְבָּא, דְּנָשַׁךְ לְשׁוּנְרָא, דְּאָכְלָה לְגַדְיָ דְּזַבִּין אַבָּא בִּתְרֵי זוּזֵי. חַד גַּדְיָא, חַד גַּדְיָא.

A slaughterer then came and slaughtered the ox that drank the water th
quenched the fire that burnt the stick that beat the dog that bit the cat
that devoured the kid that father bought for two zuzim, a kid, a kid.

The angel of death then came and killed the slaughterer that slaughtere
the ox that drank the water that quenched the fire that burnt the stick
that beat the dog that bit the cat that devoured the kid that father boug
for two zuzim, a kid, a kid.

The Holy One, Blessed be He, then came and slew the angel of death
that killed the slaughterer that slaughtered the ox that drank the water
that quenched the fire that burnt the stick that beat the dog that bit the
cat that devoured the kid that father bought for two zuzim, a kid, a kid

וְאָתָא הַשּׁוֹחֵט, וְשָׁחַט לְתוֹרָא, דְּשָׁתָה לְמַיָּא, דְּכָבָה לְנוּרָא, דְּשָׂרַף לְחוּטְרָא, דְּהִכָּה לְכַלְבָּא, דְּנָשַׁךְ לְשׁוּנְרָא, ע"ה ג"פ אלהים, דְּאָכְלָה לְגַדְיָא, דְּזַבִּין אַבָּא בִּתְרֵי זוּזֵי. וְחַד גַּדְיָא, וְחַד גַּדְיָא.

וְאָתָא מַלְאַךְ יאהדונהי הַמָּוֶת, וְשָׁחַט לְשׁוֹחֵט, דְּשָׁחַט לְתוֹרָא דְּשָׁתָה לְמַיָּא, דְּכָבָה לְנוּרָא ע"ה ג"פ אלהים, דְּשָׂרַף לְחוּטְרָא, דְּהִכָּה לְכַלְבָּא, דְּנָשַׁךְ לְשׁוּנְרָא, דְּאָכְלָה לְגַדְיָא, דְּזַבִּין אַבָּא בִּתְרֵי זוּזֵי. וְחַד גַּדְיָא, וְחַד גַּדְיָא.

וְאָתָא הַקָּדוֹשׁ בָּרוּךְ יהוה ע"ב ורבוע מ"ה הוּא, וְשָׁחַט לְמַלְאַךְ יאהדונהי הַמָּוֶת דְּשָׁחַט לְשׁוֹחֵט, דְּשָׁחַט לְתוֹרָא, דְּשָׁתָה לְמַיָּא, דְּכָבָה לְנוּרָא ע"ה ג"פ אלהים, דְּשָׂרַף לְחוּטְרָא, דְּהִכָּה לְכַלְבָּא, דְּנָשַׁךְ לְשׁוּנְרָא, דְּאָכְלָה לְגַדְיָא, דְּזַבִּין אַבָּא בִּתְרֵי זוּזֵי. וְחַד גַּדְיָא וְחַד גַּדְיָא.

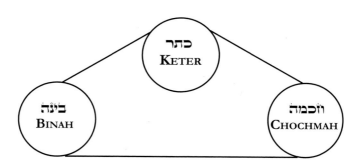

THE LOWER SEVEN SEFIROT
ZEIR ANPIN (6) + MALCHUT(1)

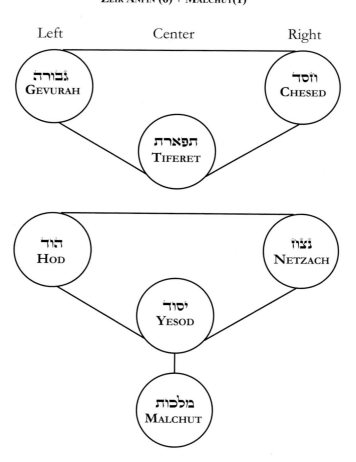

The Ten Sefirot

> conceal the blazing raw Light of the Endless World from us, a series of ten curtains filters were used. These ten curtains are known as the Ten *Sefirot*.

st as we need transformers to step down the raw naked energy coming from a nuclear ant before we can manifest it by plugging in an appliance in our home, each successive rtain further reduces the emanation of Light, gradually dimming its brilliance to a level at is almost imperceptible by our five senses. The result is our darkened Universe of aos, in which we play the game of life.

KETER - כתר - CROWN

eter, which sits like a Crown at the top above the Central Column, contains all the carnations of all the souls in existence. It embodies the Creator as unknown and nknowable and is located just below the Endless World of Infinite Light.

ill, *Keter* is the blazing intelligence that channels the Lightforce of Creation to the rest f the *Sefirot*. It functions as a super computer, containing the total inventory of what ach of us is, ever has been, or ever will be. As such, it is the genesis not only of our ves in this Earth realm, but also of every thought, idea, or inspiration we ever will have hile we sojourn here. This brings us to the subject of multiple lifetimes: past, present, d future.

eincarnation, the process through which the human soul returns to this realm again and gain until its imperfections are corrected, is a central tenet of Kabbalah. The correction rocess is called *tikkun* or karma.

he process, in which a soul is channeled down through the Ten *Sefirot* to be born in the hysical world of *Malchut*, begins in *Keter*, and no soul leaves there without the baggage it as accrued in previous lifetimes.

Jnlike the occasional flight aboard a major airline where you wind up in New York while our baggage goes to Bangkok, tikkun baggage always arrives at its proper destination. ou could never lose it in transit—even if you wanted to—because the sole purpose f your journey here is to grow and transform yourself spiritually. Most souls can lose heir self-imposed burdens of tikkun debt only through repeated trips to this plane of xistence.

he Light of *Keter* has a long way to go before it reaches us. It is as far removed from the hysical realm in which we live as an architect's first thought is removed from the building will ultimately become. *Keter* is the source of everything, an undifferentiated potential ate. The rest of the *Sefirot* are needed to transfrom that potential into something we can erceive as reality and the first to receive the power flowing out of *Keter* is:

CHOCHMAH - וֹכְמה - WISDOM

Chochmah, at the top of the Right Column, is the first depot containing all the Wisdom the Universe. *Chochmah* represents the beginning of the zodiac. It contains the totality the Light and stands as the universal "father figure." But wisdom passively contemplati itself in solitude is of no value on any plane of existence.

To be of use, wisdom must be inventoried, shipped out, and supplied to those in ne of it. To accomplish that, *Chochmah* requires connection with its corresponding "moth figure," which is:

BINAH - בינה - UNDERSTANDING

Binah, at the top of the Left Column, is a powerhouse of cosmic energy. *Bina* contains the energy of understanding that motivates the human endeavor and tugs at the earth tides that keep galaxies spinning and stars burning. When thought must be made manife into action, *Chochmah* and *Binah* meet to combine their energies.

In other words, *Chochmah* can be likened to a man who carries an encyclopedia on h back. Possession of the encyclopedia does not make the man smarter. *Binah* internalize the content so that information actually becomes part of the person.

CHESED - וֹסֶד - LOVING KINDNESS

Chesed, the most expansive of the *Sefirot*, sits below *Chochmah* on the Right Colum *Chesed* represents the pure positive energy of Sharing and Mercy and holds the sti undifferentiated seed of all that has taken place between *Chochmah* and *Binah*.

We all have seen *Chesed* run amok by sharing with no restriction. It is the ultra-liberal wh weeps more for the criminal than for his victim; it is the poor man who wins the lotter and gives every penny of his new fortune to charity, leaving his own family destitut Fortunately, *Chesed* does have a balancing counterpart, just across the way, on the Le Column, right under *Binah*. It is called:

GEVURAH - גבורה - JUDGMENT

Gevurah sits below *Binah* on the Left Column. Whereas *Chesed* gives almost to a faul *Gevurah* with its energy of Judgment is miserly. *Chesed* expands; *Gevurah* contracts. Whe *Chesed* says: "Share," *Gevurah* says: "When, how and with whom?" Where *Chesed* celebrate heroism, *Gevurah* is a disciplinarian, fearfully looking over its shoulder.

Without *Chesed's* Sharing energy, *Gevura*, too, can run amok, manifesting itself, for exampl in the tyranny of a police state. But just as *Chochma's* Wisdom cannot become manifes without *Bina's* energy of Understanding, neither can the undifferentiated seed that lies i *Chesed* ever become the differentiated tree without *Gevura's* strong hand.

That which *Chochmah* and *Binah* have put together and passed down to *Chesed*, *Gevur* brings into differentiation. This is the beginning of physicality.

Tiferet - תפארת - Beauty

iferet rests below *Keter* on the Central Column, beneath *Chesed* to the Right and *Gevurah* the Left. A thing of Beauty, whether it is a sunset, a flower, a poem, or a human mind, ust combine Wisdom (*Chochmah*), Understanding (*Binah*), and the luminosity of the ght in order to exist.

iferet is the balancing point between the Right and Left Columns, and without the mmetry of balance, there can be no Beauty. *Tiferet* thus contains all aspects of the world which we live, and it teaches us when to share and when to receive. *Tiferet* represents at elusive balance between Judgment and Loving Kindness that allows a parent to scipline a child out of love instead of out of reactive anger.

Netzach - נצח - Victory/Eternity

etzach resides on the Right Column, just below *Chesed*. A repository and storehouse of ositive energy of Victory from *Chesed*, *Netzach* radiates the *Desire to Share* and becomes e channel of that energy as it begins to approach the physical world in which we live. is analogous to the sperm that, in union with the egg, ultimately creates the individual man being.

etzach is representative of the right brain, where the eternal involuntary creative process kes place. In short, it is the artist, the poet, the musician, the dreamer, and the masculine rtilizing principle. It is where thoughts begin to manifest into physicality. s feminine counterpart, directly across the way on the Left Column, is:

Hod - הוד - Glory

od is analogous to the egg in human conception. *Hod* begins the materialization of that hich was held solely in potential in *Chesed* and *Netsach*, much as a woman manifests and ves birth to that which has been conceived in conjunction with the male fertilizing inciple. *Hod* also controls voluntary processes and left-brain activities, channeling the acticality of *Gevurah* into the human psyche. As *Netsach* is the artist, *Hod* with its energy Glory is the scientist, the logician, the math whiz, and the CPA in the brown tweed it.

Yesod - יסוד - Foundation

sod sits like a great reservoir, the Foundation, funneling and feeding spiritual Light in a anageable way into our physical world. All the *Sefirot* above pour their intellect and their tributes into its vast basin, where they are mixed, balanced, and made ready for transfer radiance so brilliant no mortal could survive its presence. Metaphorically speaking, sod is a cement truck that gathers all the raw compounds, including water and sand, ends them together, and pours out a wet mixture that will eventually harden into the ment that is our physical Universe, otherwise known as:

MALCHUT - מלכות - KINGDOM

Malchut contains the world of physicality. It is here where the cement mixture solidifie
like rock and takes on physical form and structure. It is the only one of the *Sefirot* whei
physical material seems to exist, albeit as a minuscule percentage of the whole. And
is here that a divergence in human nature spells the difference between individual live
lived in the Light and those lived in darkness. This is humankind's playing field, where v
experience, work, and transform our *tikkun* using our free will.

ZEIR - ANPIN - זעיר אנפין

The ancient kabbalists explain that of the above ten dimensions, six in particular (*Chese
Gevurah, Tiferet, Netzach, Hod,* and *Yesod*) are tightly enfolded within each other, compacte
in a dimension known as *Zeir Anpin.*

By the grace of God/Light emanating through this
Haggadah; May we all totally crush our egos and reactive
behaviors, thus eliminating chaos throughout humanity.
With love and certainty that this will happen, I dedicate
this book to The Rav, Karen, Yehuda & Michael;
and to the Chevre, for sharing the wisdom of Kabbalah
with the world. May God/Light bless you always!

Esther bat Semach v Chayah Barucha.

אסתר בת צמח וחיה ברכה